LINUX™

to go

ISBN 0-13-999269-3

90000

9 780139 992698

to go series ....

LINUX

to go

Rich Grace

Tim Parker

Editorial/Production Supervision: Kerry Reardon
Acquisitions Editor: Greg Doench
Editorial Assistant: Mary Treacy
Manufacturing Manager: Alexis Heydt
Marketing Manager: Bryan Gambrel
Art Director: Gail Cocker-Bogusz
Interior Series Designer: Rosemarie Votta
Cover Designer: Anthony Gemmellaro
Cover Design Director: Jerry Votta

The publisher offers discounts on this book when ordered in bulk quantities.
For more information, contact

Corporate Sales Department,
Prentice Hall PTR
One Lake Street
Upper Saddle River, NJ 07458
Phone: 800-382-3419; FAX: 201-236-714
E-mail (Internet): corpsales@prenhall.com

Printed in the United States of America

10 9 8 7 6 5 4 3 2 1

ISBN 0-13-999269-3

Prentice-Hall International (UK) Limited, *London*
Prentice-Hall of Australia Pty. Limited, *Sydney*
Prentice-Hall Canada Inc., *Toronto*
Prentice-Hall Hispanoamericana, S.A., *Mexico*
Prentice-Hall of India Private Limited, *New Delhi*
Prentice-Hall of Japan, Inc., *Tokyo*
Prentice-Hall of Asia Pte. Ltd., *Singapore*
Editora Prentice-Hall do Brasil, Ltda., *Rio de Janeiro*

CONTENTS

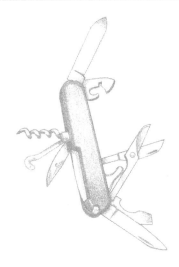

CHAPTER 3

CONFIGURING DEVICES TO WORK
UNDER LINUX 61

CHAPTER 4

FILE PERMISSIONS AND OWNERSHIP 91

CHAPTER 5

CHAPTER 6

CHAPTER 7

CHAPTER 8

CHAPTER 9

CHAPTER 10

CHAPTER 11

CHAPTER 12

CHAPTER 13

PREFACE

Linux has seen a spectacular growth curve over the last two or three years. When mail-order companies start to preload the operating system, you know it's made it to the big leagues. According to reasonable market estimates, there are over eight million Linux users in the world. Compare that to Windows's sixty-six million, and you can see that Linux has found a considerable niche in the market.

Linux's popularity has grown as the operating system has evolved from a hacker's paradise a mere six years ago to a robust, dependable, stable operating system with a friendly GUI, commercial applications, and dedicated support on the Internet. Users are no longer faced with convoluted installation and configuration processes. They don't even have to learn much about UNIX. Since Linux can work superbly on old hardware, like the 386 and 486 you replaced with your Pentium, there's no reason not to use it.

Along with the rise in popularity there has been an outpouring of books about the subject. One author has written eight books on the subject in the last five years. Yet most of the books on the shelves deal with introductory-level material for the non-UNIX user, or special configuration and programming subjects. There are no books on tricks and tips for the user who isn't a guru, but isn't a neophyte, either. You already know Linux commands, and you have the operating system running smoothly. This book addresses where to go from the basics you already understand.

The target audience for all the To Go books are users moving beyond basic knowledge levels. The series tries to cover many aspects of the subject that may be of interest, without concentrating too much on any one subject or theme. You'll find a varied assortment in these pages. Some of the subjects in this book are likely to be familiar to you; others may not be. Many veteran Linux users know the basic UNIX commands, but don't understand subjects like file permissions, using find, or configuring X properly. Thus, we've taken the subjects that most Linux users want to know about, answered many of the most commonly-asked questions, and tried to extend the typical Linux user's knowledge about the use of the operating system. Many of the subjects in this book, such as DNS, Apache, Samba, and Usenet news, have been included because of repeated requests for information from students in advanced UNIX courses. If they are curious, you may be, too.

We cover a lot of material here, from the simple to the complex. We don't try to cover every obscure aspect of Linux. We don't try to be comprehensive. We can't possibly do that in the few hundred pages you hold. Instead, we include enough detail to whet your appetite, to start you experimenting with your system, and to expand your knowledge level considerably.

We hope you enjoy reading Linux To Go. If you have suggestions for changes or additions, we'd like to hear from you. Above all else, we hope you learn something and are able to get even more from this great operating system.

BASIC INTERACTIONS WITH THE GUI

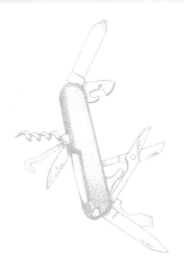

As with all major commercial versions of UNIX, Linux provides the X Graphical User Interface (GUI) as a primary visual front end for the operating system. (Although many people call this GUI X Windows, that's not the proper name. Instead, it's just called X.) Many Linux users prefer to do all their work from the command line, but there's no shame in using X. In fact, it presents its own challenges. For Linux to thrive, it must accommodate the many new users who want to use it only through the graphic interface, so that's what the bulk of this chapter is about.

BASICS OF LINUX COMMAND LINE ENTRY

Unlike Windows or the Macintosh, some command line work is almost always necessary under Linux. Whether you're in X or in the basic command line screen, command lines can be used to control virtually every Linux feature. Though X provides a basic graphic interface and offers convenience to more inexperienced users, it's possible to run every Linux feature, configure networking, and set up every device without ever seeing an icon or a color screen. Much of the power of Linux is hidden under the hood.

The names *command line* and *terminal screen* are used more or less interchangeably throughout this book. This is from historical usage where every command was entered on ASCII-based characters terminals.

Here are a few other things you should know about command line entry that will make it easier to deal with the command line.

WATCH FOR CASE-SENSITIVITY

For historical reasons, almost all of UNIX's commands are entered as lowercase, although there are some important ones that break this rule.

When you want to invoke a program mentioned in this book from the command line, type it exactly as its name appears. For example, the Xconfigurator program allows you to change X video display settings. The name of the Linux executable file is Xconfigurator, and that is precisely how it should be typed, with the capital "X." Typing it in a command line as follows will not work:

```
xconfigurator
```

This yields an error message. Typing in the next command line starts the program:

```
Xconfigurator
```

Typing most UNIX commands in uppercase causes an error, too. For example, the cal command displays a calendar for a specified month. If you type the commands in uppercase, you'll see an error. Using lowercase (the format of most UNIX commands) invokes the command properly, as follows:

```
$ CAL 12 1999

CAL: not found

$ Cal 12 1999

Cal: not found

$ cal 12 1999

    December 1999

Su Mo Tu We Th Fr Sa
          1  2  3  4
 5  6  7  8  9 10 11
12 13 14 15 16 17 18
19 20 21 22 23 24 25
26 27 28 29 30 31
```

PAY ATTENTION TO PATHS

Make sure the commands you want to execute are in the path. UNIX uses paths much like DOS and Windows. By default, most user utilities are in the /bin or /usr/bin directories, which are in the default user search path. Many system administration tools are not in these paths and the full path and command name must be specified.

You can see your current path by issuing the set command and looking for the line that contains the environment variable PATH. The output of the set command will look something like this:

```
$ set
HOME=/usr/tparker
LOGNAME=tparker
MAIL=/usr/spool/mail/tparker
PATH=/bin:/usr/bin:/usr/tparker/bin:.
PS1=$
PS2=>
SHELL=/bin/sh
TERM=ansi
```

When a command is typed, the shell looks in /bin, then /usr/bin, then in /usr/tparker/bin, then in the current directory (the period is the current directory). If the command is not found after those searches, an error message is generated. As long as the command you want to run is in the path, you need not specify the directory. On the other hand, if the command is somewhere other than a directory in your path, you need to specify the entire path to the command, like the following that gives both the directory path and the executable name:

```
$ /usr/frame/frame
```

You can modify your PATH variable contents at any time by redefining the variable. The syntax for doing so depends on the shell you are using. With bash, for example, you can redefine the PATH variable like this:

```
PATH=$PATH:/usr/mystuff
export PATH
```

The first line adds the directory /usr/mystuff to the existing PATH value, while the second line make the change effective.

USE THE COMMAND LINE HISTORY

Typing commands can be tedious, particularly when you start working with the more complex Linux commands described in later chapters of this book. Use the up and down arrow keys to scroll through all the commands in any terminal screen.

While there is command line history with the default shells Linux uses, don't assume all shells offer the same features. There are some shells that lack command line history completely (such as the Bourne shell) and some that require special instructions to be entered to allow history to be employed (like the C shell).

USE COMMAND LINES FOR SPEED

Whether in X or in the basic Linux terminal screen, it's often more efficient to type a command to get something done rather than rely on an icon to launch the command. This also provides a lot more control over what's going on in your system.

Still, Linux's command syntax is confusing. This is no surprise: Linux is very much a UNIX clone, inheriting all the complexity and intimidation that implies. Unlike UNIX, Linux goes a long way to simplify things for the average PC user, with newer versions of Linux providing easier installation routines and drastically improved device support.

More to the point, once you become used to the command line, Linux provides an almost endless series of tools, options, and features. You always know how a Linux command line appears and works, unlike the myriad X applications that all use different interface conventions. With command lines, you can keep things simple, and once you are comfortable with Linux's command syntax, you will probably prefer it to graphical interfaces for many tasks. Although Linux doesn't treat you like a kid, it's far more accessible than UNIX.

For Linux newcomers, on the other hand, it is easier and more fun to start off with X, so that is what we will discuss first.

Avoid using the root account for most of your work under Linux. When using root there is the potential to cause such serious damage to the filesystem and important files that Linux must be reinstalled from scratch. Using a regular user login, on the other hand, prevents access to most of the important system files and directories.

 X

X is the primary GUI for UNIX and Linux systems. Several years ago an enhanced version of the interface, called Motif, was also released. Motif sits on top of X and provides a more attractive and consistent interface, looking more like Microsoft Windows than anything else. Most Linux versions include X but not Motif, which is a commercial package. You can buy Motif for Linux, if you wish.

There are many advantages in using X for your interface to Linux, such as:

- ◆ Making the most of your video display system by using higher resolutions.

- ◆ Easier navigation among several different Linux shell screens as well as cut-and-paste capabilities between applications.

- ◆ A more visually pleasing screen image, offering customizable background wallpaper, color schemes, screen savers, and different third-party modifications to change the appearance of the basic GUI.

- ◆ More advanced applications for managing and configuring the network.

- ◆ Use of popular third-party programs such as Netscape Navigator and Corel Word-Perfect which have been ported from the Microsoft Windows environment.

Some disadvantages also apply when using X, such as:

- ◆ The X GUI is still a fairly rough tool under Linux, mostly because Linux is maintained by a loose network of volunteer programmers.

- ◆ User interface conventions vary from application to application.

- ◆ X is more difficult to configure than the average Macintosh or Windows interface.

Linux is and may always be a work in progress, maintained by thousands of anonymous programmers and software engineers. Inconsistencies abound throughout the operating system, although most are minor. Even when using X, you'll find yourself resorting to the command line to start many Linux programs instead of using X itself.

CHANGING X VIDEO SETTINGS

Before you begin using X, ensure that your video settings are working properly. Normally, you can type startx at the Linux command prompt to start the X interface. A default video display resolution is defined for you based on the video card and monitor settings chosen during installation. If you decide to change these settings, you need to use Linux's straightforward Xconfigurator program, which you may have seen during installation. Some versions of Linux use a program other than Xconfigurator, but all provide the same basic procedure for selecting the monitor, video card, and resolutions required to run X. If your version of Linux does not use Xconfigurator, check the documentation to determine which program you should be using. Almost all versions of the X configuration routine involve simply reading the screens, following instructions, and choosing the proper values.

Xconfigurator allows you to change GUI settings while you're actually running X, or you can quit X and invoke the program from the shell prompt. In either case, the program writes a configuration file containing all the defined settings. Whenever you change them you'll need to step through the entire process again

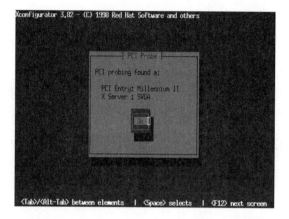

Figure 1-1   Detecting a video card under Linux.

To use Xconfigurator to reconfigure your video settings, follow the steps below:

1. To launch Xconfigurator, type the following at the shell prompt:

    `Xconfigurator`

    The program appears, displaying an introduction screen.

2. Press Enter to continue. The computer attempts to auto-detect your video card. If you have already configured X during setup, the video card type will be a familiar sight.

3. Press Enter. The monitor list appears. If you want to select a new monitor type for your display, remember that refresh rates and resolution are critically important for a monitor's display quality. The higher each of these two specifications are, the more likely it is that your monitor can support higher-resolution X GUI screens. If you make a selection that doesn't match your monitor, such as selecting a monitor type that supports much higher refresh rates and resolutions than your monitor can handle, you will be unable to display X. You could even damage your monitor if you specify settings that overload the monitor's electronics, although this is very rare. If you make a mistake, the GUI will likely become unavailable, and you will have to run Xconfigurator from the command prompt to reconfigure the settings.

4. Select a monitor from the list and press Enter. This is probably the same monitor that you selected previously during installation.

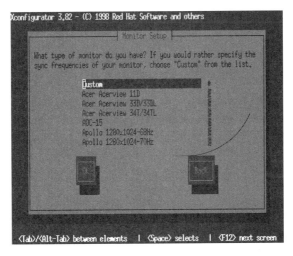

Figure 1-2   Selecting a monitor type.

Whether you are running Xconfigurator from a shell window in X or from a prompt, the program probes your system and flashes the screen several times. If X is running, it will continue running during these changes. The program then comes back with a default setting as shown in Figure 1-3.

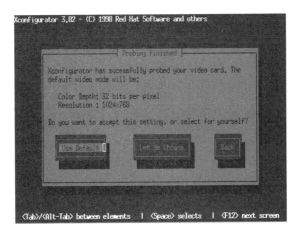

Figure 1-3   Opting for default video settings.

5. To change the video settings, select "Let me choose" and press Enter.

A few files for video support are copied from the CD to the system if they have not already been copied over during the installation routine. A Monitor Setup screen appears. This provides a list of monitors, one of which should match your monitor. If there isn't a listing for your specific monitor, you will have to make an educated guess as to which monitor best matches your own.

6. Next select the desired resolution and color depth and press Enter. Linux automatically uses the best refresh rate available. To move about, press the Tab key between columns and press the spacebar to enable the desired setting. A "You're Done!" screen appears after you have finished selecting the resolutions.

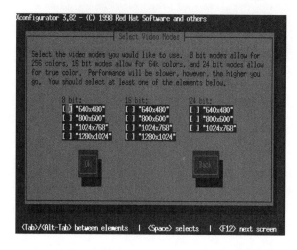

Figure 1-4   Selecting a new screen resolution and color depth setting.

7. Press Enter to write the new settings to the XF86config file. If you're in X already, quit and restart it. Otherwise, use startx to start the X interface. If you do not see the X interface, either because the screen is blank or the image looks wrong, you will need to reconfigure X. You may have to experiment quite a bit to arrive at acceptable settings for your system.

CREATING CUSTOM MONITOR SETTINGS

Xconfigurator supports the creation of custom monitor settings to match your own display. Before you do this, *consult your display's user manual for its maximum refresh rate settings at various resolutions.* You'll need to know a thing or two about your display hardware, including those all-important refresh rate settings and the amount of memory on your video card. To create custom display settings, follow the steps below:

1. Launch Xconfigurator and follow the first three steps from the previous procedure (starting on page 6).

2. When the Monitor list appears, select the default Custom and press Enter.

3. A Custom Monitor Setup screen appears. Press Enter.

4. Select the desired horizontal refresh rate and maximum resolution of your monitor from the list. The highest setting available is usually "Monitor that can do 1280x1024 @ 76 Hz" although there are some systems that support higher resolutions and refresh rates

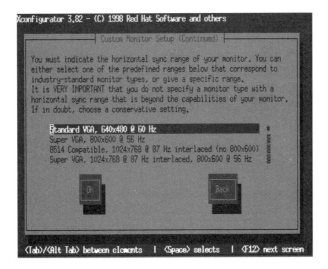

Figure 1-5   Customizing monitor setup.

Use the arrow keys to scroll down the list to see values other than those immediately shown.

5. Select OK and press Enter.

Custom Monitor Setup requires you to specify the vertical sync range of your monitor. Most current 15–17-inch monitors support at least a 50–100 Hz vertical sync range. Better monitors from ViewSonic, Sony, NEC, Nokia, Iiyama, and many others support a 40–150 vertical range.

6. Select the desired vertical sync range, select OK, and press Enter.

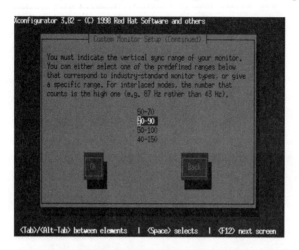

Figure 1-6   Selecting vertical sync ranges for your monitor.

7. Xconfigurator prompts that it is about to autoprobe your system. Press Enter to continue.

8. After a moment, default display settings are displayed. If you accept the default, Xconfigurator then asks about the video memory on your video card. Select the desired video memory setting and press Enter. This setting must match the amount of memory on your card. If you are not sure about the amount of RAM on your card, estimate conservatively. For example, if you are not sure if you have 2 or 4 MB video RAM, go with the 2MB setting. Most modern video cards have on-board RAM, but some older cards have none.

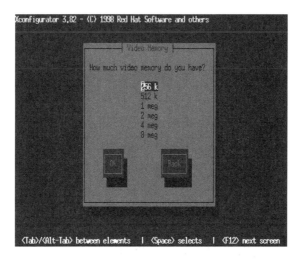

Figure 1-7   Defining the amount of video memory.

9. A Clockchip Configuration screen appears. Select the "No Clockchip Configuration" setting and press Enter. Unless you know *exactly* what you are doing, do not select anything but "No Clockchip Configuration" in this screen.

10. Select the desired resolution and color depth as described in steps 4–7 of the previous procedure (starting on page 7). If you change the video display settings after the default is provided, you will not see the video memory and clockchip settings. Press Enter. The new display information is written to the X startup file.

Once you become used to working with the Xconfigurator program, it is fairly simple. You can change X settings as many times as you need. If a particular setting doesn't work, run Xconfigurator again and try something else. It's a good idea to run Xconfigurator without running X. Xconfigurator may hang once in a while when X is running.

USING THE DESKTOP

X desktops vary with every version of Linux. One version mimics Windows 95, offering a Start menu, taskbar, and windowing gadgets, as shown in Figure 1-8. This version is displayed automatically in RedHat Linux 5.2. (The next section, "Changing the Window Manager" on page 14, describes how to switch your X desktops to other window managers for a different screen look.)

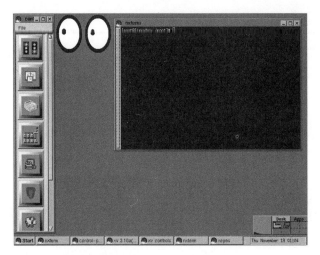

Figure 1-8   Is it Linux?

The Win95-like screen gadgets aren't actually a part of X. Instead, they're an example of a custom-programmed window manager. Many different window managers can be used with X. They essentially add new Close and Minimize gadget icons to every window's title bar and provide a control panel-like interface for some important system utilities. Figure 1-8 shows the control panel at the far left.

Linux also offers virtual desktops used automatically by X. Figure 1-8 shows an icon at the bottom right of the figure. Two virtual desktops, titled Desk and Apps, provide screen space equal to four times the resolution of the display. Clicking on a quadrant displays its contents, leaving the contents of the main screen intact. You can drag windows onto the other desktop sections or start any Linux program inside any section of the virtual desktop. Once you become accustomed to it, using the virtual desktop can be convenient and can reduce screen clutter.

To automatically scroll across virtual desktop sections, drag the mouse against the edge of the screen. After a second or less, the screen will switch to another virtual desktop section.

In any Linux X desktop environment, some conventions can be observed. To explore basic desktop actions, try these steps:

1. Click on a vacant area of the X display. A desktop shortcut menu appears as shown in Figure 1-9.

Figure 1-9   Opening the main menu.

2. To display a menu of Linux programs, right-click anywhere on the Linux screen. A Programs menu appears as shown in Figure 1-10. This is also part of the main menu, but can be accessed separately by right-clicking on the bare desktop.

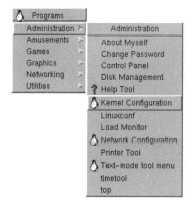

Figure 1-10   Opening the program menu. (Some Linux window managers don't provide this on the desktop.)

3. Move the mouse over any menu item and a subordinate menu provides Linux programs that can be run from the GUI. Virtually every Linux program can be run by typing its name in a terminal window or from a GUI menu, although they may run only in a terminal window.

4. To experiment with a menu item, click on the Linux screen. The main shortcut menu appears.

5. From the menu, select Programs I Amusements I Xsnow. The weather changes on your Linux screen!

6. To quit X, click on the Linux screen and select Exit Fvwm (or whatever window manager is listed there) and then Yes, Really Quit. X closes and you are returned to a Linux command screen. Simply type startx again to run X.

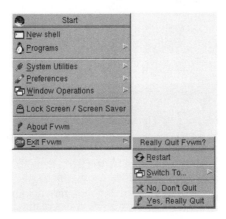

Figure 1-11   Quitting X.

CHANGING THE WINDOW MANAGER

Most flavors of Linux, including RedHat and Caldera, provide several different X front ends, called *window managers.* Window managers create distinctive appearances for the basic X GUI on your Linux computer. They can have a big influence on how you work, and they can be very confusing.

Before changing window managers, you should be used to experimenting and feel comfortable mousing around in your Linux system. Unlike Windows or the Macintosh, which present a single standard face to the world, the Linux world tends to fragment around many experimental GUIs. While this makes it difficult to train people on the system, it makes it fun to tinker with your machine. Some Linux window managers, such as the default on RedHat Linux 5.2, use a Windows 95 GUI—or what a Windows 95 GUI would look like on Dr. Frankenstein's table!

If you're fairly experienced and like to experiment, checking out different window managers is an excellent way to waste an hour or two. Be aware that different window managers change the way you use the mouse, and interacting with the desktop may completely change from one manager to another. Clicking on the screen to display the main menu in one manager may be replicated with a right-click in another.

For most versions of X, follow the steps below:

1. Click or right-click the mouse on the desktop.
2. From the main menu, select Exit and then Switch To…

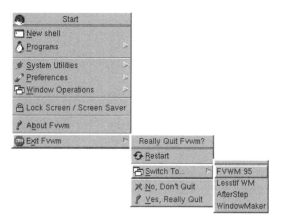

Figure 1-12   Selecting new window managers from the main menu.

3. Select a window manager type from the menu. As an example, try WindowMaker if it is available. RedHat provides this nice GUI enhancer that allows for a huge amount of display customization features.

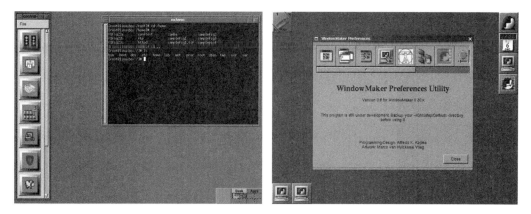

Figure 1-13   RedHat's Lesstif window manager (left), which is a default window GUI for many other flavors of Linux, and RedHat's WindowMaker GUI (right).

Caldera Linux uses a special window manager called KDE (K Desktop Environment). KDE is rapidly gaining in popularity. Check your version of Linux to see if your system supports it.

INTRODUCING XF86SETUP

Xconfigurator is an adequate tool for basic X setup. However, you may wonder why Linux lacks a graphical utility to do the same thing. Well, XF86Setup is such a tool. You can execute it while X is running or from a full-screen command line. Using XF86Setup, you work with the same settings as in the more archaic Xconfigurator program, but with a somewhat more convenient graphical setup program.

To run and begin using XF86Setup, follow the steps below:

1. From the Linux command line, type the command (exactly as it appears; remember that Linux is case-sensitive):

   ```
   XF86Setup
   ```

   The setup program appears as shown in Figure 1-14.

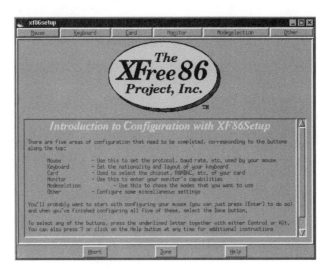

Figure 1-14   Opening XFree86.

2. To view or change your video card settings, click the Card button. The Card page appears. Along the top, notice the basic Xserver display drivers for Linux: Mono, VGA16, SVGA, 8514, AGX, I128, and so on. A few servers, such as S3 and I128, are best used with specific cards such as the Number Nine Imagine 128 series, while others, such as SVGA, are used for a wide selection of cards. The TGA server is used for Targa video boards. The S3 server is used for a common type of video chip that is used on many different cards, such as the Diamond Stealth series. SVGA is a good bet if you're not sure what type of card you have.

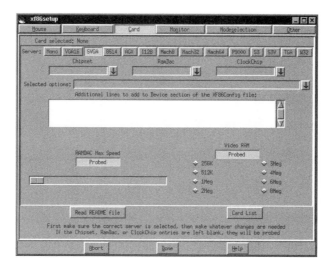

Figure 1-15   Selecting video settings.

3. To select a specific card, click the Card list button. The card list appears in a scrollable list.

4. Select the desired card from the list and click the Detailed Setup button. You return to the Card page. Your selected card is now displayed

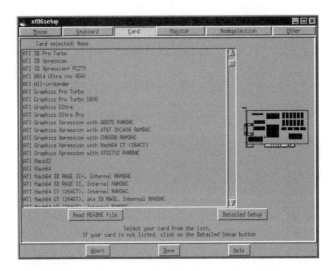

Figure 1-16 Selecting a video card.

5. Select the amount of video RAM that is built onto your video card.
6. Click the Monitor button. The Monitors type list appears.
7. Type in the horizontal and vertical refresh rates for your display *as specified in your monitor's documentation* or select a setting from the list.

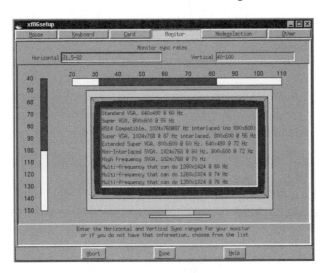

Figure 1-17 Defining monitor settings in XF86Setup.

8. Click the Modeselection button.

9. Select the desired resolution and color depth.

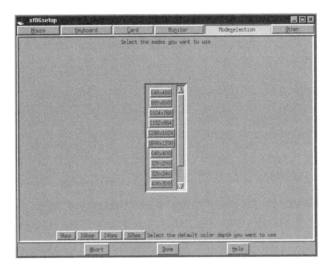

Figure 1-18   Choosing a resolution mode.

10. When you're finished, click Done, and then save your work by clicking Okay. Select Save This Configuration and Quit. Close out of X and restart it by typing startx at the prompt.

Although a feature called xvidtune may also be used under X or a command screen to adjust display settings, it's fairly crude and confusing, and not recommended for normal display use. XF86Setup provides a fairly convenient interface for changing video settings.

As seen in the figures for this exercise, you may also change the mouse and keyboard. These settings are more sensitive than those for video, and you should be careful with them if those devices already work. Also note that you can run XF86Setup from a plain-vanilla Linux command line, without ever running X.

If you don't yet have a functioning mouse, XF86Setup has a large number of options for configuring those cantankerous input devices. Whenever possible, try to define input devices during initial Linux setup, and then don't change them under X. If you do, you may have unpredictable results.

OPENING A TERMINAL WINDOW

In X, the command line is usually displayed in a separate window, called a shell or terminal screen. You may run as many terminal windows as you want during a Linux session. In fact, you'll probably become used to starting many Linux programs and processes from the command line, whether or not you're running X. The command line provides a great deal of control over how things happen in your system.

> **When you open a terminal window and start another program from it, that window must usually remain open while the program is running. If you close that terminal window, the program it spawned may also close depending on the way the application was programmed. You can place an application in background, if it doesn't require any input or output, to avoid this problem.**

To open a terminal window under Linux, follow these steps:

1. Click on any vacant area of the Linux screen.
2. From the menu, select New Shell. A new shell window appears.

Figure 1-19   Opening a new terminal window.

To display a paper-white terminal screen (which may be easier to read):

1. Click on any vacant area of the Linux screen.
2. From the menu, select Programs | Utilities | Shells | rxvt.

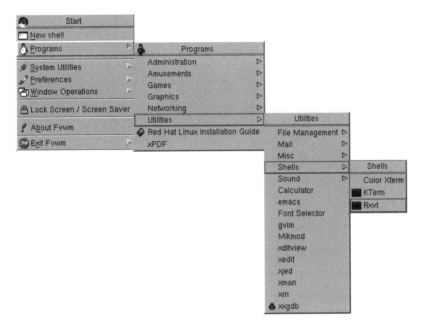

Figure 1-20   Opening a color terminal screen.

One advantage to opening a terminal window under X, as opposed to simply using the Linux text screen, is that you can drag the bottom margin of the terminal window to increase the number of lines displayed in it. This can be very helpful for displaying long lists of files in a directory that would be far too long to view in a single text screen. This can cause problems with some full-screen applications, though, such as some editors. If you start getting strange results after dragging a window to a larger size, simply close the application and restart it.

While running terminal screens in X, you can scroll up and down through their contents while the terminal displays its commands. Drag the bottom margin of the terminal window down to display more lines of text.

Using man Pages to Get Help

The man pages (for *Manual* pages) are a primary resource of online help for UNIX and Linux systems. Linux makes heavy use of man pages for virtually every command and program in the system. It is important to realize that man pages are not meant to be friendly guides for neophytes. They were written by programmers and advanced users for other programmers and advanced users who want quick references to options, arguments, and command descriptions. If you simply need to remember what the -c option does for a command, a man page is great. If you need to learn how to use the C shell, however, don't waste your time wading through the csh man page. Instead, buy a decent book on the subject!

The quickest way to obtain some kind of help on any Linux command is to type the following in any terminal window or command line:

```
man <command>
```

Typical examples may include:

```
man mount
```

```
man mkdir
```

```
man samba
```

If there's a Linux command or program you need help with, chances are there's some kind of man page for it. Of course, if you chose not to load the man pages during the installation of your Linux system, then you will only get error messages when you try to use the man command.

Use the Up arrow and Down arrow keys to scroll in a man page. This works in most versions of Linux. If the arrow keys don't perform properly, use the space bar to move from screen to screen. Using this technique, there is no way to scroll back up, though.

Starting and Using xman

The text-based man pages can be unwieldy, particularly because of the sheer number of them. Linux provides a graphical program called xman for browsing and selecting any man page in the system. Although the interface isn't exactly intuitive, xman provides a handy place to view hundreds of different man pages without having to fire up a terminal screen for each one.

To use the xman manual file browser, follow these steps:

1. From a terminal window, type xman, or from the menu select Programs | Utilities | xman. A small Manual Browser window appears at the top of the Linux screen, as shown in Figure 1-21.

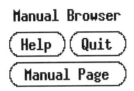

Figure 1-21   The xman startup window.

2. In the Manual Browser window, click Manual Page. The main Manual page appears as shown in Figure 1-22.

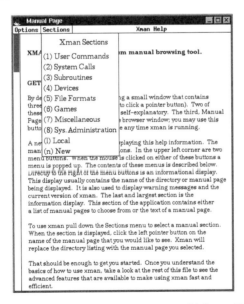

Figure 1-22   The main man page, which provides two menus at the top left.

3. To find a man page for a specific command, click the Sections menu and select a command category.

4. When the list of commands appears in the window, click on the desired command, and its man page appears.

To view the entire list of man pages in the xman window, select Display Directory from the Options menu.

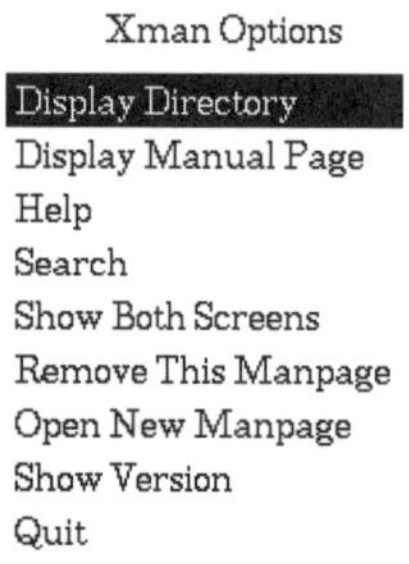

Xman Options

Display Directory
Display Manual Page
Help
Search
Show Both Screens
Remove This Manpage
Open New Manpage
Show Version
Quit

Figure 1-23   Opening the directory of man pages.

Use the Sections menu for a more manageable list of any xman page categories, as shown in Figure 1-23.

OPENING MOTIF XFM (X FILE MANAGER) AND BROWSING THE SYSTEM

If you plan to use X, you'll probably want to try out xfm as a quicker way to navigate around your system. It's not exactly Windows Explorer, but it places a lot more at your fingertips than a basic command line. The X File Manager provides graphical directory browsing and a simple way to select multiple files and directories for copying, moving, and other operations.

Do not move Linux directories and files around. Stick to files that you create, such as text and graphics files. Otherwise, you could severely damage your Linux installation.

Xfm is most handy as a means of exploring your Linux system to see what resides in the various directories.

To open and begin using xfm, follow the steps below:

1. From a terminal window, type xfm or from the menu select Programs | Utilities | File Management | xfm. The X File Manager appears as shown in Figure 1-24.

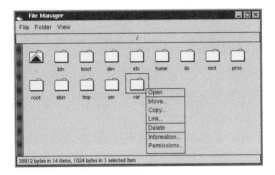

Figure 1-24   Running the X File Manager.

2. Double-click any folder to display its contents.
3. Double-click the up arrow folder to move one level up in the Linux directory structure.
4. To open any folder in a new xfm window, right-click on the folder and select Open from the shortcut menu, or simply double-click the folder. The File, Folder, and View menus provide many of the typical file management commands, such as creating new folders, selecting one or all items in a directory, and file listing and sorting options.

In Figure 1-24, also note that the directory path is listed near the top of the window. This is a handy way to check on where you are exploring within the system.

Xfm is a great way to quickly become acquainted with the contents of your system. Its weaknesses appear when you try to select multiple objects. For example, you can't use the Shift or Ctrl keys to select more than one object at a time. Also, while you can drag and drop individual items between directories, a dialog appears every time to verify that you want to perform the action.

In short, xfm is a mixed bag. It is still useful, and is much more accessible for Linux newcomers than the command line, which is discussed in the next chapter. Many command line tasks can be accomplished in a couple of mouse clicks without ever encountering the alien language of the command line.

SHUTTING DOWN PROPERLY

It's not a good idea to simply turn the Linux system off when you're finished working. In fact, it can completely corrupt your Linux system. As with any other operating system, you need to go through a shutdown process. To shut down Linux, follow the steps below:

1. Close out of X as described earlier in this chapter, assuming you are running X.
2. Type exit at the Linux prompt.
3. Press Ctrl+Alt+Delete to shut down Linux's services. When the system begins to reboot, turn your system off.

The reason you need to go through this process is simple, really. In order to speed up retrieval of files, Linux uses an i-node table to keep track of what files are on the disk, where they are, their permissions, and other types of information. Whenever you request a file or execute a command, Linux searches through the i-node table kept in memory to discover where the file is located, and then retrieves it. By keeping the i-node table in memory, Linux doesn't have to read it into memory from the hard disk every time you request something. This is a lot faster.

Every few seconds, Linux writes the memory version of the i-node table to the disk drive. When you shut off the power to the system, you may encounter a situation where the memory version of the i-node table (now lost) was not synchronized with the version on the hard drive. This results in a potentially corrupted i-node table and loss of information on the hard drive. Even worse, if the hard drive was writing to the disk at the moment power is lost, some data corruption on the disk can occur. In the worst case, this can make the filesystem unusable, although this is very rare.

The shutdown process does more than synchronize the memory i-node table with the disk's version. It also closes down all the process that are being run by the system. You'll see status messages from the kernel when you shut down the system as each process is terminated. This closes any open files, setting the filesystem in a proper state for you to use it again when you reboot.

SUMMARY

Linux can present a complex and confusing face to the world. In a lot of ways, it's easy to see why UNIX has historically been relegated to back-office environments, with its main audience being engineers and programmers.

Although Linux is essentially another form of UNIX, it is different in many ways. Some of those differences are:

◆   Markedly easier installation.

◆   More options for graphical interfaces.

◆   Better hardware device support.

◆   Easier to run on any PC, even old 386 machines.

◆   Far less expensive, even for commercial packages.

If you've ever seen another version of UNIX, such as Sun Solaris or SCO UNIX, you may understand why Linux's ease of installation and configuration is becoming so popular. Compared to the Macintosh or Windows, Linux does present more difficulties. With each new version that comes out, however, many of the usability, support, and installation problems are being addressed. Linux is a little miracle because of its freeware origins. That it continues to improve and stay affordable is a double miracle. The next chapter, "Navigating the Command Line," goes past the GUI interfaces of Linux to the core of the operating system.

NAVIGATING

THE

COMMAND

LINE

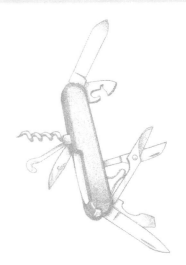

As noted briefly in Chapter 1, *Basic Interactions with the GUI,* Linux's command line is the core of the operating system. In this chapter, you will see a more comprehensive introduction to the Linux command line. This chapter focuses on task-oriented file management, without getting lost in the details. You should take away from this chapter the following:

- Basic navigation skills.
- How to read and list directories and files.
- File copying.
- File and directory renaming.
- Redirection of command output to files for future reference.
- How to mount, read, and copy a file to and from a DOS floppy.

Linux users type at what is called a *command prompt*. You see a prompt in which you type commands whenever you display the Linux text screen or open a terminal window, or a *shell*, in X. By default, on most installations the Linux prompt displays three pieces of information: the user account of the person currently using the computer, the name of the computer, and the name of the current directory. Figure 2-1 illustrates the three sections of the prompt.

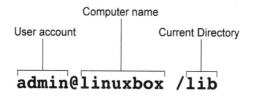

Figure 2-1   Breaking down the Linux prompt.

Linux's command prompt displays your location in the directory tree. For example, when a Linux prompt reads like the following, it indicates that you're in a directory called modules:

```
[peter@linuxbox /modules]#
```

Now, this may not be very helpful, because the modules directory is actually located in /lib/modules, and the prompt doesn't show the whole path. *The Linux prompt shows only the current local directory!* While the MS-DOS prompt shows the whole path, you can be many levels deep in the directory tree in Linux and be unsure of where you are by reading the prompt.

Type pwd at the command line to display the current path. The pwd command is short for "print working directory" and shows you the absolute path to your current directory. Note that this may not be where you think you are because links may be involved.

Not all Linux systems use this same prompt. Some customize the prompt further, while some reduce the prompt to a simple dollar sign (as used in UNIX). You can modify your prompt at any time, and set new defaults for every session when you log in. After all, customizability is one of the strong points of UNIX and Linux.

Navigating directories with the command line can be tedious, which is why the xfm file manager was introduced in the previous chapter. (See "Opening Motif XFM (X File Manager) and Browsing the System" on page 24.)

When you see a prompt like the following, it indicates that you are at the very top level of the system—the root directory:

```
[peter@linuxbox /]#
```

Every filesystem has a single root directory called "/". There is never more than one such directory on a system. Even when multiple disk drives and network-mounted drives are involved, there is still only one root directory. Don't confuse this directory with the separately named *root* directory that is reserved for the system administrator on some installations.

Always remember that the Linux command line is case-sensitive. If you use lowercase or uppercase letters the wrong way, the desired command will not execute.

Using the command line can be an intimidating experience for the new Linux user. Nevertheless, the best way to start making use of it is to begin exploring your system. By doing so, you will learn the basics of finding, copying, moving, and renaming files. You will also learn how to find out such things as free disk space and memory.

We'll start by introducing the basic Linux directory structure.

UNDERSTANDING THE LINUX DIRECTORY TREE

Linux consists of a hierarchical series of directories arranged in a tree with the root directory (/) as the top or bottom, depending on how you view the tree. When you perform a full install of most Linux distributions from CD-ROM, you wind up with over 400 MB of directories descending from the root directory.

As a rule, none of the directories that exist in Linux after installation should be moved or renamed! They tend to be linked to other directories or have dependencies with files that can cause your system to cease functioning properly.

The basic tree is shown on the next page with some selected subdirectories:

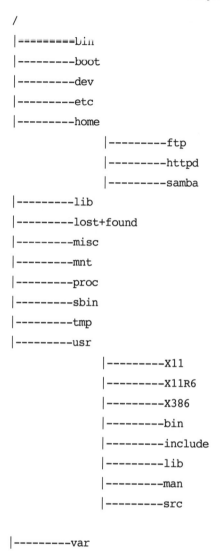

```
/
|=========bin
|---------boot
|---------dev
|---------etc
|---------home
                    |---------ftp
                    |---------httpd
                    |---------samba
|---------lib
|---------lost+found
|---------misc
|---------mnt
|---------proc
|---------sbin
|---------tmp
|---------usr
                    |---------X11
                    |---------X11R6
                    |---------X386
                    |---------bin
                    |---------include
                    |---------lib
                    |---------man
                    |---------src

|---------var
```

The directory names used by Linux are inherited from UNIX. None of the names are mandatory, but there has been a convention about directory naming and usage for the last thirty years. Why tamper with a good thing? The following are key directories and their purposes for Linux and UNIX systems:

◆ **bin**:   Many executable files are contained in this directory. These are usually in the Linux executable path and can be typed in and executed from anywhere in the system. Some executables are also place in /usr/bin, although most standard Linux utilities are kept in /bin by convention. You will become acquainted with numerous programs in this directory although there are many you will never use.

◆ **dev**: This directory contains Linux's device configuration files, including cdrom, hda1, and hda2 (disk devices), and fd0 (floppy). This is where designations in the command line such as /dev/fd0 come from.

> **The dev directory is not where the device drivers are located. This is a common misconception about Linux and UNIX. Instead, the /dev directory has information about the devices, such as the type of device and their major and minor device numbers, but the files are almost all empty in this directory!**

◆ **etc**: Key configuration files for many parts of your system, including web services (httpd), and X (X11), are located here. Most users never have to access files in this directory or its subdirectories, although system administrators will often work with its contents. This is the directory from which Linux finds much of its boot information.

◆ **home**: This contains subdirectories holding some useful information, particularly the Internet and web server httpd directory. Numerous HTML instruction files about how to use the Apache web server are located here. Not all Linux systems have a home directory, while on some systems it is empty.

◆ **lib**: This directory contains C library functions and shared library functions called by other executable programs on your system. Although this book does not discuss programming, Linux and other UNIX systems make excellent programming environments, which is why Linux is so popular with engineers.

◆ **usr**: This contains an enormous number of files for users, for configuring and running X, and for many other Linux features. Historically, the usr directory (called /u on some systems) was where any user-specific file was stored. Those files are organized into several subdirectories, such as X11R6, X11, and games. The X11/bin directory contains hundreds of individual X executable programs. The man directory is also located here, along with several subdirectories present in other UNIX implementations, such as bin and include.

◆ **sbin**: This directory contains numerous system and networking utilities, such as ifconfig, mailconf, fsck (File System Checker), and insmod (Insert Module). Not all systems have an sbin directory.

◆ **root**: This is the home directory for the Linux root administrator account. While the root directory is created for the person who has ultimate authority over the system and its configuration, other users will have their own directories just off the root level. The average Linux user should not have root access over the system; it's too easy for an inexperienced person in a production environment to cause problems on the system. This could occur when the user alters or removes an important file or changes permissions accidentally on a file or directory causing some other program or user ID to fail to work properly.

If any particular Linux executable program interests you, simply type man <command> to view help and descriptions of the program!

The following sections describe basic interaction with the Linux tree, and command line tools for manipulating files.

MOVING AROUND IN DIRECTORIES

The cd, or *change directory,* command allows you to navigate through your Linux system from the command line. Figure 2-2 shows an breakdown of the cd syntax.

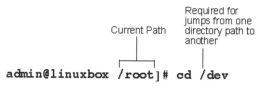

Figure 2-2   Running the CD command across devices.

If you've used MS-DOS in the past, this may sound familiar. It works the same way as in DOS—the DOS developers "borrowed" this and other commands from UNIX—with a couple of differences:

♦   Unlike MS-DOS, where the simple act of typing cd with no arguments displays the entire path in which you are located, the Linux cd command by itself will take you to your home directory immediately.

♦   Another difference is that Linux paths use the forward slash (/) instead of the backslash (\) to separate directory levels, as shown in the following example:

```
cd /usr/X11R6/bin
```

Here, you are specifying navigation from the root (/) to three levels deep in the directory tree. Each level is separated by a forward slash.

 If you use DOS or Windows systems, you likely transpose the forward slash and backslash. Always remember to use the forward slash in the Linux command line. The backslash is used by Linux to indicate a continuation on the next line. If you accidentally use the backslash and see a prompt you don't understand (usually the "greater than" sign), use Ctrl-C to return to the shell prompt.

ENTERING A NEW DIRECTORY

To enter a new directory, type the cd command followed by the name or full path of the desired directory, as shown below:

```
cd /usr
```

Another example would be the following:

```
cd /usr/X11R6
```

If you specify only a directory name, that directory must be directly below the current location. This is called *relative addressing* because you are moving relative to your current position, like this:

```
$ pwd
/usr/tparker
$ cd temp
$ pwd
/usr/tparker/temp
$ cd another
$ pwd
/usr/tparker/temp/another
$ cd
/usr/tparker
```

In the first two examples, the directory name known to be below the current directory is specified and cd moves into it. If the directory does not exist or a filename is used by mistake, an error message would be displayed. The last example shows the use of cd with no arguments to return to the home directory.

To go all the way back to the root of the Linux directory tree, simply type this:

```
cd /
```

MOVING UP ONE DIRECTORY LEVEL

Linux has two shortcut symbols that are useful when moving around directories or trying to find files. These are the single period, which means the current directory, and two periods, which means the parent directory. The parent directory is always one level higher than the current directory. Only the root directory has no parent. To go up by one directory level in the system, type the following:

```
cd ..
```

When using the cd .. command, always press the spacebar at least once between cd and .. or the command will not work!

Use more than one double period to move several levels at once, separated by slashes for each pair, as shown in this example:

```
$ pwd
/usr/brutus/book/chapter1/files
$ cd ../..
$ pwd
/usr/brutus/book
$ cd ..
$ pwd
/usr/brutus
```

MOVING FROM ONE DIRECTORY TO ANOTHER

Use either *absolute* addresses or *relative* addresses to move from one directory to another. Absolute addresses are from root, while relative addresses are from the current position. For example, to move to the /dev directory, type the following:

```
cd /dev
```

Since you are specifying exactly where, from the root directory, you want to go, it doesn't matter where you are when you type the command. On the other hand, if you are in /usr and want to go to /dev, use the same command or resort to relative addressing, like this:

```
cd ../dev
```

Experimentation is the best way to become accustomed to path navigation from the command line and to become acquainted with the various directories. Remember when lost that a simple cd / command returns you to the top of the Linux tree.

VIEWING AND LISTING DIRECTORIES

The command for displaying the contents of directories is called ls, from *list*. The ls command has options to perform a number of changes to the information returned by the command. Figure 2-3 shows a breakdown of the ls syntax.

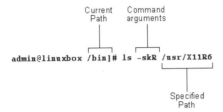

Figure 2-3   Running ls command options and complex paths.

Some of the most useful arguments are shown in Table 2-1:

Table 2-1   Arguments for ls

Argument	Description
-a	Lists all files in the current or specified directory, including hidden files. (Hidden files are indicated by a period at the start of the name.)
-F	Provides more visual clues to what kinds of items are in a directory (called the *Classify* flag). The file classifications include:
	/ Directories.
	* Executable files.
	@ Symbolic links.
	| FIFO pipes.
	= Sockets.
	Each of the classification symbols is placed at the beginning of the item name in a listing.
-k	Combined with the -s argument (as in -sk), makes ls print file sizes in kilobytes.
-r	Lists contents in reverse order by name or by time.
-s	Makes ls print the size of each file in blocks.
-S	Tells ls to list by file size, from largest to smallest.
-t	Sorts the directory listing by the time at which the files were created or modified, with the newest files first.

In general, the ls command allows for any number of options and an optional directory name. If you specify no arguments and simply type ls, you will receive a listing of the current directory. The ls command can be combined with other operations, which we'll explore later. You can list more than one directory at a time by simply adding the names of the directories, one after another, separated by spaces:

```
ls /dev /usr/tparker /bin
```

You can combine multiple ls options in the same argument, as follows:

```
ls -skR
```

This command provides a complete listing of the current directory and all its subdirectories, in order by level in the path (R), with each item's size (s) listed in kilobytes (k). It can provide a very long listing depending on the directory involved.

COPYING FILES AND DIRECTORIES

Use the cp, or *copy,* command to copy files from one directory to another or to make a second copy of a file. It operates in a similar fashion to the DOS *copy* command with a few differences. The basic syntax follows:

```
cp [options] <current file> <destination file>
```

The cp command must have two arguments for every command. If you specify only one, as you would in DOS, cp gives you an error. The cp command automatically overwrites an existing file of the specified name without bothering to warn you. This is something you become accustomed to, and you should make a habit of ensuring you know when this is going to happen by checking the directory listing first. The cp command even allows you to copy a file over itself, although this is a bad habit to get into and serves no real purpose. Rather, cp is best used for the following:

◆   Making copies of files and placing them in different directories.

◆   Making a copy of a data file in the same directory with a different name, which is a good file backup technique.

◆   Making copies of directories and placing them in new locations.

Although you can use wildcards, the cp command does not provide them in quite the same way as with DOS commands. Instead, special command options, like -r and -f, perform more complex operations. Table 2-2 provides a partial list of these cp command options.

Table 2-2   Commands for cp

Command	Description
*	Signifies that you are attempting to execute the command on all files and directories within a directory. The wildcard can also act separately on a group of files with similar names or types.
?	A wildcard character that, similar to MS-DOS, can be substituted for a single character in a file name. Multiple question marks can be used to represent several characters in a name.
-b	Backs up files in the destination directory that would otherwise be overwritten.
-f	Forces removal of any existing files in the destination directory. Be careful using this option!
-i	Forces Linux to prompt before overwriting any files in the destination directory.
-p	Preserves all file security information in copied files, including owner, user group, file access permissions, and time stamps.
-r	Recursively copies all contents of the directory, including subdirectories.
-v	Prints the name of each file during copying.

Although this is not the complete list of option, these are the options you might use most often. The * wildcard character allows you to use Linux commands on all the files of a directory, which can be a double-edged sword for the user. The * wildcard can also be used to copy, move, or otherwise operate on multiple files that bear similar names. To focus even more closely on a specific set of file names, you can also use the ? wildcard. Clear examples using the * and ? wildcards are scattered throughout this chapter. For now, simply remember that an asterisk matches everything, while a question mark matches only a single character. Figure 2-4 shows a breakdown of the basic syntax for using wildcards in file copying.

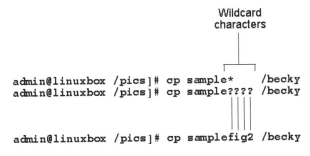

Figure 2-4   Using wildcards in file copying.

COPYING SINGLE FILES

An example of how to copy a single file to a new file in the same directory follows:

```
cp myfile myfile.old
```

This duplicates the file called myfile and gives it a different name. This prevents overwriting and creates a backup copy.

> **The cp -r command enables recursive copying of all files and directories in an existing directory.**

This example shows a file being copied from one directory to another:

```
cp /home/myfile /usr/myfile
```

This works as long as you have permission to write a file in the target directory. If you don't have access, cp returns an error message and the command fails. The command also fails if you have permission to write a file to the directory, but the directory contains a file that you cannot overwrite.

COPYING DIRECTORIES

To copy an entire directory to another, including all files and subdirectories, the syntax is as follows:

```
cp -r <directory> <destination directory>
```

Here is an example:

```
cp -r /usr/me/myoldstuff /usr/me/newstuff
```

The -r forces a recursive copy of everything in the directory. The original directory remains intact. If you wanted to copy only particular files that match a wildcard pattern you can do that, too, as shown in the following:

```
cp -r /usr/me/myoldstuff/*.c /usr/me/newstuff
```

This command copies only files ending in .c to the new directory. In all cases the names will remain the same, as we are not telling the cp command to rename the files.

To copy an entire directory's contents as a subdirectory to another, including all files and subdirectories, while viewing the list of copied files and directories, use the following command:

```
cp -r -v <directory> <destination directory>
```

The -v option forces verbose mode. This can be useful when you want to duplicate the contents of one directory in another and watch what is going on at the same time. For example, let's say you want to copy the entire contents of the /jazz directory to a new directory called /becky:

```
cp -r -v /jazz /becky
```

From the root level (as shown in the Linux prompt), this command copies the entire /jazz directory to the /becky directory, including the /jazz directory itself. This creates an additional level in the path for the /becky directory, which you may not want.

A more efficient way to copy is to *move into the directory* whose contents you want to copy, using the cd command, and then issue a slightly different cp command from the one above:

```
cp -r -v * /becky
```

Note that the command does not list the /jazz directory. Since /jazz is the current directory in which the command is executed (as shown in the prompt), and you are copying its contents, /jazz does not need to be specified in the command! It also provides a verbose display of each file and directory that is copied across to the other directory, as follows:

```
compress -> /becky/compress

cpio -> /becky/cpio

gzip -> /becky/gzip

...
```

COPYING MULTIPLE FILES

Finally, you may wish to copy multiple files of a specific type and not the entire directory. When you create text, graphic, or data files of any type, it is typical and advisable to use easy naming conventions with similar but different names, such as "samplefile1," "samplefile2," and "samplepic1." This is where the * and ? wildcards become useful.

You can move a group of files with similar names in a current directory into a new directory. An example of this follows:

```
cp samplefig* /becky
```

Another way of doing this would be as follows:

```
cp samplefig? /becky
```

This command works if all the desired files have names similar to "samplefig1," "samplefig2," and "samplefig3." In this case, the use of a single asterisk is sufficient to extract all other possibilities regardless of the length of characters. The single question mark only allows one character after the specified string to be matched.

As with MS-DOS, use the * and especially the ? character for pattern matching across multiple filenames for many different command line tasks.

For cases where you have large collections of files with similarly formatted names, such as "01fig01," "03fig07," "10fig21," and "21fig03," the question mark character proves handy for pattern matching.

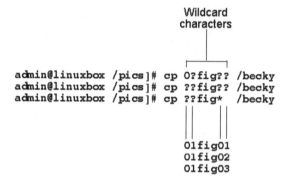

Figure 2-5   More wildcard examples when copying files.

As shown in Figure 2-5, to copy multiple files with similar patterns, try commands like the following:

```
cp 0?fig?? /becky
```

```
cp ??fig?? /becky
```

```
cp ??fig* /becky
```

Many subtleties lurk in the simplest of Linux commands, and users can become quite frustrated. After working with the cp command for awhile, the xfm (X File Manager) program starts to look a lot more attractive. With a little patience, you will become accustomed to the precision demanded by the Linux command line.

Always remember to work only with files that are non-native to the Linux operating system; in other words, files that you have created. Moving and copying other files can cause problems for your system if you don't know exactly what you are doing—and sometimes even if you do!

RENAMING AND MOVING FILES AND DIRECTORIES

The mv command renames files with or without moving them. A common misconception is that the mv command actually copies the original file somewhere else on the disk, then deletes the original, but mv is a lot cleverer than that. All it does is update the i-node table with the new name of the file (since directories do not physically exist on the disk drive). The syntax for mv is illustrated in Figure 2-6.

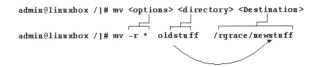

Figure 2-6   Syntax for mv commands.

You should only use the mv command with files that you create on the system, such as text or graphics files. Always keep in mind that Linux programs, and the operating system itself, almost always reside in specific directories. This is no different from any other operating system. Never casually move or delete Linux files.

File renaming and moving commands are quite similar to copying. Two arguments must be provided: the existing filename and the new filename, including any paths that need to be specified. If you don't give the mv command a path, it assumes the current location.

RENAMING AND MOVING SINGLE FILES

To rename a file, issue a command like this:

```
mv bigfile newfilename
```

This command renames the file "bigfile" to the new name "newfilename" in the current directory.

In the following examples, a sample file called "samplefig1" is used to illustrate file moving commands. To move a single file in the current directory to a new directory, type the directory name (the same filename is assumed unless you specify otherwise):

```
mv samplefig1 /becky
```

This simply moves the file from the current directory to the /becky directory.

If you're in the root level and want to do the same operation, use a command such as the following:

```
mv /home/samplefig1 /becky
```

Again, always use the prompt to keep track of your location. This also alerts you to how your command needs to be structured.

RENAMING AND MOVING MULTIPLE FILES

You can use the * or ? wildcard characters to rename more than one file at a time, as in the following examples:

```
mv /home/samplefig* /becky
```

```
mv /home/samplefig? /becky
```

This is useful when you have multiple files with similar names, such as "samplefig1," "samplefig2," and "samplefig3." The use of wildcards with the mv command is illustrated further in Figure 2-7.

Figure 2-7   *Renaming and moving files with the mv command and wildcards.*

RENAMING AND MOVING DIRECTORIES

To rename an entire directory, including all files and subdirectories, the command syntax is the same, as shown here:

```
mv dir1 dir2
```

This renames a directory called "dir1" under the current directory to "dir2." You can rename directories with a change in path, too, as shown by the following:

```
mv /usr/me/dir1 /usr/you/dir1
```

This command alters the absolute path to the directory called "dir 1" from /usr/me to /usr/you. You must have permissions to create directories in the target directory, of course. You can rename the directory while moving it, too. Since directory names and paths are kept only in the i-node table and not physically on the hard drive, the mv command provides a fast way to rename directories without the tedious process of copying files and deleting the old directories.

The command syntax for renaming and moving files is similar to copying. Once you understand copying and moving, the similarities among Linux commands start to become clearer. One good rule to follow is to never be in a hurry when you're copying, renaming, or moving things around.

> **Take care to rename and move only files related to your own work.** *Never* **rename and move operating system files!**

CREATING DIRECTORIES

As a new Linux user, establish yourself on the system by creating a directory into which you can write your data files, assuming that you don't want to use your home directory for everything. This prevents your information from becoming lost in the complicated Linux system. To create directories on your Linux system, use the mkdir command.

The command syntax for the mkdir command is basic: Simply specify the absolute or relative path for the new directory. Unless permissions prevent you from establishing directories in the new location, the directory is instantly created. Since directories don't exist on hard drives as separate entities, only as entries in the i-node table, the process is always fast.

An example of creating a new directory just below the root directory follows:

```
mkdir mygoodstuff
```

This creates a new directory called mygoodstuff directly under root. The path is thus /mygoodstuff. This command works only if you issue it from the root directory. There is no slash as the first character to indicate absolute addressing, and thus it relies on relative paths.

If you want to create a new directory called mynewstuff in an existing Linux directory, such as /home, here's how to do that:

```
mkdir /home/mygoodstuff
```

Of course, you will use your own directory names in place of the names in the examples above. Always keep the current path in mind, and if you are unsure about it, type pwd at the prompt. This example uses absolute paths to specify the location of the new directory.

The mkdir command returns error messages under two conditions: when you have no permission to create the directory or when a file or directory of the same name already exists in the target location. Examples of both error messages look like this:

```
$ mkdir /etc/example
mkdir: cannot make directory: /etc/example: Permission denied
$ mkdir temp
mkdir: cannot make directory: temp: File exists
```

In the first case, the user did not have write permission to the /etc directory, and thus could not create any directory underneath it. In the second example, a file or directory called temp exists already. Linux won't specify whether it's a file or a directory.

DELETING FILES AND DIRECTORIES

You can remove any file you've created (unless you have changed permissions to prevent you from doing so) using the rm, or *remove,* command. Directories can be removed using rm or rmdir, or *remove directory.*

REMOVING FILES

To remove a single file, simply specify its name like this:

```
rm bigfile
```

The file is removed from the directory and the space on the disk is freed up. In this case, we're assuming the file is in the current directory. Otherwise you need to specify an absolute or relative path to the file. In order to delete a file, you must have write permission to the file and appropriate directory permissions.

Wildcards are supported by the rm command, as well. For example, you can delete all the files starting with the four letters abcd like this:

```
rm abcd*
```

The rm command lets you specify multiple files to delete on one line, as long as the filenames are separated by spaces or tabs. For example, this command deletes the files "file1" and "file2" in the current directory, as well as "file3" in the directory /usr/you:

```
rm file1 file2 /usr/you/file3
```

This assumes you have permission to delete the file in the target directory.

As with any Linux command, wildcards are allowed with the rm command. For example, to delete all files ending with .doc in the current directory, issue the following command:

```
rm *.doc
```

When using wildcards, watch out for the following command:

```
rm *
```

Since the wildcard matches everything, including files starting with a period, this instantly wipes out the contents of your directory. Remember: With Linux, there is no undo command! When you delete a file, it is gone forever. Linux is not like DOS, which doesn't actually do anything to the file you erase other than modify the first bit in the File Allocation Table entry. When you delete a file in Linux, the entire entry is removed from the i-node table and the disk space is marked as available. Recovering deleted files is possible in some cases by examining the disk sector by sector, but this is time-consuming, tedious, and far beyond the capabilities of most Linux users.

REMOVING DIRECTORIES

Two Linux commands can be used to delete directories from the system: rmdir and rm. The rmdir command is more restrictive and provides more protection to the casual user. This is a traditional UNIX method of removing directories as it doesn't allow directories with files in them to be deleted. To use the rmdir command, simply specify the name of the directory you want to delete, like this:

```
rmdir /usr/tparker/foo
```

If the directory is empty, it is removed. Although you can use absolute or relative paths to delete directories, you cannot delete a directory you are currently in or one higher up in the directory tree that would leave you in limbo.

As mentioned, the rmdir command deletes only empty directories. If a directory contains any files or other subdirectories, the rmdir command does not execute. Instead you receive an error message like the following:

```
$ rmdir foo

rmdir: foo: Directory not empty
```

The rmdir command doesn't show you what is in the directory. The bottom line is that until the directory is completely empty, including all hidden file (those that start with a period), rmdir cannot remove the directory.

That's where rm comes in. The rm command can be combined with an option that results in a simple, powerful, and quite dangerous capability. The option is -r, which means recursive deletion. When rm is used with the -r option and the name of a directory, the entire contents of the directory and the directory itself are removed immediately. As you can imagine, much destruction can ensue if you misuse this command!

To remove a directory and all the files in it, issue a command likc this:

```
rm -r /usr/me/olddir
```

This removes the /usr/me/olddir directory, all the files in it, and any subdirectories and their files. Obviously, this is much quicker than deleting the files in directories and subdirectories using the rm command, and then deleting the directories using the rmdir command. On the other hand, if you use this command on directories that contain important Linux files (like the root directory, /bin, /etc, and so on), your entire system will be damaged or wiped out in seconds. If that happens you have no choice but to reinstall the software. Therefore, use the rm -r command with great caution!.

For accounts such as root, some Linux versions use a *command alias* to force the rm command to verify each deletion. This adds the -i, or *interactive*, option to the rm command. If you are running the system as the root administrator account, use the -f command option to force rm to delete files without this interaction.

If security is properly set on the Linux machine, regular users can not delete anything from the system except the files they own themselves.

FINDING FILES

The find command is one of the most powerful and useful commands available at the Linux command line. If you don't know where to find a particular file, but know the name of the file you want, or even just a piece of the name, the find command is the perfect tool. Find is also useful for locating groups of files with similar names. Using find is a great introduction to the intricacies of the Linux command line: no harm can come to any data through using it, and find makes use of many command line conventions. Review Figure 2-8 for an overview of how to use the find command.

Searching for a file and opening it in a Linux application:
```
admin@linuxbox /]# find –name samplefig1 –exec gimp {} \;
```
Searching for file patterns for a specific user:
```
admin@linuxbox /]# find –name samplefig* –user angela
```
Searching for any files created by a specific user:
```
admin@linuxbox /]# find –name *.* –user angela
```

Figure 2-8   Permutations of the find command.

The basic syntax of the find command is:

```
find startinglocation -options
```

This may seem simple, but find takes some practice. A few examples will help make the find command a little clearer. The startinglocation is the place in which find is going to start looking, and it searches recursively through the directory structure from there. The -options area is where you add options to refine your search. There are numerous options for find, most of which you'll never use. Key find options include those listed in Table 2-3.

Table 2-3   Commands for find

Command	Description
-name	Tells find to locate files whose name matches the specified pattern. This is probably the most frequently used option.
-print	Displays the entire path of each matching file in the search. (Without this option, you don't see anything!)
-user	Searches for files belonging to a specific user.
-exec *command* **{ } \;**	Allows you to automatically run a specified Linux command or program on each matching file. The brackets are added as the argument for the find option to automatically substitute the matching file. Note the presence of the backslash-semicolon pair (\;). This is called an *escaped semicolon,* in case you didn't know.
-atime <+t, -t, t>	Finds files last *accessed* more than a specified number of days ago (+t), less than a specified number of days ago (-t), or precisely a specified number of days ago (t).
-ctime <+n, -n, n>	Finds files last *changed* more than a specified number of days ago (+n), less than a specified number of days ago (-n), or precisely a specified number of days ago (n).
-mtime <+n, -n, n>	Locates files last *modified* more than a specified number of days ago (+n), less than a specified number of days ago (-n), or precisely a specified number of days ago (n).
-perm	Finds files with a specific permission level, specified as a three-digit octal code.
-type *<type>*	Locates any files of a specified type. Possible argument types include: b for block device files, c for character device files, d for directories, p for pipes, l for symbolic links, s for sockets, and f for regular files.

Now let's look at some common uses of find. To start, here is an example that illustrates the basic syntax:

```
find / -name samplefig* -print
```

This command starts searching at the root directory, descends through every subdirectory, and locates all files with a name matching the samplefig pattern. Every match is displayed on the screen. If you left off the -print option, find does the search but may not show you the results. The following shows another find example with some output from the command:

```
find /usr/tparker -name chapter01 -print

/usr/tparker/books/linux/chapter01

/usr/tparker/books/windowsnt/chapter01

/usr/tparker/books/unix/oldstuff/chapter01
```

In this case, there is no use of wildcards and there is a specified directory from which to start the search. As you can see, three matches are found. The full directory path to each match is displayed by the find command.

Not all versions of find require you to use the -print option. Some versions have been modified to automatically include this capability. If you don't use -print and you don't see any output to your find command, try the command again with the -print option. Of course, you may not see output because the search did not find anything that matched.

In the following example, which covers the entire filesystem, there are some error messages generated by the find command. This is because the user issuing the command does not have permission to access and search the listed directories. The only way around this permission problem is to log in as root.

```
$ find / -name chapter01 -print

find: cannot chdir to /dev/X: Permission denied

find: cannot chdir to /etc/rc2.d: Permission denied

find: cannot chdir to /etc/rc0.d: Permission denied

find: cannot chdir to /etc/ps: Permission denied

find: cannot chdir to /etc/sm: Permission denied

...
```

If you don't want to see the error messages, redirect them to /dev/null, like this:

```
$ find / -name chapter01 -print 2>/dev/null
```

When output is redirected to /dev/null, it is lost. Since we are directing only the standard error (file descriptor 2) to /dev/null, only the error messages are discarded. The resulting output is the matches you want and none of the permission messages.

To find files that you know have a specific extension but whose name you don't know, use the following syntax:

```
find /dirname -name *.old -print
```

FINDING AND EXECUTING PROGRAMS ON FILES

One of the beauties of the find command is its ability to execute programs on located files. Let's say you want to edit a particular configuration file but don't want to navigate through the whole system to find it. To find this specific file and execute a program on it, such as a text editor, execute a command similar to the following:

```
find / -name smb.conf -exec emacs {} \;
```

This command does two things: locates the file smb.conf and launches the Emacs text editor to edit that specific file. This is a clever way to save yourself some work and shows off the power of the find command.

The use of the curly brackets pair and the escaped semicolon are required with the -exec option for find. The bracket pair argument is used to substitute the "found" file (smb.conf) as the argument for the executable program that's specified in the find command. The \; tells Linux to close the command.

Here's another example, in which the Linux GIMP graphics editing program is invoked in the find command to open a graphics file:

```
find -name samplefig1 -exec gimp {} \;
```

FINDING FILES OWNED BY A PARTICULAR USER

To locate any files of a specific naming pattern owned by a particular user, use the following syntax:

```
find / -name sample* -user angela -print
```

This command finds all file starting with sample that are owned by the user angela. To locate *all* files of any naming pattern owned by a particular user, change the syntax as follows:

```
find /-name * -user angela
```

Remember that permission denied messages will appear if these commands, which are starting at the root directory, are run by a regular user. Instead, redirect the error messages to /dev/null and use a better starting location for the search. For example, if all the user files are in the directory /usr and the subdirectories beneath it, start the search there.

FINDING FILES OF A SPECIFIC TYPE

To find all files that end in the extension .conf in the current directory, type this command:

```
find . -name *.conf
```

Note the use of the period. This tells find to search within the current directory and any subdirectories underneath it.

USING REDIRECTION

Linux' command line provides several powerful and handy shortcuts for getting work done. The most immediately useful is I/O redirection. Table 2-4 shows some of the most common characters used for redirection.

Table 2-4   Symbols Used for Redirection

Symbol	Description
>	Sends the output of the command to a file or device.
>> <filename>	Appends the output of the command to a file.
<	Uses the contents of a file as input rather than the command line.
|	Indicates a pipe, which is a "conduit" to use the output of one command as the input of another command. Pipes can be used to connect several command actions together.

Redirection is something anyone approaching Linux can use right away. In many cases, exploring the operating system can be overwhelming. If you don't know where to find something, you can start by using the ls command. If, however, the directory is so large that it is difficult to locate the desired item, then you will need to try some other methods for searching the operating system. Here are a few of them.

SENDING OUTPUT TO A FILE

When you use the redirection operator, the output that would normally go to the screen is redirected to a file. For example, you can send the results of an ls directory listing to a file by using the following syntax:

```
ls -sR > listing
```

This command sends a complete, recursive directory listing of the current directory to a file called "listing." Note the use of the combined arguments in the ls command. This is a handy trick for viewing the contents of a huge directory, such as /usr, as a readable text file. Even though you don't see anything on the screen, the file is created. If the file already exists, the redirection operator removes the old contents and replaces it with the new output. There are no warnings generated by the system for you. This is an easy way to accidentally lose a lot of information. Thus, make sure that the file does not already exist before you redirect to a file.

Here's another example of redirection. To find all files of a particular type in any specified Linux directory, and to send the output to a text file, type a command similar to the following:

```
find /etc -name *.conf -print > conftext
```

Instead of displaying the results of the find command on the screen, the redirection argument sends the find results to a text file. If you open the new file in a text editor such as vi or emacs, you find the actual text content that would otherwise be displayed on screen. This method is a great way to preserve the results of a complicated command for further study.

APPENDING OUTPUT TO A FILE

The redirection operator, as we have mentioned, overwrites any existing content of a file that may exist. To prevent this, you can make use of the append operator. This simply tacks the output of the command on to the end of the existing file. If you specify a file that does not exist, it is created. For example, the following command appends the results of the who command (which lists everyone currently logged on the system) to the end of the file called "logfile":

```
who >> logfile
```

The logfile file is not overwritten. This provides such capabilities as writing shell programs that keep logs updated.

The append and redirect operators can be used for any Linux command that generates output. The only difference between the two commands is whether an existing file's contents are preserved or not.

USING FILE CONTENTS AS INPUT

Related to the append operator, which redirects output, is the ability to redirect input. Suppose you had a file that you wanted to mail to someone else using the Linux mail system. You could specify that file as input to the mail command like this:

```
mail tparker << myfile
```

This command will take the contents of myfile and mail it to the user called tparker. This type of redirection works with any command that accepts input (not all Linux commands do). The input almost always comes from a file, but it could be any valid device.

USING PIPES TO SEND OUTPUT TO INPUT

Pipes are misunderstood and sometimes scary for newcomers to Linux. In truth, they are remarkably simple once you understand their purpose. A pipe sends the output of one command to the input of another. For example, suppose you want to count the number of users currently logged on the system. The list of users is generated from the who command, and the number of lines in the output can be counted with the wc -l command, resulting in the number of users on the system. If we save the output of the who command to a file and then count the number of lines in the file, the process looks like this:

```
who > tempfile
```

```
wc -l tempfile
```

This works just fine, but involves two commands and a temporary file. Instead, a pipe can be used to send the output of who directly to the input of wc, like this:

```
who | wc -l
```

The result will be the number of lines in the who output equally the number of users on the system.

A couple of other examples should show the utility of pipes. Suppose you want to count all the subdirectories in a specific directory. This can be accomplished with the following command:

```
ls - lF dir1 | grep -c /
```

This may look strange at first glance, but becomes clear once you follow the logic through. The ls command displays the contents of a directory, including files and subdirectories, in this case for the directory called dir1. The l option to ls specifies a full directory listing including permissions and owners. The F option adds a slash to the end of every directory name. So, if the directory names are tagged with a slash, all we need do is count the number of lines in the output that have a slash on them. This is done by first sending the output of the ls command to the input of the grep command, which is a pattern-matching utility, and then by counting the number of lines with a slash. The -c option displays the count. The same results can be achieved by sending the output of the grep command to wc with another pipe, like this:

```
ls - lF dir1 | grep / | wc -l
```

> The key to using pipes is to remember that they work from command to command. Redirection always works from command to file or device.

Pipes and redirection can be combined on a command line. For example, saving the output of the directory counting exercise in a file is accomplished like this:

```
ls - lF dir1 | grep / | wc -l > file1
```

When you are used to Linux you will find pipes extremely handy. This is especially true if you become involved in shell programming.

USING THE COMMAND HISTORY

One of the main ways to compensate for the complexities of the Linux command line is to make heavy use of the *command history*. At the command line, press the up arrow key to view the commands you have typed previously. The command history allows you to edit and re-execute any Linux commands that you ran earlier in the terminal screen. It is possible to save yourself a lot of work when you have to issue repetitive, complicated commands.

> Although the bash, pdksh, and tcsh shells included with most Linux distributions have command history triggered by the cursor keys, don't assume all shells behave this way. Some lack history entirely and some require special commands and keystrokes to access history.

Being able to edit a command line makes repetitive tasks easier, and lets you correct logic or typing errors quickly. Some editing tricks are shown in Table 2-5.

Table 2-5   Methods for Viewing the Command History

Method	Description
Left arrow key and right arrow key	The left arrow key moves the command cursor back through the command text; the right arrow key moves the cursor to the right through the command line.
Del key	Deletes the character to the left of the command cursor.
Quick editing	Once you have edited your command, simply press Enter to execute the command. There's no need to go back to the end of the edited command to execute it. No matter how far back in the history the command originated, your newly edited version is promoted to be the last-executed command.
Automatic insert mode	When you use the command history, Linux defaults to Insert mode, which means that you can place the cursor anywhere in the command line and type in your new command text without erasing existing text.

Another highly useful technique is to use the fc command to list the contents of the command history. To list the history of the current terminal screen, type this:

```
fc -l
```

You can even use redirection to place the contents of the command history into a text file, called history in the next example:

```
fc -l > history
```

This is a great way to create permanent records of your work and can facilitate the learning process. It also allows scripts and step-by-step guides to be built for future use.

CHECKING DISK SPACE

Linux makes it easy to check the status of your hard disk. To do so from a terminal window, simply type the following:

```
df
```

The results are printed on the screen and look something like this:

```
Filesystem  1024-blocks  Used    Available  Capacity  Mounted on
/dev/hda2   1336174      893241  373885     70%       /
```

Note that the Capacity value shows the amount of occupied disk space—not the actual size of the disk! Not all systems use 1kB blocks.

To view your disk space in a more "human-readable" format, type the following:

```
df -h
```

The results are printed on the screen and look similar to what is shown below:

Filesystem	Size	Used	Available	Capacity	Mounted on
/dev/hda2	1.3G	872M	374M	70%	/

There are other commands that tell you about disk usage, but df is the easiest and most readable command included with Linux.

CHECKING MEMORY USAGE

Finding out whether the system is short of RAM is important. When you run out of RAM, the system starts using swap space on the disk, and slows down noticeably. The free command is used to tell you the amount of used RAM and free RAM. From a terminal window, type free with no arguments. The results are printed on the screen, listing the status of your system memory(in kilobytes by default). It will look something like the following:

	Total	used	free	shared	buffers	cached
Mem:	127716	48348	79368	29216	11076	26356
-/+ buffers/cache:			21924	105792		
Swap:	130748	0	130748			

To view memory status in megabytes, type this:

```
free -m
```

The results appear something like the following:

	Total	used	free	shared	buffers	cached
Mem:	128	48	80	29	11	26
-/+ buffers/cache:		22	105			
Swap:	130	0	130			

USING LINUX-BASED MS-DOS COMMANDS TO COPY FILES

File management commands and functions abound in Linux. One example is the fairly easy methods Linux provides for mounting, copying to and from, and viewing DOS-formatted floppies and other types of disks. There are a series of commands for this basic file management that harness the MS-DOS syntax, all of which begin with the letter "M" to indicate an MS-DOS command under Linux:

- ◆ **mdir**:   Display the contents of a Linux directory.
- ◆ **mcopy**:   Copy a file or selection of files.
- ◆ **mattrib**:   Display and change file attributes.
- ◆ **mdel**:   Delete a file or files.
- ◆ **mformat**: Format a floppy with the FAT file system.
- ◆ **mtype**:   Display the text of a DOS file.
- ◆ **mmount**: Mount a DOS-formatted disk onto the Linux system (supports only floppies and not CDs).
- ◆ **mmd**:   Create a new directory on a DOS-formatted disk.
- ◆ **mren**:   Rename a DOS file.
- ◆ **mcd**:   Change directory.

The commands listed here apply only to DOS-formatted disks mounted on the Linux system. If you try to apply an mdir command to a Linux-formatted disk, you will receive an error message like the following:

```
Can't open /dev/fd0: Device not configured
```

While DOS commands cannot be executed on the host Linux disk, you can, however, copy a file from the Linux hard disk to a DOS floppy.

With the "M" commands, if you have to copy a file back and forth between the two systems and don't have a network, you still have a way to do it.

> **By default, Linux uses the /dev/fd0 designation for the floppy drive. The "M" commands allow you to use the DOS-standard A: designation instead.**

MOUNTING AN DOS-FORMATTED DISK

To mount a DOS floppy diskette in your Linux system's floppy drive, issue the following command:

```
mmount --V a:
```

The mmount command enables the mounting of a DOS-formatted floppy disk in a Linux system.

CHECKING THE CONTENTS OF A DOS-FORMATTED DISK

To check the contents of the mounted floppy disk, type the following:

```
mdir a:
```

The floppy's contents (if any) are listed, as shown in Figure 1-21.

COPYING A FILE FROM LINUX TO A DOS-FORMATTED DISK

To copy a file from your Linux system to a DOS-formatted floppy, use the mcopy command, as follows:

```
mcopy <filename> a:
```

Here is an example:

```
mcopy 01fig01.tif a:
```

This is useful when you have Linux text files that you want to use in a more familiar text editor, such as Microsoft Word.

COPYING A FILE FROM A DOS-FORMATTED DISK TO LINUX

To copy a file from a DOS-formatted floppy to the current directory in your Linux system, type the following:

```
mcopy a:<filename>
```

Here is an example:

```
mcopy a:01fig01.tif
```

S U M M A R Y

In spite of the length of this chapter, we have merely scratched the surface. Throughout this book, many more command-line examples are offered for numerous tasks. There are more advanced Linux books that treat command-line subjects in detail. This chapter instead provides you with the fundamentals for how to use Linux effectively and productively.

The next chapter moves on to another important and useful topic: how to configure hardware devices to work under Linux—without programming.

CONFIGURING DEVICES TO WORK UNDER LINUX

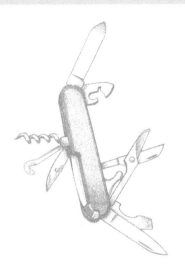

It is no fun using Linux if you cannot make some of your devices work. Items that Mac and PC users take for granted—such as modems, Zip drives, and printers—are not exactly plug-and-play under Linux. Compounding the problem, many Linux books drown the reader in detail and don't properly set the context. This is because they are written for people who already administer Linux systems or have a strong command of UNIX. Since this book isn't written for that audience, it would be incomplete without some practical methods for using hardware devices in your system.

Despite the somewhat intimidating appearance of the Linux command line, it isn't as hard as it appears to set up many normal PC devices. This book provides concrete, step-by step procedures for getting the following devices up and running under Linux:

- Floppy drives (mount, umount, mke2fs, mkfs)
- Zip drives (mount, umount, mke2fs, mkfs)
- CD-ROMs (mount, umount)
- Printers
- Network cards (make, insmod, ifconfig, route, ping)

Setting up a modem to connect to the Internet is discussed in Chapter 5, *Basic Network Administration.*

You'll also use the cat, emacs, and dmesg commands to view and edit configuration files in your system. The cat command is a simple utility for text I/O and manipulation, and can be used as a quick way to view short text files. Emacs is a powerful text editor that can be run in a Linux terminal screen or under X. Emacs is several generations beyond the ancient vi editor in ease of use, and is the standard editor used in this book.

This is not your mother's operating system. It is the dream operating system for compulsive tinkerers. There is no way to really understand how devices work under Linux (and UNIX) without having a look at some fairly obscure aspects of the system. The two preliminary items described here—device names and the fstab file system table—are not ends in themselves; they are merely tools to help you get your job done. Unfortunately, Linux doesn't provide a graphical interface for setting up disk devices. This chapter is the next best thing. By the time you finish reading this chapter, you will have a strong command of how to set up common hardware devices under Linux.

INTRODUCING LINUX DEVICE NAMES

Linux device names are organized as *device files* in your system.

Linux device files always reside in the /dev directory.

Hundreds of device files exist in the /dev directory, and the chances are good that you will never use most of them. Each file provides an abstraction layer between the operating system and a hardware device in the system. For example, the /dev/mouse file is used by Linux for reading mouse input; the /dev/modem file handles input and output for an installed modem; and the /dev/fd0 designates the internal floppy drive in the computer. This is important because when data is copied to an area like the /dev/fd0 device file, that data is actually copying to the device that is managed by the file—in this case, the floppy drive. Figure 3-1 illustrates.

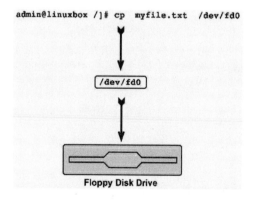

Figure 3-1   Device files provide an abstraction layer between the operating system and hardware devices.

Newer versions of Linux fully support EIDE and Ultra-DMA disk drives, including hard drives, IDE CD-ROMs, and IDE Zip drives. Those devices automatically configure themselves on the PC's BIOS when they're connected, and Linux allows you to make use of these devices almost automatically. Although SCSI devices are uncommon on home PCs due to their cost, Linux works perfectly with them, and they are ideal for UNIX and Linux servers.

You need to know the basics of how IDE works on current-generation PCs. EIDE and Ultra-DMA both support four devices on two separate IDE channels: a Primary IDE channel and a Secondary IDE channel. Each can support two devices: a Master and a Slave. If you've ever installed a disk drive in a PC, they work just the same way on the hardware level under Linux as they do under Windows.

A perfect introduction to Linux device names involves those four EIDE devices, and Table 3-1 further explains the differences between them.

Table 3-1   Four Types of EIDE Devices

EIDE Device	Linux Device Name	Typical Devices Used
Primary IDE Master	hda (/dev/hda)	Bootable hard disk.
Primary IDE Slave	hdb (/dev/hdb)	Such items as a second hard disk, CD-ROM drive, Zip drive, or tape drive.
Secondary IDE Master	hdc (/dev/hdc)	Such items as a CD-ROM drive, or second hard disk.
Secondary IDE Slave	hdd (/dev/hdd)	Such items as a Zip or tape drive.

Most PCs have a single hard drive and a single CD-ROM, usually set as the master devices on the primary and secondary EIDE chains. Each EIDE device requires a physical jumper setting. This setting is labeled on most hard disks sold today. Most hard drives and other EIDE devices have a jumper that sits on two pins, usually labelled MA for Master or SL for Slave. Having two masters or two slaves on the same chain causes conflicts and the devices will usually fail to work.

When you install Linux, you often see the listing for the CD-ROM drive as CD-ROM on /dev/hdc. This indicates a standard EIDE drive type under Linux, as noted above.

Disk drives are one of the most important parts of your system. When you install Linux, you are already successfully using devices such as /dev/hd0 and /dev/cdrom. But what if you have other disk drives that you want to use? How do you start making use of some of those hundreds of confusing device files in the /dev directory? The next step is to find out about the /etc/fstab file.

INTRODUCING /ETC/FSTAB AND FILE SYSTEMS

Information about hard drives, CD-ROMs, optical and magnetic removable devices, and other filesystem holders are all kept in the /etc/fstab file. The fstab file, which stands for file system table, is a normal ASCII file that may be altered (with care) using any editor. The fstab file is a special file in your Linux system and is necessary for the system to boot properly. The fstab must always be located in the /etc directory unless special installation configurations are employed.

The /etc/fstab file is where the device settings are created for all your disk drives, including drives that your system accesses from the network, and others that are not mounted or accessed automatically by the Linux system. The fstab table is a key part of your Linux configuration. An example from a test system is shown below:

Device	Mount point	File system type	Mount options	Dump frequency, Pass number
/dev/hda	/	ext2	defaults	1 1
/dev/hda1	swap	swap	defaults	0 0
/dev/fd0	/mnt/floppy	ext2	noauto	0 0
/dev/cdrom	/mnt/cdrom	iso9660	noauto,ro	0 0
none	/proc	proc	defaults	0 0
/dev/hdd	/mnt/zip	ext2	noauto,rw	0 0

This etc/fstab file shows all active file systems, their mount points, and their characteristics. First, the *device* is the device file in the /dev directory used as the abstraction layer between the device and the operating system.

The *mount point* is the directory used by the operating system to determine where a physical device appears; as in, a floppy disk drive appearing with the name floppy. Any name can be used, although a name that indicates the type of device is most sensible. The /mnt directory provides those mount points to your Linux system. This can become confusing, but the idea is that every disk partition used in Linux has its own special directory through which the partition's actual contents are managed. Those are the mount points. Each active partition's mount point is listed in /etc/fstab. For your Linux boot disk, the mount point is "/", or the root directory, as shown above.

The *File system type* defines what kind of file system the device or partition uses. This could be ext2 (local Linux file system), swap (Linux Swap partition), iso9660 (CD-ROM drives), msdos (DOS-formatted disks), hpfs (OS/2 drives), nfs (Network File System), and numerous others. Note that Linux's fdisk program allows the creation of many different file systems on a disk partition, and the /etc/fstab file shows the active file system type on each partition.

Mount options determine the mount type. This is whether the partition is read-only (ro), read-write (rw), and so on. This is shown in our example etc/fstab file above, along with these other mount options:

◆	**auto**:	Allows for the specified partition to be mounted automatically by Linux with a mount –a command.
◆	**noauto**:	Prevents mounting with the –a option.
◆	**defaults**:	The best choice for general operation with disk partitions, *if you know what you are doing*.
◆	**nouser**:	Prevents all but privileged users, such as root, from gaining access to the mounted partition.

This is only a partial listing of many available mount options.

Linux supports about as many disk partitions as you could possibly want in a computer. You can have dozens or even hundreds of disk partitions available to a single Linux system. This is possible because every disk partition is mapped to a specific directory on the computer, which is normally located in the /mnt directory. Paired with a device file from the /dev directory, disk devices and partitions can be accessed through the Linux computer.

Linux allows mounting of an DOS-formatted disk in the floppy drive or in other removable drives, such as a Zip. You can move and copy Linux files to and from a DOS-formatted floppy, or you can format floppies in the Linux file system.

For easiest file portability between Windows and Linux systems, specify the msdos file system type in proper entries in the etc/fstab file. For example, if you have a floppy drive and a Zip drive in your system, specifying msdos as the file system type means that you can insert a normal DOS- or Windows-formatted disk, mount it, and read and write files to it. You'll see how to do this a little later.

VIEWING CURRENT CONFIGURATIONS WITH DMESG AND EMACS

It is time to learn viewing and editing configurations. You will be working with configuration files for the rest of this chapter and throughout most of this book.

> **The cat command types the contents of a file on the terminal screen. Emacs and vi allow you to edit files. For most newcomers to Linux, Emacs is probably easier.**

When Linux boots up, the status messages might go by too quickly for you see what's happening during the process, although everything that occurs during bootup is reported on the terminal screen. It's important to keep tabs on what Linux does when it starts up. It's also important to know how to use file editing and viewing features in Linux to keep tabs on your system and to make changes to your system's configuration.

Linux stores operating system bootup messages in a file called messages, which is located in the /var/log directory. Every time you reboot, the latest set of operating system startup messages is appended to the end of the messages file. These files can become large and unwieldy. They may be saved in several different files in numerical sequence, such as messages.1, messages.2, and so on.

VIEWING MESSAGES USING DMESG

The most efficient way to view the boot messages for your system is to use the dmesg command. To begin viewing your system's messages and configuration files, type the following command at a Linux command prompt:

```
dmesg | less
```

This command uses the less viewer to enable scrolling up and down the dmesg output. Press Q to close the less program. See Figure 3-2 for an example.

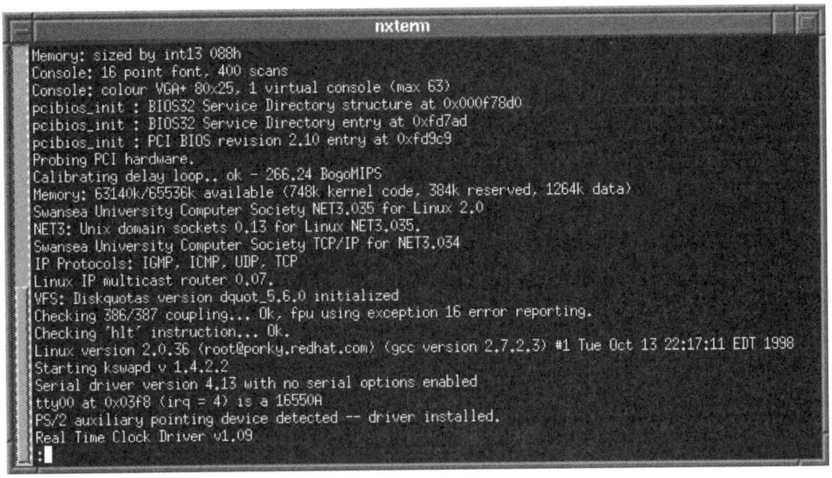

Figure 3-2 Viewing bootup messages through dmesg and less in an Xterm screen.

VIEWING MESSAGES WITH EMACS

Alternatively, you can use redirection to send the dmesg contents to a file. The following shows the syntax:

```
dmesg > bootmessages.txt
```

Run emacs to view that file by typing the following:

```
emacs bootmessages.txt
```

The editor pops up and displays the messages text file.

VIEWING THE /ETC/FSTAB CONFIGURATION FILE WITH EMACS

To view the current disk configuration in the etc/fstab file, run emacs to view it, and possibly to edit it:

```
emacs /etc/fstab
```

Emacs is probably the most usable text editor offered in Linux. Although not as simple as Microsoft Notepad, it does offer a mouse- and menu-driven interface (unlike the unintuitve vi editor), and it can be run in either a terminal screen or X. It is also an Internet News reader and an e-mail reader. You will use the Files, Edit and Search menus the most.

In emacs, once you select a menu option, you must type in its required value at the bottom of the emacs screen. For example, after selecting File I Open, you type the path and name of the file at the bottom of the emacs screen, and then press Enter to open it.

As is so typical with Linux, there are many different ways to do the same thing. You can use the more and cat commands to view the same information. For relative strangers to Linux, Emacs is more intuitive, and dmesg allows the most efficient view of your system's boot sequence.

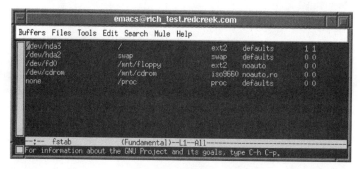

Figure 3-3   Using cat for a quick view of a configuration file.

WORKING WITH A FLOPPY DRIVE

Turning now to specific device configuration, we behold the humble floppy drive. When you learn how to work with floppy drives, you are also learning most of what you need to know to work with other types of removable disk drives. Since a floppy is by far the most common type of removable disk, that is where we start.

MOUNTING A FLOPPY DISK

The mount command is one of Linux's most important administrative commands for working with disks on the local Linux machine and on the network. The mount command's syntax works as follows:

```
mount —o <options> [-a —F —r —t …] <device name> <mount point>
```

An example is shown in Figure 3-4.

```
                                nxterm
[root@linuxbox /root]# mount -t msdos /dev/fd0 /mnt/floppy
[root@linuxbox /root]# ls /mnt/floppy
03fig013       help.exe      netware        pktdrv        winnt
diag.exe       linux         ngrpci.inf     sco
filepath.dat   mainmenu.dat  ngrsvid.exe    wfw311
help           ndis2dos      oemsetup.inf   win95_98
[root@linuxbox /root]#
```

Figure 3-4   Mounting and checking the contents of a Linux floppy disk.

At minimum, specify the mount point of the desired disk partition. An exception occurs the –a option is used. In that case, all file systems listed in the /etc/fstab file are mounted automatically. Table 3-2 explains a other commands to use with mount.

Always remember to use the umount command whenever swapping floppy disks or removable media, or you may corrupt the disk's contents.

Table 3-2   Commands to Use with mount

Command	Description
-a	Mounts automatically all file systems listed in etc/fstab.
-F	If combined with the –a option, the –F option mounts simultaneously all file systems listed in the etc/fstab file. F stands for Fork—a process that breaks out multiple instances of the mount command that execute simultaneously.
-o <options>	Provides administrative options that can be specified singly or in multiples separated by commas. A few of the many options include async, auto, noauto, ro (read-only), rw (read-write), and user (allow an ordinary user to mount the file system).
-r	Mount the file system as read-only.
-t <file system type>	Not required if the file system is specified in fstab. Specified and supported file system types include iso9660, msdos, ext2, hpfs, nfs, smbfs, proc, and umsdos. Must be used with the device name—such as /dev/fd0—if the file system type is not present in etc/fstab.
-v	Verbose execution.

Floppy drives and CDs are configured automatically to work under Linux. It takes a few simple steps to enable the use of a floppy for copying or reading files

To access a floppy disk in your Linux system, insert a floppy diskette, and type the following mount command at a Linux command prompt:

```
mount /dev/fd0 /mnt/floppy
```

This command works by default for Linux-formatted floppy disks. This tells the operating system to mount the floppy device in the directory /mnt/floppy. If you then use cd to change to /mnt/floppy, you will see the floppy's directory contents.

To mount a DOS-formatted floppy diskette, issue the following command:

```
mount –t msdos /dev/fd0 /mnt/floppy
```

Note that the –t option is required for mounting a DOS-type floppy, along with the Linux device name (/dev/fd0). If the MS-DOS file format is listed in the etc/fstab file, you wont have to do this.

Before removing the floppy diskette, type the following command:

```
umount /mnt/floppy
```

The mount command provides a large number of options and offers great flexibility. Such flexibility can be confusing. A good way to cut down on the complexity is to use the /etc/fstab file to list the file systems and device names you plan to use most often. Methods for doing this are described in a later section of this chapter.

A common error is to type unmount instead of umount when you want to unmount a device. You'll get used to using umount, but you could cheat and alias the command to unmount as well!

FORMATTING A LINUX FLOPPY DISK

You can format floppy disks for use under Linux using the mke2fs command. The mke2fs command creates Linux Native file systems on a specified disk or partition, whether that be a floppy disk, removable disk, or a hard disk partition. Under Linux, the act of creating a new file system on a disk partition renders the disk readable by the operating system. This is more familiarly called *formatting* in other operating systems.

Only privileged users, administrators, and the root account can use the mke2fs command. This helps to prevent average users from accidentally ruining a disk.

The basic syntax of the mke2fs command is:

```
mke2fs <file system> <device name> <options>
```

The mke2fs command provides a variety of options, a few of which are explained in Table 3-3.

Table 3-3   Commands to Use with mke2fs

Command	Description
-c	Performs a read-only test for bad blocks on the floppy disk before creating the file system.
-o <file system>	The -o option overrides the default file system for the mke2fs command. Typing the name of the file system after the -o option may allow the use of other file systems for formatting.
<device name>	The Linux device name as specified in the /dev directory and possibly listed in the etc/fstab file.
-L <volume name>	Adds a specified volume name to a newly-formatted disk or partition.
-v	Verbose execution.

Bear in mind that this command can be used with Zip disks and other removable drives, as will be demonstrated later in this chapter.

To format a floppy disk, you can simply place the desired floppy disk into the drive, and run the mke2fs command *without* mounting the disk! Type the following command at the Linux command prompt, as shown in Figure 3-5:

```
mke2fs /dev/fd0 1440
```

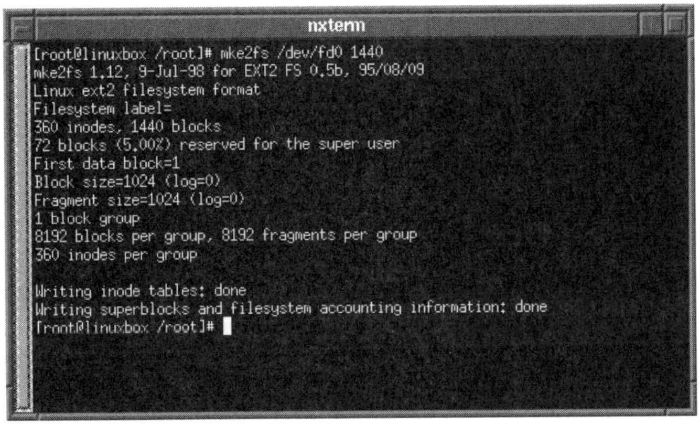

Figure 3-5   Using the mke2fs command to format a diskette.

By default, this command formats a floppy disk with the Linux Native file system. For trading files back and forth with other Linux users, this can be very handy

To view the disk's contents, mount the floppy with the command:

```
mount /mnt/floppy
```

Bear in mind that the mount command works only if the etc/fstab file is configured correctly for the appropriate file system. The default will work for this example.

Then type an ls command:

```
ls /mnt/floppy
```

Remember to run the umount /mnt/floppy command before removing the floppy!

WORKING WITH A CD-ROM DRIVE

Mounting a CD-ROM drive is similar to mounting a floppy drive. The CD-ROM entry is already in the /etc/fstab file when you first install the operating system and should never be changed. It should look something like this:

```
/dev/cdrom     /mnt/cdrom      iso9660     noauto,ro    0 0
```

To mount a CD-ROM disc, type the following mount command at a Linux command prompt:

```
mount /dev/cdrom /mnt/cdrom
```

To view the CD's contents, type an ls command such as the following:

```
ls /mnt/cdrom
```

Many versions of Linux come with supplementary CDs containing free software or trial versions of programs such as WordPerfect or Sybase. Mounting the CD enables you to read the contents of these Linux-formatted disks and access their contents.

Figure 3-6 provides an example of successfully mounting an viewing the contents of a CD.

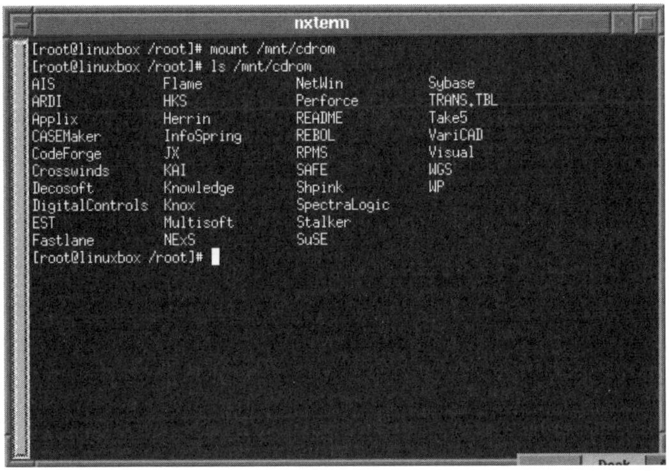

Figure 3-6   Mounting and checking the contents of a Linux CD-ROM disk.

WORKING WITH AN IDE ZIP DRIVE

In general, it is easier to work with IDE Zip drives than any other Zip type (such as SCSI or parallel port versions). Installed IDE Zip drives immediately appear in the computer's BIOS without installing other drivers (assuming the system supports EIDE or Ultra-DMA). You can immediately begin accessing a Zip through Linux's fdisk command.

The first thing to do is keep an eye on Linux while it boots. The operating system should automatically detect the presence of the Zip drive in the system. Putting a disk in the drive forces Linux to report the disk's capacity and provide it with a /dev/hddX assignment.

MOUNTING A ZIP DISK

For a quick way to mount a DOS-formatted Zip disk, without editing etc/fstab or running fdisk and mke2fs, issue the following command:

```
mount —t msdos /dev/hdd /mnt/zip
```

The MS-DOS-formatted Zip disk is mounted and you can access it normally under Linux. Other methods of doing this are also possible.

By default, Linux generally only creates two mount points in the /mnt directory: cdrom and floppy. To enable Zip operation on your Linux system, issue a mkdir command, such as the following:

```
mkdir /mnt/zip
```

This creates the new directory that can be used as a mount point for your ZIP disk. Your mount point *could* be anywhere you want on the Linux system, as long as you can always remember where it is! Placing a new zip directory in the /mnt directory works well and adheres to the same methods described for mounting a floppy and a CD-ROM. It's also easier to remember. No files need to be placed in the directory afterwards.

ENABLING PERMANENT ZIP DRIVE OPERATION

To permanently enable Zip drive operation in your Linux system, open your favorite text editor under Linux, and add the following line to the /etc/fstab file:

```
/dev/hdd    /mnt/zip    ext2    auto,rw   0 0
```

As noted earlier, /dev/hdd is the EIDE secondary slave disk designation. If necessary, change the disk designation to match your Zip drive. The mount point is /mnt/zip. Note also that ext2 is specified for Linux Native as the file system type.

Create a zip directory in the /mnt directory using the following command (make sure to keep track of your current path):

```
mkdir /mnt/zip
```

FORMATTING A ZIP DISK

Insert a Zip disk into the drive. For this exercise, make sure the contents of the disk are things you can live without.

At the Linux command prompt, type the following command:

```
fdisk /dev/hdd
```

This runs the fdisk program and forces it to operate on the installed disk in the Zip drive. Note that the disk isn't mounted yet!

Use fdisk to remove any pre-existing partitions on the Zip disk and to create a new Linux system partition. You my have to remove several oddball partitions on a Zip disk. Linux does not accurately view the partition contents of Zip disks, and will show several of them when you type "P" to display the partition table.

Next, use the mke2fs command to format the Zip disk so that Linux can read and write to it, as follows:

```
mke2fs /dev/hdd
```

Finally, issue a mount command at the Linux prompt, like so:

```
mount /dev/hdd /mnt/zip
```

You can now access the Zip drive with ls, cd and cp commands, and read or write data to the Zip disk in Linux format.

To eject the Zip disk from the Zip drive, type the following at a Linux prompt:

```
umount /mnt/zip
```

The umount command unmounts a disk's file system from Linux. In many cases, such as Zip drives, you will not be able to physically eject the disk without using the umount command.

The next section shows how to permanently set up your system for more convenient disk access to multiple formats.

WORKING WITH DOS-FORMATTED DISKS

If you own any kind of removable device and it connects to an IDE channel, the chances are good that you will be able to make use of it under Linux using the same methods described in this chapter. This includes IDE SyQuest drives, Sony high-capacity floppies, and many others.

Bear in mind that you won't be able to use the DOS-type "M" commands, such as mdir and mformat, on removable drives other than a floppy diskette.

To check the mounted file systems on your systems, simply type mount at the shell prompt.

USING /ETC/FSTAB TO ACCESS DOS-FORMATTED DISKS

Using some of the tricks from earlier sections in this chapter, you can do something that PCs normally can't do: read different types of floppies on the same system. Although the mount and umount processes under Linux are fairly laborious, Linux does allow you to read DOS and Linux floppies and removable disks from within the same devices.

The mount, mkfs, and mke2fs commands require administrative or root privileges under Linux.

In earlier sections, you learned to use the mount command to mount a disk of any format with a single command. In the long run, however, you will probably want greater convenience in managing disks under Linux. The key is to have a properly edited /etc/fstab file. For example, the complete contents of the author's fstab file are shown below.

Device	Mount Point	type	options	Pass number
/dev/hda	/	ext2	defaults	1 1
/dev/hda1	swap	swap	defaults	0 0
/dev/cdrom	/mnt/cdrom	iso9660	noauto,ro	0 0
none	/proc	proc	defaults	0 0
/dev/fd0	/mnt/floppy	ext2	defaults	0 0
/dev/fd0	/mnt/dosfloppy	msdos	defaults	0 0
/dev/hdd	/mnt/zip	ext2	defaults	0 0
/dev/hdd	/mnt/doszip	msdos	defaults	0 0

Notice how the /dev/fd0 and /dev/hdd device files are used twice in the fstab table. One table entry is used for accessing ext2 (Linux Native) disks, while another is used for accessing msdos-formatted disks.

Also notice how the mount points are named according to their disk type to eliminate confusion. You *must* still unmount each disk before removing and inserting another one.

 Always **use the umount command before removing a disk from a Linux drive. Failure to do so can cause i-node table corruption on any new floppy or disk you put in that drive.**

In the following series of steps shows how to set up your system to access DOS-formatted floppies.

1. Using a text editor, add the following line to the /etc/fstab file in your system:

   ```
   /dev/fd0   /mnt/dosfloppy   msdos   noauto  0 0
   ```

2. Create a new subdirectory in the /mnt directory called "dosfloppy," like so:

   ```
   mkdir /mnt/dosfloppy
   ```

3. Insert a DOS-formatted diskette into the floppy drive. To verify that this works, you may want to have a some sample files on the floppy.

4. Issue a mount command, as follows:

```
mount /mnt/dosfloppy
```

After a moment, the disk is mounted and the prompt returns.

At this point, you are able to use standard Linux syntax to access the DOS floppy such as ls, mkdir, cp, and all the rest. You won't have to use the "M" commands to work with DOS floppies after modifying the etc/fstab file as described above.

This technique works the same way with Zip disks and other removable devices. Just create a new directory in the /mnt directory (or any other place in the filesystem for that matter) as a mount point for DOS-formatted Zip disks, add the proper entry to the fstab file similar to the one shown above, and you are ready to go.

FORMATTING DOS-FORMATTED DISKS

The mkfs.<file system builder> command may be employed to format disks in several Linux-supported file systems. Examples include mkfs.ext2 (for Linux Native), mkfs.msdos (for MS-DOS disk formatting), mkfs.hpfs, mkfs.nfs, and mkfs.minix.

> You can also format disks with the DOS file system under Linux using the mkfs.msdos command. The mkfs in these commands stands for Make File System, and these commands are typically used by administrators and root.

All the file system choices can be found in the /usr/src/linux-2.0.36/fs directory, or whatever directory name is used with your Linux distribution. Newer version of the Linux kernel may include even more file systems, such as version 2.2 which supports symmetric multiprocessing and other new features.

Linux provides a set of utilities called *file system builders*. Using the mkfs command combined with the specific file system builder as its suffix, you can format a mounted disk with that operating system's file system. The mkfs.msdos command is combined with the actual device name from the /dev directory, as shown here:

```
mkfs.msdos /dev/fd0
```

The following is an example for zip disks or other removables:

```
mkfs.msdos /dev/hdd
```

Once a disk is formatted, you can mount and access it normally. When you unmount the disk and insert it into a Windows machine, it will be readable by that system.

> **Be very careful using this command! If you specify the wrong device, such as /dev/hda, you may wind up reformatting your Linux system partition!**

CONFIGURING A NETWORK INTERFACE CARD

Ideally, you should set up at least one networking card when installing the operating system since Linux is very much a network operating system. Linux also supports multiple network interfaces, which means you can set up any Linux computer as a router. Routers can be complex devices, but the basic definition of a router is a device that connects at least two separate networks together and sends data back and forth between them. If a computer can run two or more networking cards in its chassis, and the operating system supports it, it can be set up as a router.

When setting up a network card, one primary piece of advice applies: use a similar type of network interface card (NIC) for each connection to a network from your machine. Although Linux supports running as many drivers in the kernel as necessary, it is much easier to use a single driver to support two or more cards of the same type. This is especially true of the actual types of cards that Linux supports, and Linux runs reliably with most of the major networking cards from 3Com, Intel, and Novell/Eagle, among numerous others. This is not a hard-and-fast rule. There is nothing to stop you mixing network cards at all, but your system will have to load separate device drivers for each. By keeping to the same type of card, you minimize the amount of RAM these drivers require.

For example, if you have a Novell/Eagle NE2000 networking card defined as eth0 in your system and you want to add a second card, it is more RAM-efficient to use another NE2000 card. (NE2000s are rock-solid 16-bit ISA networking cards that are widely regarded as 'old reliable' devices.) If you happen to have a PCI Fast Ethernet networking card based on the DEC 21140 chip, such as the inexpensive NetGear FA310TX, use a second card of the same kind. Many DEC-chip Fast Ethernet cards, such as the Net-Gear, use Linux's Tulip driver, and that is the example used in this section.

Don't assume that because the NICs are made by different manufacturers that you need different drivers. Many cards are OEMed (Original Equipment Manufacturer). This means that one company makes the card and sells it to other companies. The other companies silk-screen their logo on the card, package it in a different box with their name on it, and treat it like a competitive product. In many cases, dozens of cards use the same drivers like the Tulip driver. This is especially true of inexpensive 10Mbps and 100Mbps Ethernet cards. There are very few manufacturers of these cards, but many OEM versions are available.

As mentioned, the foremost reason for sticking to one type of card is so that you only have to load one NIC driver into the Linux kernel. Thus, setting up the second card is easy: the Linux kernel usually automatically detects the second card and dynamically assigns it as /dev/eth1. If you have a driver that works well for the card you have, using a second card of the same type eliminates any potential problems. If you use a different card, you will have to load a new driver alongside the one already in the system.

Some users may need to set up their first networking card under Linux. You still need to know what type of card you have, particularly if your Linux installation does not detect your network card during installation. For example, Caldera OpenLinux's installation frequently does not detect the network card. If this happens to you, don't panic. This section describes exactly how to set up a networking card on an existing, functioning Linux system. Although we will go into more detail in a moment, the process requires four basic steps:

1. Compile the driver from a basic source code file (gcc) or compile the driver file into a loadable module with a bundled makefile (make) if a compiled driver is not available from the manufacturer.

2. Insert the loadable network card module into the Linux kernel (insmod).

3. Set up Linux to permanently install the module.

4. Configure the card's IP address (ifconfig).

To do this, you will encounter some new commands: gcc, make, and insmod. A brief overview of these commands follows.

◆ **gcc**   If a network card maker supports Linux, they usually write the driver in the C or C++ programming language and distribute the source code on their web site or bundle the driver with the available versions of Linux. It is up to the user to compile the C file—called, for example, tulip.c— into a loadable kernel file (*.o) using the gcc command. Linux's C compiler is gcc (GNU C Compiler) and it is a major application for creating C programs under Linux. It's not too difficult to do this when setting up a networking card, although it can require a bit of detective work.

When all you have is a C source file for a driver, scroll through the file to locate the compilation instructions. The tulip.c file, for example, contains compilation information at the end of the source code. We'll use this as an example of what to do to install a new driver or update an existing driver.

> If the driver developer has even the slightest inclination to be helpful, compilation instructions are written into the source code, usually at the beginning or the end of the driver file.

◆   **make**:   Some manufacturers write their Linux drivers and distribute the source code along with another file called a makefile. In this case, all you need to do is copy the source file and the makefile into the same directory and type the make command at the prompt. This instructs Linux to run the compiler with all the correct instructions. Next, insert the .o file, also called a *module*, into the Linux kernel using the insmod command.

The make command compiles C code into loadable modules that can then run within the Linux operating system kernel.

◆   **insmod**:   This command (Insert Module) loads an object module (*.o) into the kernel.

Both gcc and make are complicated commands that provide a huge number of options, but this book does not explain them in any great depth. They are often used by C programmers, but for our purposes a few simple steps are all you need. For updating or installing a driver, both gcc and make are simply tools to help you get the job done.

MANUALLY INSTALLING A LINUX DRIVER FOR A NETWORKING CARD

To manually install a networking card into a Linux system, here are the steps to take:

1. Locate the driver file. It may be on a web site, on your Linux CD-ROM, on the driver diskette bundled with the network card, or on the Modules diskette bundled with your operating system (Caldera does this, for example). Normally, the driver is in the form of a C source file, such as tulip.c.

2. Create a new directory on your system and copy the driver file source code into it.

3. Open the source code file using your preferred editor, such as vi or emacs.

4. Locate the line in the source file labeled "compile-command" and select it, as shown in Figure 3-7.

Figure 3-7   Locating the required source code statement for compiling a module.

It may be labeled slightly differently and several different compilation lines may be written here, so be sure to select the right one.

5. Copy the selected line to a new file and strip out any extraneous text. The statement should read something like the following:

```
gcc —DMODULE —D__KERNEL__ —I/usr/src/linux/net/inet —
Wall —Wstrict-prototypes —O6 —c tulip.c
```

6. Save the statement into a new text file in the same directory as the source code. Call the file something like "compile." This creates a simple compilation script.

7. Run the script as shown in Figure 3-8. The statement should be similar to the following with compile being the name of your script file. Note that the dot-slash tells Linux to look for the compile program in the current directory in case it's not in the search path and tells Linux to avoid executing any other program called compile:

```
./compile
```

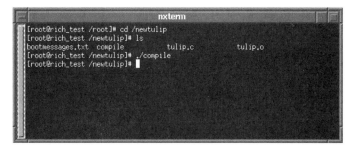

Figure 3-8   Executing a compiler script.

Alternatively, you can copy and paste the compiler line onto the shell command prompt and simply run it that way, as shown here:

```
/sbin/insmod <driver name>
```

A new object module file should be created (tulip.o, for example).

8. Still within the same directory, type this command:

```
/sbin/insmod <driver name>
```

The insmod command resides in the /sbin directory, and the full path must be specified as above. An example of this command follows:

```
/sbin/insmod tulip
```

Substitute the name for your driver. No file name extension is necessary. This command compiles the C-language driver file into a loadable module, and a new .o file is added to the directory. *This requires a makefile bundled with the source file or written by the user!* If the driver source code file comes with a makefile, continue with steps 9–11. If you don't have a makefile, things become much more complicated. You need to invoke the C compiler with a mess of options. Instead, take the time to find a precompiled version on the web: you'll save yourself a lot of trouble.

9. Copy the source code file and makefile to a new directory.

10. Change to the new directory containing your driver, and type something like the following:

```
make
```

11. Then, execute the /sbin/insmod command noted in step 8.

After insmod executes, the installed device is scanned on the PCI or ISA bus and registered with the kernel. You should see a message on the screen reporting the status of the module load. Now, use ifconfig and ping to test out your card, as described in a later section of this chapter.

The steps above are great for testing out a networking card and driver in your system, but there is one drawback: the module is not permanently installed in the kernel. If you reboot, the network card is once again unavailable! The next section shows how to permanently install a network card driver into your system.

AUTOMATICALLY EXECUTING A LINUX DRIVER FOR A NETWORKING CARD

It's always good to know how to compile and insert a new or updated module into the Linux kernel, because hardware makers frequently update their drivers. Still, it is tedious to manually install the driver every time you want to use it. To permanently activate a network driver in your system, follow these steps:

1. If you haven't obtained the driver update or need to install the network card driver, follow steps 1–3 from the exercise in "Manually Installing a Linux Driver for a Networking Card" starting on page 80.

2. Using the following command, copy the driver module (the *.o file) to the following directory:

```
cp tulip.o /lib/modules/2.0.36/net
```

If you're running a different version of the kernel, the "2.0.36" directory will be named differently. Just substitute the name of the subdirectory under /lib/modules corresponding to the Linux kernel version you are running.

3. Move to Linux's /etc/sysconfig/network-scripts directory, like so:

```
cd /etc/sysconfig/network-scripts
```

4. Using your preferred text editor, create a new text file called ifcfg-eth1, as shown in Figure 3-9. Call the text file ifcfg-eth0 if this is the only networking card you are installing.

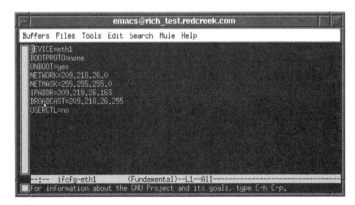

Figure 3-9   Editing the ifcfg-eth1 file for a second network card.

5. Edit the file to use values similar to the following:

```
DEVICE=eth1

BOOTPROTO=none

ONBOOT=yes

BROADCAST=172.16.1.255

NETWORK-172.16.1.0

NETMASK=255.255.255.0

IPADDR=172.16.1.120
```

For the IP address information shown above, substitute the values for your network. Use the correct broadcast, network, subnet mask, and IP address values.

The broadcast address is the final numeric address for the network. Since a Class C network has 256 addresses (0–255), the broadcast address would be x.x.x.255. For a Class B, it would be x.x.255.255.

If you have a networking card installed in your system, an ifcfg-eth0 file is already resident in the /etc/sysconfig/network-scripts directory, and the eth0 network card's IP values are already written in that file.

6. Next, using your preferred text editor, edit the etc/conf.modules file as shown in Figure 3-10. Add an entry similar to the following if you are adding a second networking card:

```
alias eth1 tulip
```

Figure 3-10   Editing conf.modules.

Note that in Figure 3-10, two different networking cards are specified. If this is your only networking card, enter instead something like the following:

```
alias eth0 tulip
```

7. Save your work, shut down, and restart Linux. The networking cards initialize and configure during bootup.

After setting up your networking cards, keep an eye on Linux as it boots. It will announce the presence of each network interface card and its interrupt and I/O memory port settings. With any luck, neither card will conflict. Linux will configure them at the hardware level and you can set up the second card for IP networking.

All your networking cards can be configured this way. Once the cards are installed and initialized, configure the cards by editing the ifcfg-ethX files or by using the more convenient and more powerful ifconfig command described in the next chapter.

Current versions of Linux supports up to four networking cards in the same system. This lets you use a Linux box as a router, gateway, or firewall connecting up to three local area networks to the Internet, or up to four local area networks together.

CONNECTING TO A PRINTER

Linux printer support improves constantly. New device drivers appear almost daily, and if your printer isn't officially supported by Linux, try to keep an eye on manufacturers' web pages and Linux user groups for new or updated drivers. A few Epson Stylus Color inkjet printers are supported, as are many standard HP LaserJet printers. Printing from a Linux machine is normally quite simple. Printers are treated in a fairly generic fashion and can be accessed as one of four different types:

♦ **Local**: A printer directly attached to the Linux system. The Linux computer must run the lpd daemon. The lpd daemon is the "line printer daemon," which is a driver that sets up and handles printing using the properly chosen printer type. This is the simplest option for most users.

♦ **Remote**: A printer attached to another system (Linux or UNIX) that runs an lpd daemon in the kernel. This requires an IP address and rights to access the printer.

♦ **SMB**: A printer attached to a Windows 9x/Windows NT server and shared across the network. This is a popular option. It requires an IP address, rights to access the printer, and a network connection to the Windows networking system.

♦ **NCP**: A NetWare-type printer connected to a NetWare print server. This requires the IPX/SPX protocol.

Printers can be configured only by the Root account although any user ID can access the configured printers (unless the system administrator sets access restrictions).

The /dev directory contains a set of device files used to control the printer device, numbered starting at zero: /dev/lp0, /dev/lp1, /dev/lp2, /dev/lp3, and so on.

CONNECTING TO A PRINTER ON A NETWORK

During installation, you are offered the option to install a printer. If you want to set up a printer in a functioning Linux system, the possibilities are almost endless. As an example, RedHat Linux offers a graphical utility in its Control Panel to perform simple printer connections. To do this, follow the next set of steps.

1. Under RedHat Linux open X, and click the Printer Configuration icon in the Control Panel. (See Figure 3-11.) The Print System Manager window appears.

Figure 3-11   RedHat's Control Panel.

2. In the Print System Manager, click Add, as shown in Figure 3-12. The Add a Printer Entry dialog appears to select among the four printer types listed earlier.

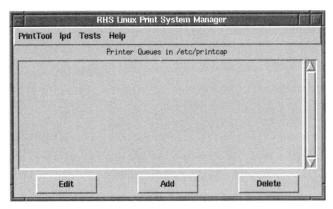

Figure 3-12   Opening RedHat's Print System Manager.

3. To connect to a Windows-networked printer, select Lan Manager Printer (SMB) and click OK, as shown in Figure 3-13).

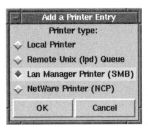

Figure 3-13   Selecting Lan Manager Printer (SMB) in the Add a Printer Entry window.

4. A warning screen appears. Click OK. An Edit Printer Entry window appears as shown in Figure 3-14. For printing from the Linux system, keep the Names and Spool Directory the same as the default values.

Figure 3-14   Using the Edit Printer Entry window.

5. Enter the print server name, which is a standard NetBIOS computer name. It is "riohobox" in the Figure 3-14; yours will differ.

6. If the name of the print server is correct, you should not need the IP address. If desired, though, you can enter its IP address here.

7. Type in the proper user name and password for an account that has permission to access the printer. It should not be the root account; this would cause a gaping security hole.

8. To choose the correct printer driver, click the Select button next to the Input Filter field. The Configure Filter dialog appears as shown in Figure 3-15.

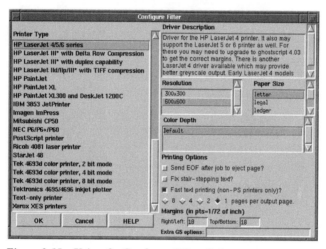

Figure 3-15   Using the Configure Filter dialog.

9. Select the correct driver, DPI setting and other choices for your printer, and click OK when done.

10. Run a test print by selecting the new printer in the Print System Manager list. Then, select the Print ASCII Test Page option or the Print PostScript test page option from the Test menu.

CONNECTING TO A LOCAL PRINTER

Setting up a local printer is even easier.

1. Click the Add button in the Print System Manager (Figure 3-12).

2. Select the Local Printer type and make sure the printer is connected properly.

3. Click OK. A message window appears, displaying the list of printer ports detected by the operating system. Typically, the parallel port is set to /dev/lp0 or /dev/lp1.

4. Click OK again. When the Edit Local Printer Entry window appears, leave the defaults as they are, as shown in Figure 3-16.

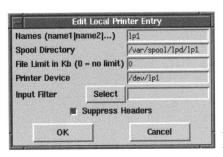

Figure 3-16   Using the Edit Local Printer Entry window.

5. Choose the correct Input Filter as described in the previous step 8 and Figure 3-15.

It's much easier to set up printing in X, particularly in RedHat. RedHat Linux version 5.2 irons out a lot of the kinks in hardware support and actually makes printer support—and significant network management features—almost plug-and-play. While it's not perfect (what operating system is?), the potential of Linux has come a long way in a very short time.

SUMMARY

Linux hardware support is now much less of a fantasy and much more of a reality. It's becoming increasingly practical for the average intelligent computer user to approach Linux and, armed with a few tips like those conveyed in this chapter, start making some real progress in mastering this alien operating system. The next chapter provides a significant change in focus, describing basic network management such as creating and maintaining user accounts, and describes key network configuration and troubleshooting tools.

FILE

PERMISSIONS

AND

OWNERSHIP

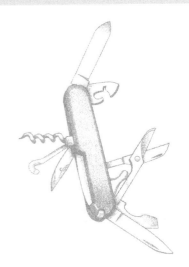

A ny Linux system requires at least a cursory amount of administration. If two people in a home share a Linux computer, the chances are good that both users are
running the root account. This isn't a good idea. Even if you are not concerned about
the complex issues of computer security or restricted file access, it is still important to
ensure that key files and services in your system cannot be overwritten or removed
accidentally.

If you are running Linux for the first time, it is a good idea to create an alternate
account for yourself that allows you to do the things you want in the system, while preventing fatal mistakes that are all too possible with the root account. You will find out
how to do that in this chapter, and will be able to decide what kind of account you want.

This chapter provides a straightforward introduction to user management and file
permissions under Linux. Among the topics discussed in this chapter are the following:

◆   Creating user accounts (adduser and passwd; editing etc/passwd).

◆   Creating new groups and adding users to them (editing etc/group).

◆   Modifying file and directory permissions (chown, chgrp, chmod).

Enormous Linux and UNIX books exist that spend hundreds of pages preaching the
vital necessity of good security techniques. Here, it is boiled down to the basics and
focuses on key tasks that even average Linux users eventually have to perform.

INTRODUCING LINUX USER ADMINISTRATION

Under Linux, *user permissions* are a key way to enforce security in a network. Linux uses permissions to determine how groups and users interact with shared devices and files in the Linux file system. The basic rules for Linux administration include:

◆ The root account password should never be given out.

The root account is the top-level administrative account on any Linux machine and on any network controlled by a Linux machine. Anyone with access to the root account's password can do anything they want in the Linux computer and some- times on other systems in the same network, including formatting the system hard disk partition. The root account is the presumptive account for the most experi- enced and skillful administrator in the network.

◆ All accounts should have a password.

User accounts should not be accessible by simply pressing Enter at the password prompt—especially for root! Even if Linux is running on a home system, remem- ber that your eight-year-old could manage to press Enter and start playing around on your computer. When you come home, you might find the Linux system that took you months to build being destroyed by an inadvertent disk formatting com- mand from the hands of your child. Do yourself a favor: make sure all accounts on your system have at least some kind of password. (Corporate Linux users don't have to be told this; eight-year-olds are often in short supply in that environment.)

◆ Don't use passwords such as *guest, administrator, password, secret*, or *user*.

If your Linux system is sitting on your desk at home, password security probably sounds like a joke. If it is sitting on your desk at work, password security starts to become much more important. People like simple passwords and don't like to change them. If people use their last names for a password, or the names of Greek gods and goddesses or the like, naming conventions become a little too obvious.

One classic password-breaking scheme is called the *dictionary attack*. The hacker compiles a 100,000-word or so text file from A to Z, and then fires it off as an auto- mated password logon script to try to break into someone's system (usually a cor- poration or government agency). On a home system, all this is not quite as important (except for the eight-year-old factor).

Here are some key terms to know:

◆ **UID** and **GID**: User ID and Group ID are numeric values Linux uses to help keep track of accounts within the system. Linux prefers numbers instead of the full alphabetic names simply because computers are much better and faster at handling numbers, and they take up less space.

◆ **Home directory**: This is the location for the user's personal files on the system and point in the file system at which the user logs on to the computer. Home directories should be arranged in a simple, logical manner to minimize work and confusion for the administrator. Most systems place home directories in a directory called /usr or /u.

◆ **Group**: A group is a collection of user accounts labeled something like "Admins," "Backup Admins," "Local Users," "Sales," "Marketing," and the like. Groups offer the advantage of potentially providing uniform user permissions to all accounts in the group. The root administrator for the Linux machine determines how all user accounts and groups behave. Users can be in any number of groups, but a user is active in only one group at a time.

CREATING NEW USER ACCOUNTS

User accounts can be created in two ways: in the Linux GUI or by using the adduser command. GUI utilities, while convenient, are inconsistent between different Linux implementations, whereas every version of Linux provides adduser. This is the primary tool for creating and maintaining user accounts. The adduser command options include those shown in Table 4-1.

Table 4-1   Commands for adduser

Command	Description
-c	A comment field for the new user's password file.
-d <home directory>	Allows you to specify the location of the new user's home directory. If not specified, home directories for each new account are created automatically in the /home directory.
-e <date>	The date on which the account expires in MM/DD/YY.
-f <days>	The number of days after a password expires that the account is disabled. The default value is -1, which means the account is immediately disabled.
-g <group name>	The name of the user account's initial or default login group. This group must already exist and can be added to the system by editing the etc/group file.
-G <group names>	Additional groups to which the user account may belong. Each is listed with a comma and no spaces between each group name, as in "sales,marketing,remoteusers".
-k	RedHat option that allows copying of default home directory files from an admin-specified directory other than etc/skel. This requires use of the -m option.
-m	Forces creation of a home directory, if one does not exist, with the admin-defined files copied automatically from the etc/skel directory or from another location, which requires use of the -k option.
-n	By default, creates a group having the same name as the user through the Adduser command. Otherwise, create new groups by editing the etc/group file and then use the -g option. (RedHat only: Use the -n option to turn this feature off.)
-r	Creates a system account with a UID lower than 500.
-s <shellname>	Specifies the type of login shell for the user. The default is /bin/bash.
-u (UID)	Specifies the user ID number of the account. If not specified, adduser takes the first available number after 500—the first account you create automatically uses 500 as the UID. (Note that some versions of Linux use different starting points for UIDs.)

CREATING A NEW ACCOUNT USING /ETC/SKEL

Network administrators often want to automatically copy certain files and default directories to the user's home directory. This provides a navigation path for the user, and allows for useful items such as help text files, collections of symbolic links to different programs in the Linux system, and directories for organizing user documents. Linux does not create those default files and directories for you. The administrator must create those files and default directories and place them into the /etc/skel directory. (Skel stands for skeleton, and the /etc/skel directory is presumed to have a "skeleton" of directories and files that may be reproduced in every user account's home directory.) Then, as the admin creates accounts, the -m command option is used to ensure that the default files and directories copy over to the new user's home directory. Not all versions of Linux support the /etc/skel capabilities.

To create a new account using a home directory with the properly created contents of the /etc/skel directory, issue the following command (with a different name for your desired account, of course):

```
adduser rich —m
```

It's as simple as that. If you have a special set of default directories and files in /etc/skel, they are replicated in the new user's home directory.

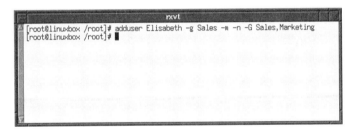

Figure 4-1   Running the adduser command to create a new account.

CREATING A NEW ACCOUNT WITH GROUP MEMBERSHIP

There is a root group, as well as the root account, to which you may want to add accounts. To add a new account to the Linux system's root group, issue a command such as this:

```
adduser rich —g root
```

To create this new account with an expiration date of 02/28/01, run a command such as the following:

```
adduser rich —e 02/28/01 —g root
```

To create an account with membership in multiple groups and default home directory content, issue a command like this:

```
adduser —m —G Sales,Marketing,EngQA,Techpubs rich
```

Note the use of the uppercase G for this particular option, and that the new user's account name appears at the end of the command.

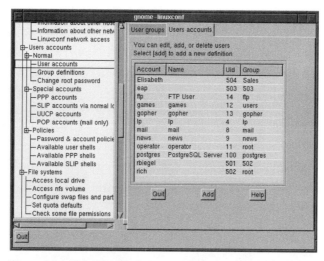

Figure 4-2   Using RedHat's Linuxconf to manage user and group accounts.

Once the accounts are created, you *must* create their passwords. Unfortunately, adduser doesn't provide options for this important task, and it must be done separately using the passwd command.

Removing users from your system is a matter of removing their entries from the /etc/passwd and /etc/group files. Any ASCII editor can be used to remove their entries from these files.

CREATING USER PASSWORDS

Once a user account is created, the next step is to run the passwd command for that user name. The syntax for this simple command is as follows:

```
passwd <username>
```

To create a password for a new account, follow these steps.

1. At the prompt, type the following command, substituting the proper user name where appropriate:

```
passwd rich
```

2. Type in the desired password. Be sure you spell it correctly; Linux does not display the password value on screen. Then, press Enter.

   If the password is a simple word, a message appears as shown in Figure 4-3, stating "BAD PASSWORD: it is based on a dictionary word." A password based on a dictionary word is easy to crack. Creating a password with numbers mixed into it makes it much safer, although more difficult to remember. The passwd program will accept the "bad" password, but always provides this message when a password is deemed unsafe.

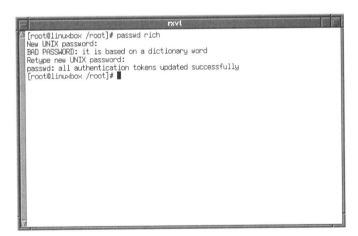

```
[root@linuxbox /root]# passwd rich
New UNIX password:
BAD PASSWORD: it is based on a dictionary word
Retype new UNIX password:
passwd: all authentication tokens updated successfully
[root@linuxbox /root]#
```

Figure 4-3   Running the passwd command.

3. Retype the password at the prompt and press Enter. If the two passwords match, the account's authentication tokens are updated and the account is ready for use. If you mistyped either password, you have to repeat the whole process again.

To view the results of your work, type the following command:

emacs /etc/passwd

Figure 4-4 shows that the root, rbiegel, eap, and rich accounts all have encrypted passwords added to their entries in the /etc/passwd file. Also note that each account's home directory, and user ID is listed in their entries.

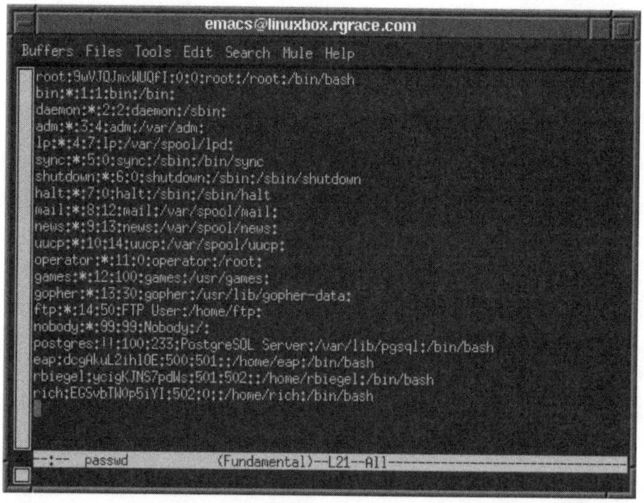

Figure 4-4   Viewing the contents of the etc/passwd file.

As you can see in your /etc/passwd file, there are seven fields for each line, each field separated by a colon. Each line corresponds to a single user ID. The fields, from left to right on each line, are:

◆   user name: This is the name the user types to log in to the system. Some user IDs are reserved for the system's use and are not really logins. Instead, they are used for tracking and ownership purposes

◆   password: The password is always encrypted and decrypting it is very difficult. Usually passwords have varying length that bear little resemblance to the password used for that account. If there is no character between the first and second colon, that account has no password. If + or x appears in the password field, it means one of two things: NIS (Network Information Services, formerly called YP for Yellow Pages) is used for user logins or a shadow password file is employed by the system. A shadow password file is a file usually called /etc/shadow that has extremely restrictive permissions, preventing anyone but root from looking at the encrypted passwords.

◆ user ID: The UID is used by Linux to track everything the login does.

◆ group ID: The GID indicates the group that the user starts in. The /etc/group file contains all the group information.

◆ comment: This field is for comments and usually contains the user's full name or contact information.

◆ home directory: The directory in which the user is placed when they log in.

◆ startup program: The program executed when the user logs in, usually a shell.

There is little variation in the way these fields are presented within all the versions of UNIX and Linux available today. The differences are mainly in the number conventions for UID and GID, as well as the way passwords are stored.

CREATING GROUPS

The method for creating and modifying groups differs from user accounts. Under Linux, groups are created by editing the /etc/group file. This is usually a manual task, although there are some scripts available to provide automated group maintenance. Even a new Linux system has a significant groups file, as Figure 4-5 shows. Groups are created with a new group ID number (GID).

Figure 4-5   Editing the /etc/group file to create or change group information.

Typical entries in the /etc/group file read something like the following:

```
Root::0:root,rich
```

...

```
Sales::51:rich,rbiegel,eap
```

```
Marketing::52:rbiegel,eap
```

The first item is the group name, followed by a pair of colons that could contain a password required when you change into that group, the group ID number, and then a comma-separated list of all user names that are allowed in that group. Simply type in the new groups in the same format as shown above, using your preferred text editor. When you create new user accounts for the Linux system, you add them to desired groups as described in "Creating a New Account with Group Membership" on page 95. After that, the user's name appears in the group's entry in /etc/group.

Working with text files and command-line features can be very tedious, particularly on a busy Linux server that may be accessed by dozens or even hundreds of people. Because of Linux's increasing maturity, better tools are evolving that help address repetitive tasks. For example, RedHat's Linuxconf is a flawed but still useful program that offers significant user and group management features, as shown in Figure 4-6.

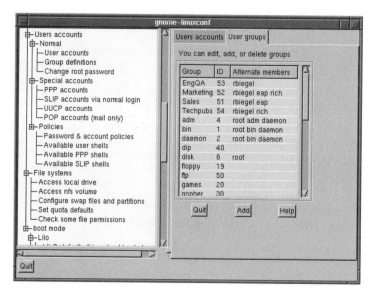

Figure 4-6   Using RedHat's Linuxconf program to manage user and group information.

The same information written in the /etc/passwd and /etc/group files is replicated in Linuxconf. The left pane provides a hierarchical list of services and features while the right pane provides the management for each service. Clicking on Group Definitions displays the list of groups in the system. Linuxconf has serious deficiencies as a management tool, primarily due to its amateurish GUI. Still, if you make changes to group or user settings, you can easily check the results by viewing the passwd or group files manually.

Once your groups and user accounts are all set, you need to work with Linux file permission features to ensure that your users and groups have appropriate access to what they need—and no more. File access permissions are a key aspect of system security, and are discussed in the following sections.

USING GROUPS

If you have set up your /etc/groups file properly, you may be a member of more than one group. For example, you may be a member of a group called admins and a group called programmers. However, you are only ever in one group at a time, according to Linux. That's because Linux can keep only one GID (group ID) number associated with you and your files at any one time. So how do you change groups?

When you logged in, you were assigned to whichever group you are supposed to be in according to the /etc/passwd file's fourth column. You can change groups at any time by issuing one of these two commands:

```
newgrp GID
```

```
newgrp groupname
```

The newgrp command accepts both a Group ID and a group name. When you issue the command, newgrp checks the /etc/group file to see if you are a member, and if you are, changes your GID to match that group. There is no confirmation of the change.

The only way to tell which group you are in is to save a file and check the file permissions. For example, the following user started in the group students and used newgrp to change to the group admins. By saving a file and checking the permissions, the user can see which group they are in at the moment:

```
# cal > /tmp/foo
# ls -l /tmp/foo
-rw-r--r--   1 tparker students 538 Apr 24 17:02 /tmp/foo
# cal > /tmp/foo
# newgrp admins
# ls -l /tmp/foo
-rw-r--r--   1 tparker admins 538 Apr 24 17:03 /tmp/foo
```

UNDERSTANDING ACCESS PERMISSIONS

As noted earlier in this book, the Linux file system is fairly conventional, based on a simple tree structure of files and directories. (If you need a refresher, Chapter 2, *Navigating the Command Line,* describes the Linux tree structure.) File access permissions are a primary security mechanism within Linux.

As you might expect, Linux offers numerous ways to influence how users interact with files and directories. Every file in your Linux system possesses a set of *access permissions.* You manage file security and permissions directly in the Linux file system. To check any file's permissions, the quickest way is to issue an ls –l command. An example output appears below:

```
-rwxr-xr-x   1 root  root      2864   Oct 13  21:44 arch

-rwxr-xr-x   1 root  root     62660   Aug 28  16:43 ash

-rwxr-xr-x   1 root  root    153752   Aug 28  16:43 ash.static

lrwxrwxrwx   1 root  root         4   Aug 28  16:43 awk -> gawk

drwxr-xr-x   1 root  root         4   Aug 28  16:43 applications
...
```

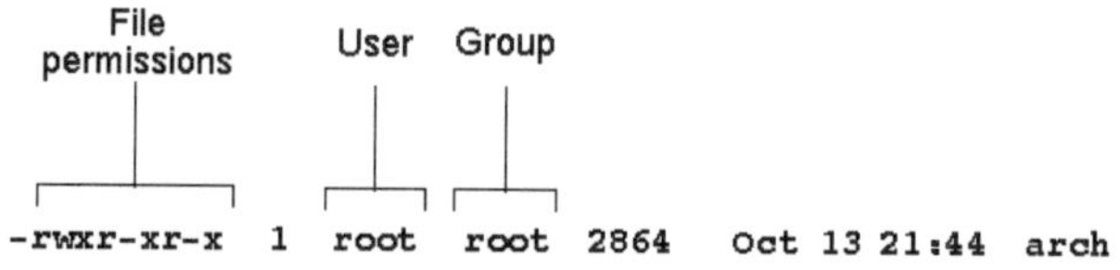

Figure 4-7   Fields in file listings from the ls –l command.

As shown in Figure 2-7, the entries on the far left are the set of access permissions for each file. The letters and dashes determine how the file behaves in different users' hands. Table 4-2 and Table 4-3 explain the privileges and file types that some of these entries symbolize.

Table 4-2   Basic Access Privileges

Permission character	Meaning
-	Disabled.
r	Read-only.
w	Write: can modify, delete, and save changes to the file.
x	Execute the file.

Table 4-3   File Types (first bit only)

First bit of permission block	Meaning
-	Indicates normal Linux file.
l	Indicates symbolic link.
d	Indicates directory.
b	Indicates block mode device file.
c	Indicates character mode device file.

As described in Table 4-3, the first dash or other character in the set of ten characters indicates the file type. If you see a dash (-) as the first character of a file listing, that indicates that the listing is a normal Linux file. For a contrasting example, look at the fourth listing above, which indicates a symbolic link. The other nine bits are split into three equal parts: the user octet, the group octet and the world octet. Their positions are shown in Figure 4-5.

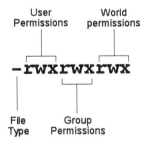

Figure 4-8   Dissecting file system permissions.

Pay attention to the user, group and world octets in the file access permissions. Those values are modified using the chmod command.

The term *octet* is used to describe a three-bit binary number that ranges from 000 (0) to 111 (7) in value. Each of the three bits in the user, group, and world octets can be toggled to 1 by inserting an r, w, or x setting in order from left to right. A dash (-) indicates that the bit is set to zero.

Sample Octet Values		Binary Equivalent
rwx	7	111
rw–	6	110
r––	4	100
–––	0	000

The characters in the three octets (user, group, and world) set their values for Read, Write, and Execute in order from left to right. A dash is used to disable a bit if the particular right is not permitted. Another example follows:

```
-rw-r--r--  1 rich  admins 712704  Feb 6   21:44 coredump
```

In this example, "coredump" is a normal Linux file, indicated by the leftmost dash in the listing. The next three characters (rw-) indicate that the user (the account "rich," in this case) has both Read and Write permission for this file, but no Execute privileges, since the file is not an executable in any case. The second and third octets (r-- and r--, respectively) indicate that the other members in the group admins and any other accounts in the network, have only read privileges for the file. So, after the initial dash, the three octets have a value of 644.

```
-rwxrwxrwx  1 rich  admins 712704  Feb 6   21:44 coredump
```

Here, coredump has access permissions that grant read, write, and execute permissions to all users: the owner account, the group accounts, and anyone else in the system or network. The three octets have a value of 777.

The trick to understanding how to read permissions is to always remember that there are three groups of three letters. They are for user, group, and world from left to right. The permissions are always read, write, and execute, in that order.

Now that you understand how to read access permissions, you may wonder how to change such permissions for your users and groups. File permissions are changed by using the chmod command described in the next section. User and group ownership methods also are described a bit later.

USING CHMOD TO CHANGE FILE ACCESS PERMISSIONS

After you have set up your users and groups, you need to set some file access permissions. You do so using the chmod (change mode) command. Some of the arguments used in chmod commands are shown in Table 4-4.

Don't use chmod to change access permissions for utilities and executable programs in the Linux system. There are many programs that should not be touched by anyone except the root administrator.

Table 4-4　Commands Used with chmod

Command	Description
r	Read-only.
w	Write: This allows users to modify and delete the file.
x	Execute the file.
s	Set user or group ID. This allows use of chown or chgrp on the file.
t	Set sticky bit. This enables the file to be permanently loaded into memory after the first execution while the system is running. For frequently-loaded programs, this can save execution time. Make sure you have plenty of memory to use this.
a	Set action to apply to all items in the current directory.
g	Group permission. This can be enabled or disabled.
o	Other or world permission. This applies to everyone else in the network or the system.
u	Current user permission. This can be enabled or disabled. It enables the command to be applied to the file or files a specific.

The basic syntax for the chmod command is as follows:

```
chmod <a/g/o/u><-/+/=><r/w/x/-> filename
```

The -, +, and = operators are used to disable, enable, and set values for the accounts. The a, g, o, and u options determine whether the settings for user/owner, group, or world are affected by the command. For example, using the a argument affects the permissions for all entities associated with the file. Some other examples are shown below.

CHANGING PERMISSIONS FOR FILES

Changing permission settings for all files in a directory is easily accomplished with chmod. For example, to change the settings so that all users have read-only permissions, issue the following command:

```
chmod a=r-- *
```

Since the equals sign is used, the permissions are set explicitly to read only. No write or execute permission is available to user, group, or world. This would set the permission block to look like this:

```
r--r--r--
```

To add write permission for user and group to a file with these permissions you would issue a chmod command like this:

```
chmod ug+w filename
```

This would change the permission block to look like this:

```
rw-rw-r--
```

Finally, to add execute permission for user, group, and world, we could issue either of these two commands:

```
 chmod ugo+x filename
```

```
 chmod a+x filename
```

The permission block would then look like this:

```
rwxrwxr-x
```

Let's take away permission for anyone in the group that owns the file to read, write, or execute the file. The command is:

```
chmod g-rwx filename
```

The resulting permission block looks like this:

```
rwx---r-x
```

Permissions for directories are set the same way as permissions for files, but read, write, and execute mean something different:

◆ **read**:   An ls can be performed on the directory.

◆ **write**:   Files can be added or removed from the directory.

◆ **execute**:   You can cd into that directory.

The permissions for directories sometimes conflict with permissions for a file. For example, a directory may not allow you to write (add or remove files) from a directory, but you could have write access to the file. Whether file or directory permissions take precedence often depends on the version of Linux, although directory permissions usually override the file permissions.

You don't have to use the letters u, g, and o for chmod. This is a method called *symbolic addressing* and is easier to remember when you are learning permissions. You can use absolute addressing, which uses octal numbers to specify the user, group, and world permissions directory. An example follows:

```
chmod 444 *
```

Each of the three octets (user, group, and world) has a single digit applied to its settings. Note the use of the wildcard to enable permission setting for all files in the current directory. The results appear as shown here:

```
-r--r--r-- 1 rich  admins 712704   Feb 6  21:44  coredump
-r--r--r-- 1 rich  admins  74764   Feb 6  21:44  coretest
-r--r--r-- 1 rich  admins   1324   Feb 6  21:44  corefinal
...
```

To change the permission settings for all files in a directory so that all users have only read and write permissions, issue a command like the following:

```
chmod a=rw- *
```

Another example is shown here:

```
chmod 666 *
```

The results appear as follows:

```
-rw-rw-rw- 1 rich  admins 712704   Feb 6  21:44  coredump
-rw-rw-rw- 1 rich  admins  74764   Feb 6  21:44  coretest
-rw-rw-rw- 1 rich  admins   1324   Feb 6  21:44  corefinal
...
```

Note how all three octets change their values.

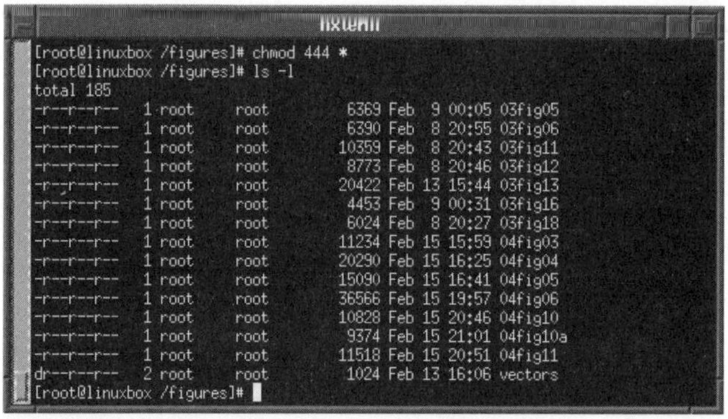

Figure 4-9   Using chmod to change access permissions for all files in a directory.

SETTING THE STICKY BIT FOR A PROGRAM

Setting the sticky bit for a particular program caches it in the program's code in memory for future executions. If you want to set this for something like the emacs text editor, issue a command like this one:

```
chmod +t emacs
```

The results appear as shown below:

```
-rwxr-xr-t   2 root  root 2989940   Oct 6    21:44 emacs
```

When the t value is set, it takes its place in the execute bit for the world octet, thereby ensuring that anybody who has permission to access the Linux system can run the emacs editor from the server's RAM memory.

Of course, in all the preceding examples, modify the commands to suit your own directories or files. Compare the permission settings to the numbers specified in each command, and the pattern starts to become clear.

If you want to run X, the xfm file manager program offers the same file access permission features in a somewhat more convenient form. Run xfm, locate the desired file or directory, and right-click on its icon. From the pop-up menu, select Permissions, and the Change Permissions window appears as shown in Figure 4-10. Do the settings shown look familiar?

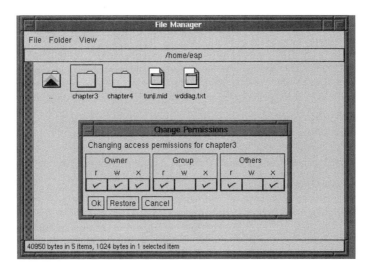

Figure 4-10   Using Linux's xfm file manager to change permissions under XWindows.

The next section describes how to define user and group ownership settings for files in the Linux system.

USING CHOWN AND CHGRP TO MODIFY FILE OWNERSHIP

The commands chown and chgrp are closely related to chmod. All three commands modify the properties of files in the Linux file system. The chown command changes the ownership of one or more files, while the chgrp command changes the group ownership of files. Now that you know how user and group accounts are created, chown and chgrp are the tools to help apply that knowledge to files and directories in your system.

The following syntax for chown shows that it is quite simple:

```
chown <options> username filename
```

Table 4-5 shows some arguments that can be used with chown, and the chgrp command options are shown in Table 4-6.

Table 4-5   Commands Used with chown

Letter	Meaning
-c	Show changes to each file on screen.
-f	Don't print error messages.
-v	Verbose mode. This shows information for all files on which chown is operating. Error messages are also shown.
-R	Recursive option. This performs the operation on the contents of all subdirectories. Be careful with this option!

Table 4-6   Commands Used with chgrp

Letter	Meaning
-c	Show changes to each file on screen.
-f	Don't print error messages.
-R	Recursive option. This performs the operation on the contents of all subdirectories. Be careful with this option!

CHANGING INDIVIDUAL OWNERSHIP OF A FILE OR FILES

To change ownership of an individual file to a new owner such as "eap", with on-screen verification, issue a command such as the following:

```
chown -v eap chapter1.doc
```

If the user account isn't yet created, an error message is shown.

Don't issue a chown –R <name> * command from the root directory or you'll change the ownership of every file on the system!

To change ownership of all files in a directory *and all subdirectories* to a new owner, issue a command such as the following:

```
chown -v eap *
```

Your results will be similar to those shown in Figure 4-11. The -R (recursive) option can save an enormous amount of work—just be sure you don't issue this command from the root directory!

```
                                    rxvt
chapter3     chapter4      tunji.mid    wddiag.txt
[root@linuxbox eap]# chown -v -R eap *
owner of chapter3 changed to eap
owner of chapter3/03fig05 changed to eap
owner of chapter3/03fig06 changed to eap
owner of chapter3/03fig11 changed to eap
owner of chapter3/03fig12 changed to eap
owner of chapter3/03fig13 changed to eap
owner of chapter3/03fig16 changed to eap
owner of chapter3/03fig18 changed to eap
owner of chapter4 changed to eap
owner of chapter4/04fig03 changed to eap
owner of chapter4/04fig04 changed to eap
owner of chapter4/04fig05 changed to eap
owner of chapter4/04fig06 changed to eap
owner of tunji.mid changed to eap
owner of wddiag.txt changed to eap
[root@linuxbox eap]# ls -l
total 41
drwxr-xr-x   2 eap      root       1024 Feb 15 20:34 chapter3
drwxr-xr-x   2 eap      root       1024 Feb 15 20:33 chapter4
-rwxr-xr-x   1 eap      root      28078 Feb 15 20:38 tunji.mid
-rwxr-xr-x   1 eap      root       9800 Feb 15 20:38 wddiag.txt
[root@linuxbox eap]# █
```

Figure 4-11   Using chown to change individual ownership of files in a directory.

Only root change the ownership of any file on a Linux system. If you are logged in as a user, you can change only the ownership of files you already own. You can't take ownership of a file you do not own unless permissions are specifically set to allow you to do so.

CHANGING GROUP OWNERSHIP OF A FILE OR FILES

The chgrp command operates in similar fashion. Notice that in Figure 4-11 all the files and folders have an eap owner but their group is still root. To change this group ownership of all files in the directory *and all subdirectories*, issue a command such as the following:

```
chgrp —v —R Sales *
```

The command changes group ownership of all files and subdirectories, in the documents folder, to the Sales group. With the Verbose option, each file is accounted for on the screen.

```
                              rxvt
owner of wddiag.txt changed to eap
[root@linuxbox eap]# ls -l
total 41
drwxr-xr-x   2 eap      root      1024 Feb 15 20:34 chapter3
drwxr-xr-x   2 eap      root      1024 Feb 15 20:33 chapter4
-rwxr-xr-x   1 eap      root     28078 Feb 15 20:38 tunji.mid
-rwxr-xr-x   1 eap      root      9800 Feb 15 20:38 wddiag.txt
[root@linuxbox eap]# chgrp -v -R Sales *
group of chapter3 changed to Sales
group of chapter3/03fig05 changed to Sales
group of chapter3/03fig06 changed to Sales
group of chapter3/03fig11 changed to Sales
group of chapter3/03fig12 changed to Sales
group of chapter3/03fig13 changed to Sales
group of chapter3/03fig16 changed to Sales
group of chapter3/03fig18 changed to Sales
group of chapter4 changed to Sales
group of chapter4/04fig03 changed to Sales
group of chapter4/04fig04 changed to Sales
group of chapter4/04fig05 changed to Sales
group of chapter4/04fig06 changed to Sales
group of tunji.mid changed to Sales
group of wddiag.txt changed to Sales
[root@linuxbox eap]# 
```

Figure 4-12   Using chgrp to change the group ownership of files in a directory.

LOCATING FILE TYPES WITH THE FILE COMMAND

This section provides yet another type of interaction with the Linux file system: file classification. Linux file names are usually in lowercase and provide no filename extensions (such as .exe, .doc, and others common in DOS/Windows computing). Directories are often named the same way, and it may be hard to distinguish between them You can run ls –l to discover which names refer to what files or directories. Still, with hundreds of different files in a Linux system, it can be difficult to keep track of them. This is especially true if many users interact with the system and save files there.

The file command allows you to quickly search and classify files of various types in the system, and lists the output on the terminal screen. Search criteria are defined by means of a "magic" file, which defines the file types that Linux is able to search and classify. In RedHat Linux, the magic file is located in /usr/share/magic; it may be elsewhere in other Linux systems.

Try the following locations in your Linux distribution:

◆ /usr/share/magic

◆ /usr/lib/magic

◆ /etc/magic

The /usr/share/magic file provides the Linux file classifications in your system. This tool can be used for numerous other tasks, such as modifying access permissions for large collections of files in a busy Linux server.

If nothing else works, run the command "man file" to find the documented location of the magic file on your system.

The basic syntax for the file command is as follows:

```
file <options> <filename or wildcard>
```

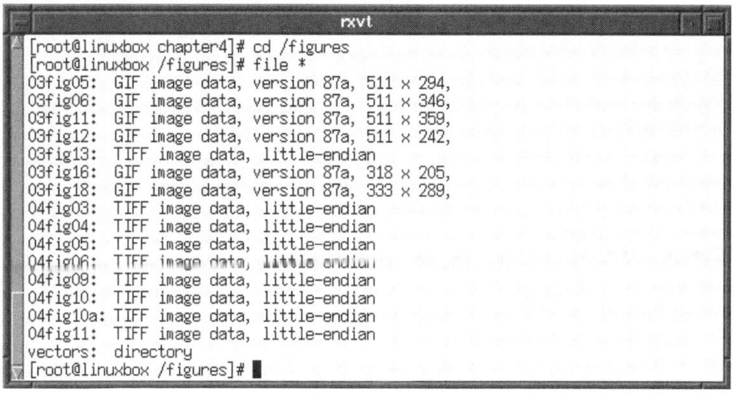

```
rxvt
[root@linuxbox chapter4]# cd /figures
[root@linuxbox /figures]# file *
03fig05:   GIF image data, version 87a, 511 x 294,
03fig06:   GIF image data, version 87a, 511 x 346,
03fig11:   GIF image data, version 87a, 511 x 359,
03fig12:   GIF image data, version 87a, 511 x 242,
03fig13:   TIFF image data, little-endian
03fig16:   GIF image data, version 87a, 318 x 205,
03fig18:   GIF image data, version 87a, 333 x 289,
04fig03:   TIFF image data, little-endian
04fig04:   TIFF image data, little-endian
04fig05:   TIFF image data, little-endian
04fig06:   TIFF image data, little-endian
04fig09:   TIFF image data, little-endian
04fig10:   TIFF image data, little-endian
04fig10a:  TIFF image data, little-endian
04fig11:   TIFF image data, little-endian
vectors:   directory
[root@linuxbox /figures]# ▊
```

Figure 4-13   Running the file command to classify all files in a directory.

File classifications recognized by the file command include, but are not limited to:

- ASCII text.
- Bourne shell script text.
- C program text.
- C-shell commands.
- Data.
- Empty.
- Standard MIDI data.
- ELF 32-bit LSB executable (Linux executable).
- The tcpdump capture file.
- GIF image data.
- TIFF image data.
- Symbolic link.
- Directory.

To run the file command on a directory, use the following syntax:

```
file *
```

All items within that directory will be listed and classified as shown in the extract below. Unfortunately, this command can't be run recursively on subdirectories.

```
Main.dt:        ascii text
Personal.dt:    ascii text
bin:            directory
cdrom:          directory
dev:            directory
etc:            directory

...
```

SUMMARY

Many Linux users totally ignore file and directory permissions until they become a problem. Many users also use the root account for everything. It is these users who end up reloading their systems frequently because they deleted or corrupted an important file. If you plan to use your Linux system properly, set up user accounts and understand file permissions. Neither task is difficult, and they add a whole new dimension to your Linux knowledge.

chapter 5

BASIC

NETWORK

ADMINISTRATION

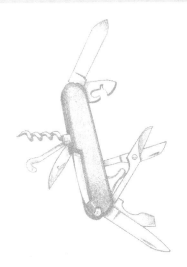

A Linux system can run quite well as a stand-alone machine not connected to the Internet or a local area network. However, the real fun in using an advanced operating system like Linux comes when you start networking. Although you may fear networking and the complicated protocols that go with it, you will be surprised at how easy networking is to set up and configure properly.

USING IFCONFIG TO SET UP YOUR NETWORK INTERFACES

Let's take a closer look at an integral part of Linux networking: setting up your network interface's IP address and checking its operation. If you have two or more networking cards installed in your system, the same rules apply. Also, if you plan to run two networking cards, some basic steps have to be followed in order to make the two cards operate together. For our purposes, we assume in this section that you have one or two networking cards installed.

Linux and networking are virtually synonymous. Linux is built from the ground up to be a pure network operating system. Once you have your basic file security tasks in order, it's time to begin opening the Linux server up to the network.

The ifconfig (interface configuration) command is a critical Linux tool for setting up network interfaces The ifconfig command supports configuration of the many networking protocols under Linux, some of which are shown in Table 5-1.

Table 5-1   Networking Protocols Supported by ifconfig

Protocol	Description
ddp (AppleTalk)	Linux can be used as a server and a router on AppleTalk networks. It operates based on *zones* that contain up to a thousand networked devices in a network segment. AppleTalk routers are supported by major router manufacturers, such as Cisco. Although AppleTalk is a fairly inefficient and chatty networking protocol compared to TCP/IP, it is common and easy to work with.
IPX	Linux supports the Novell NetWare protocol for NetWare version 3 and version 4. This is not discussed in this book. NetWare 5 natively supports IP, so IPX is almost obsolete.
inet6 (IPv6)	Linux supports this next-generation Internet protocol that drastically expands the IP address space from 32 bits to 48 bits. It adds two more octets to the typical IP address number. This sounds like no big deal until you realize that every IP address is now defined by a number 2^{48}, instead of 2^{32}, making life a lot easier for the average administrator. The downside is that routers and general internetworking hardware will need major upgrades to work with this new protocol.
inet (IPv4)	This is the standard supported in this book. It provides Class A, Class B, and Class C address ranges within a 32-bit address space. (Class D and Class E also exist but are not used for general networking tasks.)

If there was no other reason to build a Linux machine than to set it up as a simple router, that would be reason enough to dedicate a cheap PC with two networking cards to the task. Linux can work as an AppleTalk, IPX, or IP router with a few simple commands. IP is the network protocol used in this book as it's the most common and is also used on the Internet.

The ifconfig command offers a huge number of options, many of which require knowledge of IP networking. The most commonly used are shown in Table 5-2.

Table 5-2   Commands Used with ifconfig

Command	Description
<IP address>	The primary address value assigned to the network interface card. (This assumes you are running IP and not another protocol.)
<interface>	The device name for the interface card. This value is required for proper card configuration. Typically, the first card in your system is called eth0; the second card is eth1; a third card is eth2, and so on.

Table 5-2, continued.

Command	Description
broadcast <broadcast IP>	The broadcast IP address for the interface card. This value is configured automatically by Linux when you assign a new IP address to a card; you should not have to specify this value.
(-) promisc	Specifies whether promiscuous mode is on or off. Under Linux, promiscuous mode is used for monitoring IP packet traffic through a network interface.
(-) arp	Specifies whether the arp protocol for the selected interface is on or off. Address Resolution Protocol (arp) maps physical network addresses to IP addresses. Systems using the arp protocol broadcast *arp requests* to known IP addresses in the network, which respond with their physical hardware address, often called a MAC address on network cards. In this way, IP addresses can be assigned to a hardware address that never changes. Arp capabilities are enabled by default. Since arp requests can add to overall network traffic, some administrators disable this feature.
mtu N	Specifies the Maximum Transfer Unit (MTU) in bytes. The default value for physical network interfaces is 1500 bytes. If transmitted packets are larger than the MTU of a destination interface, they are fragmented during transmission and reassembled at the destination.
Up/Down	Enables or disables the interface. Specified at the end of an ifconfig command.
netmask <subnet mask value>	The subnet mask value for the network connected to the interface. This defines the number of possible nodes in the local network. This value is set automatically by Linux when you declare the IP address for the card (255.0.0.0 for a Class A, 255.255.0.0. for a Class B, and so on). The value can also be entered by the user.
(-)allmulti <multicast enabled or disabled>	Enables or disables multicast capability for the selected interface. If enabled, the interface receives copies of packets transmitted in multicast mode, which is useful for limiting IP broadcast traffic.

Table 5-2, continued.

Command	Description
irq <value from 0-15> io_addr <value> media type <10baseT, AUI, 10base2, 100baseTX, auto>	These three values allow the user to change the interrupt value, I/O port, and physical connection type for the network card. Many devices don't allow the hardware configurations to be changed in the operating system. When you type ifconfig to check your configuration, the program displays the interrupt and I/O port addresses.

IPv6 addresses can also be attached to an interface, although most public networks don't support it yet.

The basic syntax for ifconfig is as follows:

```
ifconfig <device name> <up> <node IP address> netmask
<mask value> broadcast <broadcast IP value> <other
options>
```

The broadcast and netmask values are strictly optional. Linux reads the octets comprising the IP address and extrapolates the mask and broadcast addresses without additional input.

ENABLING AN INTERFACE CARD AND DEFINING IP ADDRESSES

To enable an interface card and define its IP address, issue an ifconfig command with the following options:

```
ifconfig eth0 up 10.0.0.1
```

You would replace the 10.0.0.1 with whatever IP address you are using. If you want to change the IP address of an interface, just give the new address to ifconfig and the command handles the other values automatically. The up argument is the key. Linux is smart enough to know what the correct subnet mask and broadcast IP values are supposed to be. Thus, the command above is sufficient to set up the card. The command below is the equivalent:

```
ifconfig eth0 up 10.0.0.1 netmask 255.0.0.0 broadcast
10.255.255.255
```

To check your system's configuration, type ifconfig again and press Enter. The results appear on your terminal screen as shown in Figure 5-14.

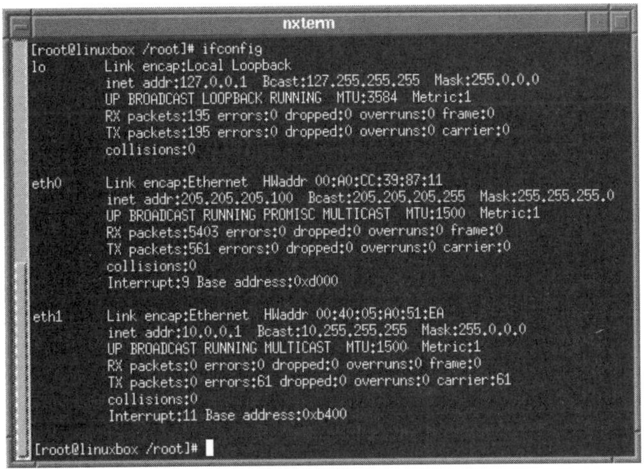

```
                            nxterm
[root@linuxbox /root]# ifconfig
lo        Link encap:Local Loopback
          inet addr:127.0.0.1  Bcast:127.255.255.255  Mask:255.0.0.0
          UP BROADCAST LOOPBACK RUNNING  MTU:3584  Metric:1
          RX packets:195 errors:0 dropped:0 overruns:0 frame:0
          TX packets:195 errors:0 dropped:0 overruns:0 carrier:0
          collisions:0

eth0      Link encap:Ethernet  HWaddr 00:A0:CC:39:87:11
          inet addr:205.205.205.100  Bcast:205.205.205.255  Mask:255.255.255.0
          UP BROADCAST RUNNING PROMISC MULTICAST  MTU:1500  Metric:1
          RX packets:5403 errors:0 dropped:0 overruns:0 frame:0
          TX packets:561 errors:0 dropped:0 overruns:0 carrier:0
          collisions:0
          Interrupt:9 Base address:0xd000

eth1      Link encap:Ethernet  HWaddr 00:40:05:A0:51:EA
          inet addr:10.0.0.1  Bcast:10.255.255.255  Mask:255.0.0.0
          UP BROADCAST RUNNING MULTICAST  MTU:1500  Metric:1
          RX packets:0 errors:0 dropped:0 overruns:0 frame:0
          TX packets:0 errors:61 dropped:0 overruns:0 carrier:61
          collisions:0
          Interrupt:11 Base address:0xb400

[root@linuxbox /root]#
```

Figure 5-1   Viewing interface configurations with ifconfig.

Note that the IRQ and memory I/O port addresses also are reported.

CHECKING THE OPERATION OF AN INTERFACE CARD

To check your interface's operation, issue a ping command. Ping commands send a status message to the interface and time how long it takes to receive a reply. An example follows:

```
ping 10.0.0.1
```

Use your own IP address for the ping command. The ping command is a powerful tool and is used in the next section of this chapter.

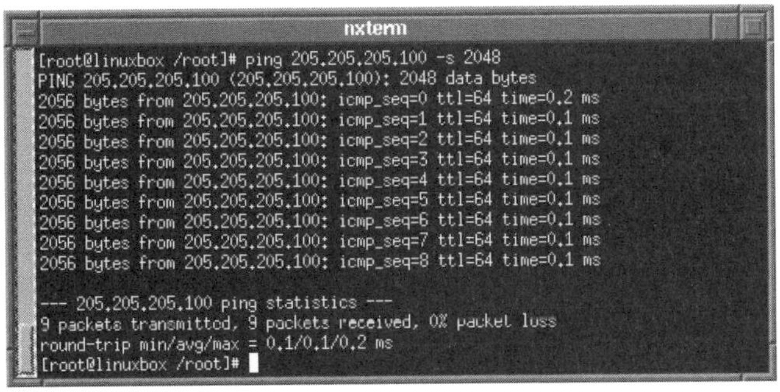

```
                            nxterm
[root@linuxbox /root]# ping 205.205.205.100 -s 2048
PING 205.205.205.100 (205.205.205.100): 2048 data bytes
2056 bytes from 205.205.205.100: icmp_seq=0 ttl=64 time=0.2 ms
2056 bytes from 205.205.205.100: icmp_seq=1 ttl=64 time=0.1 ms
2056 bytes from 205.205.205.100: icmp_seq=2 ttl=64 time=0.1 ms
2056 bytes from 205.205.205.100: icmp_seq=3 ttl=64 time=0.1 ms
2056 bytes from 205.205.205.100: icmp_seq=4 ttl=64 time=0.1 ms
2056 bytes from 205.205.205.100: icmp_seq=5 ttl=64 time=0.1 ms
2056 bytes from 205.205.205.100: icmp_seq=6 ttl=64 time=0.1 ms
2056 bytes from 205.205.205.100: icmp_seq=7 ttl=64 time=0.1 ms
2056 bytes from 205.205.205.100: icmp_seq=8 ttl=64 time=0.1 ms

--- 205.205.205.100 ping statistics ---
9 packets transmitted, 9 packets received, 0% packet loss
round-trip min/avg/max = 0.1/0.1/0.2 ms
[root@linuxbox /root]#
```

Figure 5-2   Using the ping command.

CHECKING NETWORK BEHAVIOR

If you have two networking cards installed in the same Linux system, you must set up IP forwarding. With IP forwarding, the networks connected through each card can send data between them. IP forwarding enables a Linux system with at least two network interfaces to act as a router. Once your network cards are running, you can start checking their operation using two important commands: ping and tcpdump.

USING PING TO VERIFY CONNECTIVITY

Use ping to verify your connections. The ping command sends what are called *ICMP echo requests* and receives *echo replies* from the tested IP address. Every time a ping command is issued, a packet of test data is sent to the IP address specified in the command. If the destination is reachable, an echo reply is sent back and the results are displayed on your screen. Linux defaults automatically to send continuous pings to the specified IP address until you hit Control-C to stop it. The basic syntax of ping follows:

```
ping <ip address> <options>
```

Some ping options include, but are not limited to, those shown in Table 5-3.

Table 5-3   Commands Used for ping

Commands	Description
-c <number>	Sends a specified number of ping packets to the destination.
-f	Forces a "flood ping" that sends IP packets one hundred times a second or as often as packets come back from the destination, whichever is greater. This can be a brutally fast ping setting on faster computers. This is not recommended on active networks, but is great for testing.
-i <number>	Specifies waiting a desired number of seconds between pings. This is incompatible with the -f option.
-s <packet size in bytes>	Specifies a packet size for the ping operation. The default size is 56, which combined with packet header information creates a packet of 64 bytes for every ping. Specifying 2048 forces a ping of 2 Kilobytes.
-R <filename>	Records the route to the destination IP and *may* display the route in each return packet. Many pinged host types ignore this option. This is a useful troubleshooting feature that emulates a trace function. IP packets cannot contain more than nine route values.

To quickly enable IP forwarding, issue the following command:

```
echo > 1 /proc/sys/net/ipv4/ip_forward
```

Some versions of Linux provide an X-based network management tool where this feature can be turned on with the click of a mouse. Using the echo command to set the value works just as well. Pinging the interface from the local Linux machine doesn't mean that the system's basic routing capabilities are working.

Other UNIX and various Windows systems all support ping. If you have one of these systems or another Linux system connected to one of your Linux interfaces, simply issue a ping command from that system to the other interface—the one to which the external system is *not* connected. (See Figure 5-16.) The syntax would look something like the following:

```
ping 10.0.0.1 -R
```

On Windows, it could also look like something like this:

```
C:\> ping 10.0.0.1 -r 2
```

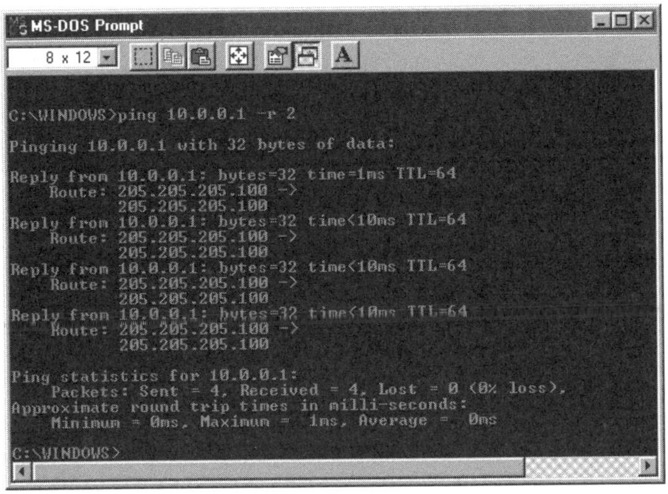

Figure 5-3   Using the ping command from a remote system to check IP forwarding in a Linux system.

USING TCPDUMP TO VERIFY INTERFACE BEHAVIOR

The tcpdump command can be used in combination with ping to check the behavior of any network interface in the Linux system. If you run ping to a network interface's IP address from another system and then run tcpdump to view the results, some interesting things can happen. This is a great way to ensure that both of your network cards are working.

The basic syntax of tcpdump follows:

```
tcpdump <options> <network interface>
```

Some tcpdump command options are shown in Table 5-4.

Table 5-4 Commands Used with tcpdump

Command	Description
-c <number>	Stops capturing packets after receiving a specified number.
-e	Displays the MAC addresses of the involved network interfaces in the network packet transaction.
-l	Ensures that the captured packet data can be viewed in the terminal screen directly from the capture buffer.
-i <interface>	Specifies the network interface on which to listen.
-n	Displays IP addresses instead of DNS hostnames.
-w <filename>	Writes raw captured packets to a specified file.

To view packet traffic as it travels through any network interface in the Linux system, issue a tcpdump command at the command prompt during a ping operation, as shown in Figure 5-17.

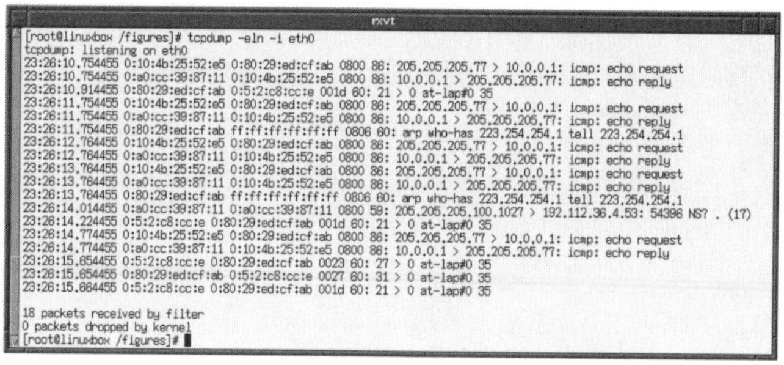

```
rxvt
[root@linuxbox /figures]# tcpdump -eln -i eth0
tcpdump: listening on eth0
23:26:10.754455 0:10:4b:25:52:e5 0:80:29:ed:cf:ab 0800 86: 205.205.205.77 > 10.0.0.1: icmp: echo request
23:26:10.754455 0:a0:cc:39:87:11 0:10:4b:25:52:e5 0800 86: 10.0.0.1 > 205.205.205.77: icmp: echo reply
23:26:10.914455 0:80:29:ed:cf:ab 0:5:2:c8:cc:e 001d 60: 21 > 0 at-lap#0 35
23:26:11.754455 0:10:4b:25:52:e5 0:80:29:ed:cf:ab 0800 86: 205.205.205.77 > 10.0.0.1: icmp: echo request
23:26:11.754455 0:a0:cc:39:87:11 0:10:4b:25:52:e5 0800 86: 10.0.0.1 > 205.205.205.77: icmp: echo reply
23:26:11.754455 0:80:29:ed:cf:ab ff:ff:ff:ff:ff:ff 0806 60: arp who-has 223.254.254.1 tell 223.254.254.1
23:26:12.764455 0:10:4b:25:52:e5 0:80:29:ed:cf:ab 0800 86: 205.205.205.77 > 10.0.0.1: icmp: echo request
23:26:12.764455 0:a0:cc:39:87:11 0:10:4b:25:52:e5 0800 86: 10.0.0.1 > 205.205.205.77: icmp: echo reply
23:26:13.764455 0:10:4b:25:52:e5 0:80:29:ed:cf:ab 0800 86: 205.205.205.77 > 10.0.0.1: icmp: echo request
23:26:13.764455 0:a0:cc:39:87:11 0:10:4b:25:52:e5 0800 86: 10.0.0.1 > 205.205.205.77: icmp: echo reply
23:26:13.764455 0:80:29:ed:cf:ab ff:ff:ff:ff:ff:ff 0806 60: arp who-has 223.254.254.1 tell 223.254.254.1
23:26:14.014455 0:a0:cc:39:87:11 0:a0:cc:39:87:11 0800 59: 205.205.205.100.1027 > 192.112.36.4.53: 54396 NS? . (17)
23:26:14.224455 0:5:2:c8:cc:e 0:80:29:ed:cf:ab 001d 60: 21 > 0 at-lap#0 35
23:26:14.774455 0:10:4b:25:52:e5 0:80:29:ed:cf:ab 0800 86: 205.205.205.77 > 10.0.0.1: icmp: echo request
23:26:14.774455 0:a0:cc:39:87:11 0:10:4b:25:52:e5 0800 86: 10.0.0.1 > 205.205.205.77: icmp: echo reply
23:26:15.654455 0:5:2:c8:cc:e 0:80:29:ed:cf:ab 0023 60: 27 > 0 at-lap#0 35
23:26:15.654455 0:80:29:ed:cf:ab 0:5:2:c8:cc:e 0027 60: 31 > 0 at-lap#0 35
23:26:15.664455 0:5:2:c8:cc:e 0:80:29:ed:cf:ab 001d 60: 21 > 0 at-lap#0 35

18 packets received by filter
0 packets dropped by kernel
[root@linuxbox /figures]#
```

Figure 5-4 Viewing network traffic with the tcpdump command.

The command should look like the following:

```
tcpdump -eln -i eth1
```

The tcpdump command is most definitely an administrator-only program.

Press Control-C when you've captured enough packets to view easily. It is much easier to do this in X and run tcpdump in a separate terminal window than to occupy the entire screen with a confusing jumble of TCP/IP packet information.

To view packet traffic in a somewhat less verbose fashion, and limit the number of packets captured, issue a tcpdump command such as the following:

```
tcpdump -ln -c 20 -i eth1
```

```
rxvt
[root@linuxbox /figures]# tcpdump -ln -c 20 -i eth0
tcpdump: listening on eth0
23:05:30.014455 205.205.205.100.1027 > 202.12.27.33.53: 54398 NS? . (17)
23:05:30.354455 205.205.205.77 > 205.205.205.100: (frag 36842:57601480)
23:05:30.824455 23 > 0 at-lap#0 35
23:05:31.854455 205.205.205.77 > 205.205.205.100: icmp: echo request (frag 36898:148000+)
23:05:31.854455 205.205.205.77 > 205.205.205.100: (frag 36898:57601480)
23:05:31.854455 205.205.205.100 > 205.205.205.77: (frag 6691:57601480)
23:05:31.854455 205.205.205.100 > 205.205.205.77: icmp: echo reply (frag 6691:148000+)
23:05:32.854455 205.205.205.77 > 205.205.205.100: (frag 37154:57601480)
23:05:33.144455 21 > 0 at-lap#0 35
23:05:34.354455 205.205.205.77 > 205.205.205.100: icmp: echo request (frag 37410:148000+)
23:05:34.354455 205.205.205.77 > 205.205.205.100: (frag 37410:57601480)
23:05:34.354455 205.205.205.100 > 205.205.205.77: (frag 6692:57601480)
23:05:34.354455 205.205.205.100 > 205.205.205.77: icmp: echo reply (frag 6692:148000+)
23:05:35.354455 205.205.205.77 > 205.205.205.100: (frag 37668:57601480)
23:05:36.564455 27 > 0 at-lap#0 35
23:05:36.564455 31 > 0 at-lap#0 35
23:05:36.574455 21 > 0 at-lap#0 35
23:05:36.854455 205.205.205.77 > 205.205.205.100: icmp: echo request (frag 37922:148000+)
23:05:36.854455 205.205.205.77 > 205.205.205.100: (frag 37922:57601480)
23:05:36.854455 205.205.205.100 > 205.205.205.77: (frag 6693:57601480)
[root@linuxbox /figures]#
```

Figure 5-5   Viewing packet traffic with tcpdump.

If you use ping and tcpdump correctly, you can troubleshoot a lot of network problems. For a fuller understanding, significant IP networking knowledge is necessary, but it doesn't take a doctorate to figure it out. By following the steps in this section, you will absorb much essential TCP/IP information from your computer. If you're an advanced user, the odds are you are just looking for a refresher.

Some versions of Linux also provide X GUI-based networking utilities that can make your life considerably easier. RedHat, for example, provides an application called Linuxconf that displays every setting for almost every networking service and feature in the operating system. RedHat also provides a Control Panel with separate networking and printing setup applications that take much of the work out of configuring connections, including turning on IP forwarding.

SUMMARY

Setting up a network card and verifying its operation is a step-by-step process, as you have seen. While not quite as easy as plug-and-play under Windows, Linux does make this process quite smooth. If you have more than one machine in your home or office, setting up a network is a fast and fun way to share files, as well as give you the feeling that you really are a technical guru!

CONNECTING

TO

THE

INTERNET

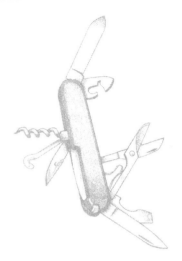

G etting online is one of the major uses of Linux, both from a user's perspective for accessing e-mail and browsing the World Wide Web, as well as from a server's perspective for offering up web pages to others. This chapter explains what you need to do to get your system online, whether it be installing a modem or configuring the network protocols.

Even if you don't plan to set up your own web server, this chapter explains everything you need to do to access the Internet from your Linux system. You can also access bulletin boards, FTP sites, and other computer servers once your system is properly configured. Because Linux's roots are in UNIX, and UNIX itself was instrumental in the creation of the Internet and TCP/IP, it is not surprising that Linux is particularly well suited for accessing the Internet. All of the tools you need are included with the basic Linux distributions, although properly configuring the system is often difficult if you haven't been through the process before. Fortunately, the steps to take are straightforward and methodical, as this chapter demonstrates.

INSTALLING A MODEM

There are a bewildering number of modems available these days, practically all of which work with Linux. For simplicity, we'll concentrate on those that support asynchronous speeds up to 56 Kbps, or analog modems, although Linux will work with synchronous modems, cable modems, and modems supporting technologies like ISDN, and ADSL. Asynchronous analog modems have come a long way in the last twenty years, from 50 baud to today's 56 Kbps units. There are many standards used in the analog modem world, each defining a particular speed. Most of today's modems support one of the high speed standards like V.32 or V.90. (If you're confused about what these numbers mean, the section "Modem Standards" on page 131 explains the standard number and the speed to which it corresponds. Fax standards are also covered.)

For our purposes, analog modems fall into two categories: internal and external. Linux can be configured for either. Whatever type of modem you use, you need to have an available IRQ for the modem. With external modems, a serial port is necessary, too. Internal modems, of course, do not need a serial port, although they should be configured so as not to conflict with an existing serial port. Most PCs are shipped with two serial ports: COM1 and COM2 in DOS terminology. Up to four serial ports (COM1 through COM4) can be supported on a PC without using special multiport serial cards. Since there are only two IRQs available for the serial ports, COM1 and COM3 share one IRQ, while COM2 and COM4 share another. They are differentiated from each other by their I/O address. See Table 6-1 for typical configurations for serial ports.

Table 6-1   IRQ and I/O Addresses for PC Serial Ports

Port	I/O Address	IRQ
COM 1	3F8	4
COM 2	2F8	3
COM 3	3E8	4
COM 4	2E8	3

Linux doesn't use the COM1 through COM4 nomenclature for the serial ports. Instead, the ports are named based on whether they are sending or receiving data. The major and minor device numbers for the ports are different, too, depending on whether the device is sending or receiving data. Table 6-2 shows the DOS and Linux names, as well as the most commonly used major and minor device numbers for the four serial ports. The Linux device names have their origin in incoming terminal device names (tty) and outgoing lines used with the cu (call UNIX) utility. When Linux was installed, it created these devices for you automatically. Since Linux treats both the ttyS and cua devices exactly the same, you can configure with either name. Many administrators like to use the ttyS name to indicate that it is a serial device, while others prefer cua to indicate that it is a modem device. You are also not limited to only four modems on a Linux system. Even though there are only four COM ports, Linux's use of devices allows for there to be an unlimited number of modems attached through multiport serial cards or remote access servers.

Table 6-2   DOS and Linux Serial Port Names

DOS Name	Linux Name	Major Device Number	Minor Device Number
COM 1 Incoming	/dev/ttyS0	4	64
COM 1 Outgoing	/dev/cua0	5	64
COM 2 Incoming	/dev/ttyS1	4	65
COM 2 Outgoing	/dev/cua1	5	65
COM 3 Incoming	/dev/ttyS2	4	66
COM 3 Outgoing	/dev/cua2	5	66
COM 4 Incoming	/dev/ttyS3	4	67
COM 4 Outgoing	/dev/cua3	5	67

The first step in configuring Linux for access to the Internet or other dial-in services is to complete the modem installation. The steps are a little different depending on whether you are using an internal or external modem. To install your external modem, simply attach the modem to an available serial port using a modem cable that adheres to the RS232C standard, as almost all modem cables do. After connecting the modem, power up the modem and the Linux system. The Linux system may already be running, since there is no need to power down the system to attach an external modem.

If you are using an internal modem, you have to perform slightly different steps depending on whether the modem is plug-and-play or not. The steps to install an internal modem are:

1. Power down your system.

   You should never attempt to install cards or other devices into a system that has power. A short may result causing serious damage to your system. You can also expose yourself to a shock. After powering down the Linux system, disconnect the power cord and wait a few seconds for any residual charges to dissipate.

2. Remove the system's cover.

   Most systems have a set of four or six screws on the back plate that hold the cover in place. Remove the screws and the cover, and then locate an available PCI or ISA slot for the modem, depending on your modem and motherboard's type. Remove the back panel plate, if necessary, which is usually held in place by a screw or is a knock-out panel.

3. Set the IRQ and I/O address.

   If the modem has jumpers or software that allows you to set the IRQ and I/O address or the COM port number, choose a setting that is not already installed in the PC. This is typically COM3 and COM4 (see Table 5.1 for more information). If your modem is plug-and-play, these parameters should be set automatically when the system reboots. This will happen if your machine has a Plug-and-Play BIOS. If not, you will need to use a utility to set the parameters.

4. Replace the cover and reboot the machine.

5. Create a link to /dev/modem.

   Most utilities that use a modem try to find it at the device name /dev/modem. This device doesn't exist until you create it. To create the link between your actual modem device and the /dev/modem device, use the following command:

   ```
   ln /dev/cuaX /dev/modem
   ```

   In this command, cuaX (or ttySX) is the device name for the modem you added.

By default Linux sets modem device (/dev/ttyS and /dev/cua) permissions to allow only root to access them. If you want all users to be able to access the modem, follow these steps:

1. Log in as root.

2. Change to /dev.

3. Issue the commands:

   ```
   chmod go+rw /dev/ttyS*

   chmod go+rw /dev/cua*
   ```

These commands change all the modem devices to allow access for all users. If you want to restrict access to a particular device, such as /dev/cua2, use that name instead of the wildcard.

There is no special configuration program to tell Linux that modems are attached. Instead, the utilities that use the modems check the device and configuration files and assume there is a modem at a particular device name.

MODEM STANDARDS

Analog asynchronous modem standards and the speeds they define are shown in the following tables: Table 6-3, Table 6-4, and Table 6-5. Most modems will support all standards below their advertised maximum speed. Thus, a V.34 modem is capable of all speeds below 28.8 Kbps. Some standards have more than one name in common use. When this occurs, the alternate name is shown in parentheses. If more than one standard defines a particular speed (such as 1,200 bps), the standards are not usually compatible and are therefore shown separately. Although there is a difference between bits-per-second (bps) and baud, there is no conversion shown here since most modems are now rated in bps.

Table 6-3   Data Modem Standards

Standard Name	Speed (bits per second)
V.90 (V.PCM)	56,600
V.FC (V.Fast Class)	28,800
V.34 (V.Fast)	28,800
V.32 terbo	19,200
V.32 bis	14,400
V.32	9,600
V.22 bis	2,400
V.22	1,200
Bell 212A	1,200
V.21	300
Bell 103	300

Table 6-4   Data Compression Standards

Standard Name	Compression Ratio
V.42 bis	4:1 compression to 115,200 bps on a 28,800 bps line.
MNP5	2:1 compression algorithm used in older modems.

Table 6-5   Fax Standards

Standard Name	Speed (bits per second)
V.17	14,400; 12,000; 9,600; 7,200
V.29	9,600; 7.200
V.27 ter	4,800; 2,400
V.23	1,200
V.21 Channel 2	300

TESTING YOUR MODEM WITH MINICOM

Linux includes a utility called minicom that provides a text-based emulation of a Digital Equipment VT102 terminal. The minicom utility can be used for dialing out to other systems but cannot show web pages or other graphical information. Minicom is well suited for testing the modem you just installed. To use minicom to test your modem, follow these steps:

1. Log in as root and set access permission to minicom.

   If you want all users to be able to use minicom, edit the file /etc/minicom.users and add a line with the word "ALL" on it. Although this is most likely the default configuration of the file, you should verify that it is. If you want to restrict access, list the logins that are allowed to use minicom—one name per line—and remove any line with "ALL" on it.

2. Start minicom by issuing the command:

   ```
   minicom -s
   ```

   This will create a global configuration file (/etc/minirc.dfl) for minicom if one does not already exist. If a configuration file exists, you do not need the trailing –s option. The minicom utility assumes that a modem device is /dev/modem unless specified otherwise.

3. Configure the modem and dialing strings.

   A dialog appears that allows you to configure several aspects of minicom. Choose the Modem and dialing option. Another menu with a list of settings is displayed. These contains command codes for the modem. By default the commands use the AT command set originally developed by Hayes and subsequently adopted by most other modem manufacturers. If you think your modem is AT command set compatible, leave these settings as they are. If the modem doesn't work properly, the first things to check are these settings. Use the documentation that came with your modem to enter the proper command strings.

If you want to change the default modem device from /dev/modem, choose the Serial Port Setup option and enter the device name in the proper field.

4. Save the settings.

To save the configuration file, return to the main minicom menu and choose Save Setup as dfl. This will write the configuration information. Whenever minicom starts, this file's command codes are used to control the modem.

5. Call another number.

Linux's protocols haven't been set up to connect to your ISP, but you can still test your modem by telling minicom to dial a number. Choose your own phone number, for example, even though it won't answer properly. This ensures that the modem device is found properly and minicom can dial out using it. To dial a number, choose the Exit option from the minicom menu. If minicom could find the modem device, it will clear the screen and display a welcome message. To dial a number, enter the string:

```
ATDT number
```

The number should be the telephone number you want to dial. After hitting Enter, you will probably hear the modem click, then a dial tone, and then the dialing digits. Some modems suppress these noises, which makes it hard to diagnose any problems. Your documentation will tell you how to turn up the volume.

6. Exit minicom.

To exit minicom use the Alt-Z sequence to bring up a menu, and then select X for exit. Some versions of minicom use a different command than Alt-Z; the default settings are usually shown on the screen when you leave the minicom menu.

SETTING UP PPD FOR FULL-TIME DIAL-OUT

There are two protocols used to connect to an Internet Service Provider (ISP): SLIP (Serial Line Interface Protocol) and PPP (Point to Point Protocol). Of the two, PPP is faster, more advanced, and in use by most ISPs. Some ISPs still support the older SLIP system. Unless your ISP specifically doesn't support PPP, it is best to use PPP for all Internet connections. You will notice an appreciable difference in performance.

To use SLIP or PPP, two IP addresses are involved: one for your machine and one at the other end of the connection (usually the ISP's server). Both SLIP and PPP are incorporated as part of the Linux kernel. When you installed Linux, you may have been asked if you want to add SLIP or PPP support. If you were not asked, support may have been linked in automatically. To check whether PPP or SLIP is active on your system, issue this command to display the system start-up messages:

```
dmesg | more
```

Look for a line that starts with PPP, like this one:

```
PPP: version 2.2.0 (dynamic channel allocation)
```

The line for SLIP could look like this:

```
CSLIP: code copyright 1989 Regents of the University of
California
```

```
SLIP: version 0.8.4-NET3.019-NEWTTY-MODULAR (dynamic
channels, max=256)
```

If neither PPP nor SLIP lines appear in the output of dmesg, then they are not loaded as part of the kernel. To add PPP or SLIP support to Linux, use a configuration tool like RPM or change to the source directory for your Linux version (such as /usr/src/linux or /usr/src/redhat) and run the following command:

```
make config
```

When asked, answer Yes to the question about linking in PPP or SLIP support. The prompt for PPP, for example, looks something like this:

```
PPP (point-to-point) support (CONFIG_PPP) [M/n/y/?]
```

Relink the kernel, reboot, and you should see the lines shown earlier starting with PPP or SLIP in the output of the dmesg command.

Since PPP is the dominant protocol used to connect to ISPs, we'll focus on configuring the PPP daemons on your system. The way PPP is used is to connect to the Internet is straightforward. First, a modem calls the ISP's number and logs in using a login name and password. Then, PPP starts up and takes over the connection, passing information to and from your computer to the ISP. Take the following steps to configure PPP:

1. Configure a chat script.

   A chat script is used by the chat program to tell your connection what to expect from the ISP and what to send in reply. This is nothing more than a macro that sends the login name and password at the appropriate times. Save the chat script in a file that you then call from the command line.

The format of the chat script is always in sets of two parts. The first tells your system what to expect, while the second tells it what to send. If nothing is expected or sent, a pair of quotation marks with nothing in them is used to skip that component. Here's a typical chat script:

```
"" ATZ OK ATDT 2370400 CONNECT "" ogin: ppp word:
password
```

This script tells the chat utility to expect nothing from the remote system, and then send "ATZ" which receives the modem's attention. The chat script receives an "OK" from the modem, and then sends the dial string "ATDT 2370400". Of course, you should use your own ISP's phone number. When the carriers are synchronized and after a CONNECT message from the modem, the chat script sends nothing. The script waits for the remote system to send something ending in "ogin:" (we ignore the first letter to avoid case problems), and then you send your account login name. After receiving the "word:" string (from password:) from the remote system, send the password. Following that, you should be logged in and the modem is then handed over to PPP. In this example we used the login ppp, which many ISPs use to indicate an incoming PPP connection request. Your ISP may provide a different login name which should be embedded in the chat script instead.

Chat scripts can have many other commands in them to handle error conditions and busy signals. Although most of these add-ins are going to be more complicated than you need, there are a couple of simple modifications you should save in your chat script:

```
ABORT BUSY 'NO CARRIER' "" ATZ OK ATDT 2370400 CONNECT
"" TIMEOUT 10 ogin: ppp word: password
```

This modification tells chat to abort the login process if the modem responds with a BUSY string or NO CARRIER (the single quotes are used to make sure chat interprets the two words as a single string). The TIMEOUT command can be used anywhere and tells chat to wait ten seconds for the login prompt.

After you have written your chat script and saved it in a file, you can launch the script with the following command where filename is the name of the chat script:

```
chat -f filename
```

You will see how to simplify this process, along with the start-up of PPP, a little further on.

2. Set up ppd.

To start the PPP protocol, the pppd daemon is used. The command line used to start pppd looks like this:

```
pppd /dev/ttyS3 28800 crtscts defaultroute
```

This line tells ppd to start up using device /dev/ttyS3 and connect at 28800 using hardware handshaking (crtscts) and to use the local machine's IP address for the local end of the connection. Normally two IP addresses are supplied, separated by a colon. The first is your machine's assigned IP address, and the second is the remote machine's IP address. If your ISP assigns you an IP address for your connection, you can use it in place of the defaultroute entry on the command line. This IP address can be different than your machine's local area network IP address: it is used only for the pppd connection. However, since most ISPs use dynamic IP addresses assigned when the connection is made, you most likely will need to tell pppd to use whatever IP address the ISP sends you. You can do this like using the following command:

```
pppd /dev/ttyS3 28800 crtscts some_IP:
```

In this command, some_IP is the local machine's IP address (even 127.0.0.1 or 0.0.0.0). The colon followed by nothing tells pppd to translate the ISP-supplied IP address to the local address.

3. Set up a pppd configuration file.

   The pppd process can read a configuration file, if it exists, to control how it behaves. Most of the time the pppd configuration file is stored as /etc/ppp/options. Although the contents of the options file change with the version of Linux, the file usually has one or more lines in it. A good options file contains these entries:

```
domain foobar.com

auth              # turns on authentication

usehostname       # use local hostname for authentication

lock              # use UUCP-style file locking
```

   The first line defines the local domain name (if there is one). The second and third lines control machine authentication, which allows PPP to be sure which machines are using the connection. The last line controls how pppd locks files to prevent multiple use. If your ISP does not support authentication over PPP, you can ignore the second and third lines. If you don't have a domain, or don't want to use one in your connection, ignore the first line. All /etc/ppp/options files should have the lock line in them.

4. Combine the chat and ppp commands into a shell script.

   Since you don't want to manually enter both the chat and pppd lines at the shell prompt every time you connect to the Internet, you can simplify the process by combining the two commands into a shell script. The pppd command can contain the chat script, but it is often easier to leave two separate commands for faster debugging. To create the shell script, save the chat and ppd command lines into a file, call it something simple like "internet," and make the file executable. Simply typing the filename will now connect you to the ISP.

5. Test the PPP connection.

   Test your PPP configuration by running the commands to connect to the ISP and by ensuring that the modem dials out properly. After a connection is established, issue the following command:

   ```
   ifconfig
   ```

   You should see diagnostics about the connection. Look for a section labeled ppp0, which is the first PPP connection. If you don't get any ppp0 diagnostics, the connection failed. Check the command lines and make sure the modem is dialing out to the ISP. If you know the IP address of a different machine on the Internet, another way to test the PPP connection is to ping that machine.

6. Terminating the PPP session.

   The PPP connection will remain up until one end terminates it and the other finishes. To stop PPP, you can kill the pppd process, or wait for the other end of the connection to hang up. Many versions of Linux include a script called ppp-off (usually located in /usr/sbin) that will terminate the pppd daemon on demand.

CONFIGURING LINUX FOR DIAL-IN

By default Linux sets up modems for dial-out access only. You might want to dial in to your Linux system from somewhere else or allow others to access your system through the modem. To do so, you need to set your modem to allow dial-in. Since normal Linux logins are required, leaving a Linux system set for dial-in is not a major security problem. Only those who know a valid login and password will be granted access to your system. To allow dial-ins, tell Linux to activate a program called uugetty that watches the modem port for any incoming call. When one is detected, the login program is launched. To set up a modem for dial-in access, follow these steps:

1. Log in as root and edit the /etc/rc.d/rc.serial file

   The /etc/rc.d/rc.serial file is read by another script that is started by init. You can put the name of all serial devices that have a uugetty processes associated with them in this file. Since many systems will not have an /etc/rc.d/rc.serial file, you can create one from scratch. For each modem device that is to be used for dial-in access, add a line to the rc.serial file like the following, replacing the device name with your modem device name:

   ```
   /bin/setserial /dev/ttySX spd_hi
   ```

The spd_hi (speed high) option allows Linux to communicate with the modem much faster than the normal speed used to connect to other systems. This is useful when using 56 Kbps modems, as Linux was designed with an upper modem speed of 38400 bps. For even faster modems, such as ISDN or cable modems, use the spd_vhi (speed very high) option instead. You can always reset modems to the slower normal speed using the following command from the shell prompt:

```
setserial /dev/modem spd_normal
```

Some modems allow hardware handshaking instead of software. If your modem supports the RTS (Request to Send) and CTS (Clear to Send) signals, use them by adding the following line to the rc.serial file, again replacing the device name with the proper modem device name:

```
/bin/stty crtscts < /dev/ttySX
```

Since hardware handshaking is faster than software-controlled handshaking, this is a useful method for improving modem communications.

2. Tell /etc/inittab to start uugetty.

The /etc/inittab file tells Linux what processes to start when it boots. To have a dial-in modem answer calls, uugetty is best started from the /etc/inittab file. By default, uugetty is not usually in the /etc/inittab file. Thus, you will have to manually add it. To start uugetty from /etc/inittab, add the following lines (the first line is a comment line; replace the device name with your modem device name):

```
# start uugetty on /dev/ttyS3
```

```
s3:235:respawn:/sbin/uugetty ttyS3 F28800 vt100
```

The command line tells ttyS3 to start uugetty on run levels 2, 3, and 5 using the F28800 specification from /etc/gettydefs. The line will default to a vt100 terminal emulation, and will restart itself whenever the process terminates, or *respawns*.

3. Edit the /etc/gettydefs file.

To set up the uugetty process for each modem device that will receive dial-in calls, edit /etc/gettydefs by adding a line like the following:

```
# F28800 fixed baud rate modem entry
```

```
F28800# B28800 CS8 CRTSCTS # B28800 SANE —ISTRIP HUPCL
CRTSCTS  login: #F28800
```

You may find a line like this already in /etc/gettydefs, or you can copy a similar line and edit it. This line sets up a getty that communicates only at 28800 bps. To step down to different speeds, the last entry is changed to the next-lowest speed. B28800 sets the baud rate, CS8 sets eight-bit characters, CRTSCTS sets hardware handshaking, and HUPCL tells uugetty to hang up the line when it is cleared.

4. Edit the /etc/default/uugetty file.

To tell uugetty how to set up the modem and behave for incoming calls, the /etc/default/uugetty file is used. Individual uugetty files can be customized for each modem, by saving the configuration as /etc/conf.uugetty.ttySX where ttySX is the device name. Some Linux systems have a template uugetty file, while others do not. The contents of a simple /etc/default/uugetty file and the meaning of each line appended as a comment looks like the following:

```
INITLINE=cua2   # the device name to initialize (leave
off /dev/)

TIMEOUT=60      # number of seconds to forced
disconnect if idle

INIT="" \d+++\dAT\r OK\r\n #add modem autoanswer string
here

WAITFOR=RING    # wait for a ring

CONNECT="" ATA\r CONNECT \s\A# detect a connect
response from modem
```

If you do have an existing /etc/default/uugetty file, you will find these commands embedded in it along with a lot of comments.

5. Test the modem.

After making these changes, you can verify the setup works properly. The easiest way to ensure the configuration files are reread is to reboot the system. You can also issue the following command to tell init to reread /etc/inittab:

```
init q
```

To test the dial-in modem, dial the modem's telephone number from a standard phone or from another modem. When the phone line rings, the modem should answer and, unless the volume is turned down, you will hear the carrier sounds. If you are calling from another computer, you will receive a Linux login.

PROVIDING PPP CONNECTIONS ON A DIAL-IN LINE

You can configure your Linux system to provide PPP services to callers dialing in to your system. This is handy if you are setting up your system to be an Internet server or to provide other services to friends. The steps to set up PPP to handle incoming calls are simple:

1. Create a PPP account.

   To manage security and ownership, set up a special login to handle the PPP dial-in. You can edit the /etc/passwd file directly for this account, since it has no home directory, or you can use whichever user maintenance scripts came with your version of Linux, such as useradd. A typical entry in /etc/passwd for the PPP login looks like the following:

   ```
   ppp:*:250:52:PPP dial-in account:/tmp:/etc/ppp/ppplogin
   ```

   This line sets the login to ppp with no password. This line also sets the user ID to 250, which must be unique, and the group ID to 52, which must exist. The next part of the line is a comment explaining the use of the login, sets the home directory to /tmp, and executes the /etc/ppp/ppplogin script when an attempt to login as ppp is made. The account doesn't have to be called ppp; any name will do.

2. Set up the /etc/ppp/ppplogin script.

   The ppplogin script starts the PPP daemon for the incoming call. The script looks like the following:

   ```
   exec pppd —detach silent modem crtscts
   ```

   This line tells pppd to start up and not detach itself from the line. The silent option tells pppd to wait for the other system to connect to yours. The modem option tells pppd to monitor all configured modem lines for an incoming call, and to use hardware handshaking (crtscts) to talk to the modem.

SETTING UP PAP AND CHAP

Security is an important consideration with PPP. There are two security protocols used with PPP called PAP (Password Authentication Protocol) and CHAP (Challenge Handshake Authentication Protocol). CHAP is more secure than PAP, but both are in common use. Both PAP and CHAP rely on two interconnected systems for sending authentication messages to each other at intervals. This ensures that the machines are allowed to be on the connection and that nothing has broken in to the session. CHAP is invoked by using the auth option in the pppd command line or in the /etc/ppp/options file (as shown in the previous section of this chapter). The files CHAP and PAP use to contain the authentication information are called /etc/ppp/chap-secrets and /etc/ppp/pap-secrets, respectively. The format for both files is the same. The following is an example chap-secrets file:

```
# client             server                      string
merlin.foobar.com    brutus.animalhouse.com     "secret
login"
merlin.foobar.com    goof.cats-r-us.com          "meow
meow meow"
```

The file is in three columns, the first for the local host name, the second for the remote machine name, and the third for the authentication string. In this case, the local machine is merlin.foobar.com and any time the remote system goof.cats-r-us.com connects, CHAP expects the remote machine to supply the string "meow meow meow" to prove it is the machine it claims to be.

If your machine has to answer a challenge, the columns are reversed. To connect to the machine bigboys.rugby.com from merlin.foobar.com, you have an entry like this:

```
bigboys.rugby.com merlin.foobar.com    "tackle hard"
```

Whenever the bigboys machine asks your machine to authenticate itself, it sends the string "tackle hard." Since this is used at both ends, the two machines exchange this secret string to prove they are who they claim to be. If the string doesn't match, the protocol fails the authentication.

PAP and CHAP allow wildcards to be used so that entire domains or subnets can be authenticated with one chap-secrets line, instead of having to add many names for each possible access point. Asterisks are used to indicate complete domains, like this:

```
*.rugby.com        merlin.foobar.com    "tackle hard"
```

This line tells your machine that any machine on the rugby.com domain requires the "tackle hard" authentication. The same applies for the other column, too.

```
merlin.foobar.com *"this is a secret"
```

This line tells CHAP that any connection to your machine must have the specified authentication string.

SUMMARY

As you have seen, setting up your modem to work with Linux is simple. Configuring the dial-out and dial-in ports, as well as PPP, is a little more complex. Still, following the step-by-step instructions shown in this chapter will guide you through the process. While these commands are not intuitive, they are consistent with all versions of Linux (and UNIX).

INN AND NNTP: CONFIGURING LINUX FOR NEWS

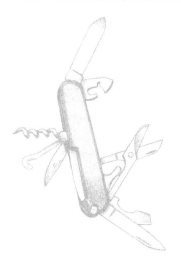

I nternet newsgroups are a popular source of information, gossip, troubleshooting advice, and just plain fun for many people. All this despite the fact that newsgroups are character-based in this GUI-centric decade. Usenet, the source of newsgroups, now provides over 100,000 newsgroups delivering hundreds of megabytes of information daily. Downloading all this data is unrealistic for most Linux systems, but the ability to download and browse through the newsgroups of interest to you is well within the grasp of all Linux users with an Internet connection. This chapter shows you how to download and post newsgroups information.

HOW USENET WORKS

You probably already know that Usenet is a collection of newsgroups, all grouped into subcategories like recreation (rec), computers (comp) and science (sci). Inside each high-level category are breakdowns to more explicit levels, such as comp.windows for Windows users and comp.mac for Macintosh users. There are more levels below these that further break down subjects, such as comp.lang.c for the C language and rec.auto.antiques for old cars. The number of newsgroups is vast, numbering over 100,000, and they cover any subject you can imagine.

Newsgroups are made up messages called *articles*. Usually these are ASCII text, but some newsgroups accept and handle binaries using UUENCODE or similar binary-to-ASCII converters. When you select to download a newsgroup, the newsgroup software figures out when you last downloaded articles and requests everything since then in a stream from the supplier. The supplier is usually an ISP for smaller systems. Sometimes the stream is limited by size, by the number of articles, or by the number of previous days you can retrieve. In other cases, you can retrieve all the articles ever posted to the newsgroup. When your system connects to a newsfeed, it uses a system called *ihave/sendme* to specify which articles it wants. This works when only a few newsgroups are involved, but when you are downloading megabytes of material, a different technique called *batching* is employed. With batching, everything in a newsfeed is sent in one block and your system sorts out duplicates later. Some newsgroups are limited to particular companies and physical areas, some are worldwide.

When someone writes a new article to a newsgroup, it is sent to one Usenet server which then uses a technique called *flooding* to send it to all other Usenet servers. In this way, your article joins the newsgroup along with all the other articles. Connections to a Usenet server are called *newsfeeds*, and most ISPs have one.

Two terms associated with Usenet newsfeeds are *pulling* and *pushing*. These are used with smaller systems that use the ihave/sendme system of transferring information instead of batching. When your system requests a particular newsgroup or even specific articles inside a newsgroup based on the date, it is pulling the news. When your system downloads the newsfeed without regard to the date, it is pushing the news.

GETTING NEWS

There are two ways to read newsgroups from your Linux system. The first is to forego downloading newsgroups to your system, and to instead connect to an ISP and read the news on their system. The option most users choose, however, is to download newsgroups directly to their Linux system, browse through them at their leisure, and post their own articles later. Since reading news on an ISP's system requires nothing more than a telnet or PPP link, as long as your ISP allows you to read on their system, there is nothing special you need do to Linux. On the other hand, if you want to download newsgroups to your system, you have some choices to make.

There are three ways to set up Linux to handle newsgroup downloads: C News, INN (Internet News), and NNTP (Network News Transfer Protocol). C News is designed to work best over UUCP connections to other UNIX hosts, and since most people now use TCP/IP to connect to ISPs, this approach is not covered here. INN and NNTP allow you to download newsgroups to your Linux system over a TCP/IP connection. INN is the most widely used approach for Linux systems because it is more configurable and flexible. Unfortunately, it is also a more difficult to set up than NNTP, the older of the two systems. Some Linux distributions include both INN and NNTP. Most, however, offer only the former because it is the newest and most capable newsgroup handler. Since INN is the most common choice for news access, it is the focus of the main part of this chapter. We will examine NNTP in its own section after looking at INN.

Be wary of disk space with newsgroups: a full feed of Usenet takes up over 1GB of disk space a day. Even downloading a small number of newsgroups can fill your disk. Each time you download ten average nonbinary newsgroups, for example, several megabytes of disk space are used, which quickly multiplies if you do not clean out old articles. Before you know it, your disk is full!

As for connection methods to download newsgroups, downloading a few megabytes a day takes a long time with a slow analog modem. If you move to the binary newsgroups, downloading a single newsgroup can take all day on a 56K modem! Use common sense and select newsgroups that can be handled easily by your system's connection to the Internet.

Of the many thousands of newsgroups on Usenet, there are more than a few of interest to Linux users, system administrators, and developers. The following newsgroups are exclusively about Linux, or are in some way related. Check them out!

◆ comp.os.linux.answers	HOWTOs and FAQs about Linux and utilities.
◆ comp.os.linux.announce	Moderated official Linux announcements.
◆ comp.os.linux.development.*	Linux development and applications.
◆ comp.os.linux.	Hardware questions and answers.
◆ comp.os.linux.networking	Networking questions and answers.
◆ comp.os.linux.x	Linux-specific X questions and answers.
◆ comp.os.linux.misc	Anything that doesn't fit anywhere else.
◆ comp.os.linux.*	Other newsgroups that come and go about Linux.
◆ comp.os.unix.*	UNIX questions and answers, often of interest to Linux users.
◆ linux.dev.kernel	Linux kernel development.
◆ linux.dev.*	Linux application development.
◆ comp.windows.x.*	X questions and answers for all platforms.
◆ gnu.*	GNU utilities and applications.
◆ gnu.emacs.*	GNU emacs questions and answers.

INSTALLING INN

INN is included with most versions of Linux, including RedHat, SlackWare, and Caldera. With most current versions of Linux, the INN binaries are compiled for you, although there are source code archives available on many FTP and web sites. The pre-compiled version is much easier to install, since you don't have to worry about modifying makefiles and running the compilers. Unfortunately, no decent documentation exists for INN yet, although there are FAQs included with the CD-ROM versions of INN, called INN-faq_part1 through INN-faq_part9.

There are no special hardware or software requirements to use INN. Essentially, any system that can run Linux can run INN, although the more RAM the better. Having some swap space allocated on your system for INN is wise, since the available memory may fill up quickly when articles are downloaded. If you are planning only on downloading a few newsgroups, then this is unnecessary.

Next, let's step through an install of INN on a typical Linux release. Some extra work is involved with some Linux releases, and is noted in the steps below:

1. Check whether INN is already installed. Some versions of Linux install INN during the original Linux installation. One easy way to find out if INN is installed is to check for the existence of the files /etc/rc.d/init.d/innd and /etc/rc/d/rc.news. The paths mentioned are the defaults for most versions of INN, although you may want to use the find command to make sure the files are not installed in some obscure location. If you are running a package installer like RedHat's RPM, you can check to see if the INN package is installed with a command like this:

    ```
    rpm —q inn
    ```

    Of course, if INN is already installed, skip the rest of these steps.

2. Check the /etc/passwd file for a user called "news". This exists in some versions of Linux and is missing in others. This user ID owns the INN files and newsgroups and should be set up if it doesn't exist. If the news user is missing, add it to /etc/passwd manually or through a user maintenance tool. The user ID is the important part: the home directory and startup shell do not matter, as they are not used.

3. After making certain there is a user called "news", a group of the same name is needed, too. Check /etc/group and add the "news" group if it isn't already there. There should be only one user of this group: "news".

4. Use whichever package installer your version of Linux supports, such as RPM, to install the INN software. By default INN is installed into /usr/lib/news which is where most newsreaders expect to find this information. If you want to install into another directory, set up symbolic links to /usr/lib/news to prevent problems in the

future. If you are not using a package installer, the INN archive should have a file that instructs you how to launch the installation routine. This is slightly different for each release of INN.

5. Start the INN daemon innd by issuing the command:

```
/etc/rc.d/init.d.innd start
```

The INN daemon often sends mail to the news user ID, so you may want to redirect it to another login. Do this by creating an alias in the mail system to root or any other user ID to which you want to redirect mail. Mail aliases are usually kept in a file like /etc/aliases. If you make a change to the file, reboot or run the command "newaliases" to make the changes take effect right away.

The INN program will have copied some files into the cron directory. These are used for cleaning out the news files on a regular basis. The files involved are usually placed in the /etc/cron directory, although some versions place them in /usr/spool/cron. The cron files have names like /etc/cron.daily/inn-cron-expire and /etc/cron.hourly/inn-cron -nntpsend. The latter file is responsible for sending any articles you generate to the news server on an hourly basis, unless you modify the default settings.

INN uses two daemons to control the news system. The first, called innd, handles the INN system itself. The nnrpd daemon provides the newsreader capability on your machine. Normally, innd is configured to start when your system boots, while nnrpd is started whenever a user invokes the newsreader. There is no advantage to keeping nnrpd running all the time.

CONFIGURING INN

If you needed to configure INN from scratch, an entire book would be required to explain the process and the available options. Fortunately most of the configuration is done for you with the Linux-distributed versions of INN. The defaults are set for most systems, and all you need to do is customize the configuration files. This section explains the most common configuration modifications.

◆ Check the /etc/news/inn.conf file and verify the accuracy of the local host name and an optional organization name that will append to the headers of your posted articles. The format of the lines in the inn.conf file is always a keyword followed by a colon, then white space, then the value. There are many keywords allowed with INN, most of which you won't want to use. A typical Linux inn.conf file looks like this:

```
server: localhost
organization: TPCI
```

You can also specify a domain name in the inn.conf file, although INN reads this from /etc/hosts if there is no domain line here. Note that some distributions of Linux do not use /etc/news as the path to the INN files, using /usr/lib/news instead.

◆ Edit the /etc/news/hosts.nntp file to provide the IP addresses of all your newsfeeds. Although more than one newsfeed is allowed, you will most likely have only one. The format of the /etc/news/hosts.nntp file is the IP address or DNS-resolvable name of the newsfeed followed by a colon and any password required to log in to that machine for the newsfeed itself. Many newsfeeds don't bother with passwords. The sample file below lists two newsfeeds, one requiring a password and the other not.:

```
205.150.89.1: gimmenews
47.1.1.306:
```

The simplest form of hosts.nntp will just have the localhost entry on a line, assuming you retrieve your newsfeed from some other utility, like this:

```
localhost:
```

◆ If you are going to allow other machines to access your Linux machine to read and post news, specify which machines and users are allowed in the /etc/news/ nnrp.access file. The format of this field is described further on in this chapter, along with some examples.

◆ Customize the expire.ctl file to specify how long to keep articles. This file is discussed later in this section.

CUSTOMIZING THE /ETC/NEWS/NNRP.ACCESS FILE

The /etc/news/nnrp.access file contents follow a particular format. This file is read whenever someone tries to use INN to use the news system. Each lint in the nnrp.access file has the same format, shown in here:

```
machinename:permissions:userID:password:newsgroups
```

In this syntax, machinename is the name of the machine on which the user is allowed to access the news system, permissions are the permissions allowed for that user, userID and password are used to authenticate the user's ID before articles are posted, and newsgroups are the newsgroups that the user is allowed to access.

The machinename field allows the use of entire subnets and domains using wild-cards or the use of single machine names including fully qualified domain names. The permissions are one of the following values:

- **Read**:   Provides read-only access.
- **Post**:   Allows posting of messages.
- **Read Post**:   Provides both Read and Post permissions.

If a user ID and password are not specified, then all users on the machine named in the line are allowed. If specific names are provided, only one user ID and password can be specified on each line.

The newsgroups field is used to allow access to specific newsgroups based on names and wildcards. For example, the entry sci.* allows access to all newsgroups starting with "sci". An exclamation mark prevents access to a group. For example, !comp.* prohibits access to any newsgroup starting with comp.

By default the nnrp.access is set to prevent all users from accessing news. The following nnrp.access file shows a variety of different setups:

```
*.tpci.com:Read Post:::
pluto.space.com:Read:guyl::!alt.
pluto.space.com:Read Post:roym::comp.*
```

This nnrp.access file allows anyone on the domain tpci.com to read and post newsgroup messages. There are no login and password checks, and no restrictions on the newsgroups to which users have access. The machine pluto in the domain space.com has several restrictions, though. The user guyl can read anything from the machine pluto.space.com except the alt hierarchy of newsgroups. He can't post to any newsgroups, because he does not have Post permission. The user roym can access the newsgroups from the same machine, and can read and post to any newsgroup starting with comp. Neither user has a password check performed by nnrp.access.

You can simplify this file enormously if you have no connections to other machines. In this case, only the localhost need be listed, like this:

```
localhost:Read Post:::*
```

When setting up the system, you can choose to limit newsgroups access to specific users, using nnrp.access to uniquely identify each user. You can instead open the domain wide, as the first line in the example above shows. Alternatively, you can even allow anyone connecting to your system from anywhere to read and post newsgroup articles from your machine by replacing the domain with an asterisk.

CUSTOMIZING THE EXPIRE.CTL FILE

The expire.ctl file is included with most distributions of Linux. It specifies how long to keep newsgroup postings. Without an expiration date, after which these files are deleted, your disk space would fill up quickly. The format of the two types of lines in the expire.ctl file are:

```
/remember/:14

pattern:flags:keep:default:purge
```

The first line occurs only once in the expire.ctl file and is usually set to fourteen. The second line occurs any number of times, setting expiration information for different newsgroups. An example from an expire.ctl file will help explain what's happening here:

```
/remember/:14

*:A:4:4:5

control:A:1:1:2

junk:A:1:1:2

comp.os.linux.*:A:1:7:7

alt.*:A:1:2:2
```

The fields in these lines, from left to right, specify the newsgroup patterns to be matched, a flag to indicate which newsgroups in that hierarchy (A for all, M for moderated, U for unmoderated), the minimum number of days to keep postings, the maximum number of days to keep postings, and the number of days after which postings are purged from the files. The file above starts by setting all newsgroups—shown by the asterisk and the A flag—not specifically mentioned later in the file to be kept for four days, and then deleted. The control and junk lines following this are used for INN internal tracking purposes, and postings there are kept for one day and purged on the second. Following the junk line is a specific instruction to keep comp.os.linux.* newsgroup postings for seven days and to keep all alt.* postings for only two days.

All INN information about newsgroups and the postings that are currently on the system are kept in the file active, usually in /etc/news. This file has a strict syntax of the newsgroup name followed by the highest and lowest article numbers currently kept by INN, followed by a flag to indicate whether local postings are allowed. This file is strict about syntax and any changes you make using an editor may cause INN to lose track of newsgroups. For this reason, you should never manually edit the active file.

INSTALLING NNTP

NNTP is included with some distributions of Linux and can be downloaded as source code from many UNIX archives. Because there are several site-specific details that must be linked into the binary, NNTP is rarely distributed as a binary file. Therefore, a compiler is needed to compile and link the NNTP programs. NNTP consists of two client programs, one for pulling the news and the other for pushing, as well as the server program. The server is called *nntpd* and, as the name suggests, it is a daemon that runs all the time on your Linux system.

Before installing and compiling NNTP, set up a directory in which the newsfeed will store articles. By default NNTP expects this to be /usr/spool/news/.tmp and the directory is owned by the user "news" and the group "news". The user and group entries are set up the same way as with INN, discussed previously, starting on page 146. You can accomplish the creation and permission-setting steps with two commands:

```
mkdir /usr/spool/news/.tmp

chown news.news /usr/spool/news/.tmp
```

You now have to make a decision about whether nntpd will be running all the time, started from the rc files when Linux boots, or whether it will be managed by inetd and started only when needed. The latter reduces the system load, except when news is downloaded. To set up nntpd in the inetd.conf file, add this line with an editor:

```
nntp  stream  tcp  nowait  news  /usr/etc/in.nntpd  nntpd
```

There is often a line like this already in the inetd.conf file, but commented out. If this is the case, simply remove the comment symbol. If you are setting up nntpd to be started by rc, make sure there is no nntpd line in the inetd.conf file. Instead, nntpd is started from one of the rc directories, usually rc.inet2.

As a final step before installing NNTP, add this line to the /etc/services file:

```
nntp 119/tcp readnews untp
```

This makes sure a TCP port is dedicated to nntpd. This line probably already exists and is commented out. In that case, simply remove the comment symbol.

After you have obtained the NNTP source code from the CD-ROM or a web archive, install the software using whatever script is supplied. This does not compile NNTP, though, and to begin the installation and configuration routine, you must run the file conf.h containing the configuration routine for NNTP. The default location on most systems is /usr/lib/news/common/conf.h although your location may be different. To be sure of the location of the NNTP files, use the find command to locate conf.h, as shown here:

```
find / -name conf.h -print
```

Run the conf.h program by changing into the directory and executing the shell script. The macros ask questions about your system, and then prepare NNTP.

After conf.h finishes compiling the NNTP binaries, provide more configuration information in the file /usr/lib/news/nntp_access (the default location), which is similar to the nnrp.access file discussed with INN. The format of the nntp_access file is:

```
machinename read-permissions post-permissions newsgroups
```

In this format, machinename is the name of the machine the line refers to, read- and post- permissions specify the permissions for reading and posting respectively, and newsgroups specifies the newsgroups to which access is granted or denied.

The read permissions are more complex than INN's nnrp.access file. There are four values allowed:

- **read**:   Can retrieve articles (pull the news).
- **xfer**:   Can send articles (push the news).
- **both**:   Can send and receive articles.
- **no**:   No access to articles.

The post permissions have only two values:

- **post**:   Can send articles.
- **no**:   Cannot send articles.

The newsgroups specify the newsgroups the line refers to in the same way as nnrp.access. Here is a sample nntp_access file:

```
default xfer no

linux.tpci.com  both post !alt

brutus.woof.com read no comp,sci
```

This file uses a default entry when no specific line matches. The default in this file is to allow pushing of the news, but no posting. No restrictions are posted on the newsgroups. Users on the machine linux.tpci.com can push and pull the news, as well as post articles, but can't access the alt newsgroups. Users on the system brutus.woof.com can pull news on the comp and sci newsgroups, but can't post to them. If a specific match for a system name is not found, no access is allowed. Access could be allowed if there is a line marked default that matches all remote machines not otherwise specified. Partial matches for names and domains are allowed in nntp_access.

NEWSREADERS

There are many newsreaders available to Linux users, most ported from UNIX. These range from the original limited-capability newsreaders, to threaded newsreaders, to the latest GUI-based tools with multiple window support. One keyword with many newsreaders is *threaded*, which means they are able to work with newsgroups that support threads. A thread is like a subject title that is propagated from message to message. The ability to use threads means that when you are reading messages about a subject, you can follow from message to reply to re-reply and so on without having many other subjects interspersed. Threads make reading newsgroups friendlier and easier.

If you are using a GUI-based browser on your Linux machine, such as the latest releases from Netscape, you may not need to install a dedicated newsreader. This is because many browsers have newsreader capabilities built in. An example of Netscape running newsgroups is shown in Figure 7-1.

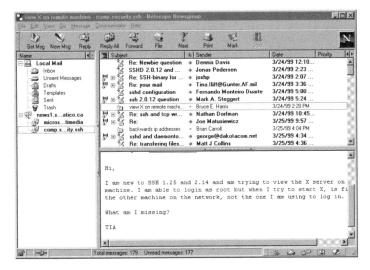

Figure 7-1   Netscape can be used to read newsgroups instead of a character-based newsreader.

The two most popular character-based newsreaders are trn and tin. A few other newsreaders are bundled with Linux, too, such as pine. The choice of newsreader is usually a personal one, balancing features against ease of use and ease of configuration. Most people will prefer a graphical newsreader such as Netscape Navigator, but character-based systems tend to be faster, and for those people who grew up on UNIX systems, more familiar.

USING TRN

The most popular non-GUI newsreader for Linux is trn, or *threaded read news,* which is a superset of the rn (read news) program used for many years. Although trn is old, it has the advantage of being fast, easy, and efficient. The trn newsreader is included with most CD-ROM versions of Linux that include the INN package.

The easiest way to install trn is with one of the package installers like RedHat's RPM. You can determine if trn is already installed by using the query command with RPM, as shown here:

```
rpm —q trn
```

If trn is not installed, load it off the CD-ROM. To install trn using RPM, issue the following command, replacing the RPM package name with the correct version from the CD-ROM:

```
rpm —i trn-3.6-12.i386.rpm
```

You can search for the trn release on the CD-ROM by mounting the CD and using the find command, like this:

```
mount /dev/cdrom /cdrom

find /cdrom — name trn —print
```

Note the package name that the find command returns.

If you are not using RPM or a similar package handler, install trn from an archive or tar file. Usually a script is included for the installation process, which involves copying the trn files to the default locations.

After installation there is no configuration required for trn unless you changed the location of the news files from the default of /usr/lib/news.

To use trn to read threaded newsgroups, you must tell trn how to build the threads. A thread database is constructed specifically for trn by a utility called *mthreads,* which is normally stored in /usr/local/bin/rn/mthreads, although several other locations are common. The mthreads utility reads all the messages in a newsgroup and builds the threads based on message numbers in the articles. This allows trn to follow from message to message in a single thread, or to ignore entire threads you are not interested in. The thread database doesn't have to exist for trn to work, but trn will not be able to follow threads without the database.

The best way to run mthreads is to place it in a crontab file and let it build the thread database after downloading news. You can always run mthreads from the command line if you want to force a thread database rebuild. The normal action is to build the threads of all the downloaded newsgroups. To specify a newsgroup for which to have the thread database built, provide the name of the newsgroup after the command, like this:

```
mthreads alt.humor
```

Or you can index an entire hierarchy by specifying the higher level newsgroup name, such as the following which indexes all the alt newsgroups:

```
mthreads  alt
```

To exclude newsgroups or hierarchies of newsgroups from the database build, use an exclamation mark. The following command indexes all the alt newsgroups, but ignores the alt.rec newsgroups:

```
mthreads alt,!alt.rec
```

To index everything in the downloaded newsgroups, use this command:

```
mthreads all
```

This is the command normally placed in the crontab file.

If you download multiple newsgroups, or you update frequently, launching mthreads from a crontab file may not work well, since the thread database quickly becomes dated. Fortunately, mthreads can be run in daemon mode, where it is active all the time. This mode does consume system resources, of course, but your threads are always in place and up to date. When in daemon mode, mthreads checks the newsgroups every ten minutes. To launch mthreads in daemon mode, use this command to reindex all the newsgroups:

```
mthreads —d all
```

You can specify and exclude specific newsgroups, as well, the same way as you would using mthreads from the crontab file or the command line.

USING TIN

Instead of depending on the mthreads-trn combination, you can choose a newsreader that doesn't need to have thread indexes rebuilt prior to use. One popular newsreader, called *tin*, rebuilds the indexes only when you need them. This only moderately slower, the delay when a newsgroup is entered being only a second or two unless the newsgroup is very large.

The tin newsreader is supplied with some distributions of Linux and is available on many Linux web sites and FTP archives. Installing tin involves copying the files into a directory in the search path. The tin newsreader is started by typing the name on the command line, or you can specify a newsgroup like this:

```
tin comp.os.linux.announce
```

When tin is launched with a newsgroup specified, it indexes the newsgroup and stores the index in a directory under the user's home directory, such as /usr/tparker/.tin/index/newsgroup_name where newsgroup_name is the name of the newsgroup. Since the .tin directory starts with a period it doesn't show up with normal ls commands.

The size of the newsgroup index directory can quickly grow if you read multiple newsgroups. This multiplies if there are several users on the system, as the newsgroup indexes are not shared in any way. For this reason, you may want to force tin to use a single location for all newsgroup indexes. Do this by setting up tin as the owner of news, and the group news, as shown in the following, providing the full path to tin:

```
chown news.news tin
```

This way, when tin executes it is as the user news, and the indexes are stored under news's home directory (make sure you specify a home directory in the /etc/passwd file).

By default, tin works with all the newsgroups you download. If you don't specify newsgroups, you will retrieve them all. Using a newsreader like tin, you can select newsgroups to download, and others to ignore.

If you do a lot of newsreading and find the delay while tin builds each index annoying, you can put tin in daemon mode which keeps all the indexes current. There is a daemon called tind which does this, and it is supplied with some versions of Linux. Since tind is usually distributed as source code, it will need compiling.

S U M M A R Y

Setting up your system for Usenet access is not difficult, although a little time-consuming. However, if you have ever been hooked on reading newsgroups on a regular basis (and it can be very addictive), the effort is worthwhile. It is also handy to be able to share your newsfeed with friends. There are many interesting newsgroups available, and a wide number of newsreaders. You will eventually find the one that you stick with, and until then there is plenty with which to experiment and experience.

USING

FTP

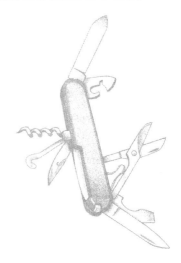

The last chapter looked at setting up your Linux system to use the Internet. E-mail and the World Wide Web are the reasons most people connect to the Internet. Another major use of the Internet, and the reason why it was originally developed, is transferring files from one machine to another. There are several ways to move files from one system to another, but the most common and the fastest is File Transfer Protocol (FTP). In this chapter we look at how to set up and use FTP on your Linux system.

THE BASICS OF FTP

The File Transfer Protocol (FTP) is used to move files over a TCP/IP network. While FTP is character-based, there are a few GUI interfaces to FTP. FTP uses two TCP ports: port 20 is used to transfer data and port 21 is used to transfer commands. Linux reserves these ports for FTP when it sets up the TCP/IP services.

When you request a file from another machine, your machine is asking for a service. Your machine is the client, and the other machine is the server, since it is servicing your requests. If someone requests files from your Linux machine the roles are reversed: your machine is the server and the remote machine is the client. Your machine can act as both client and server at the same time.

To handle FTP requests coming to your machine, a server daemon called ftpd is kept running at all times (it is launched from /etc/inetd.conf). Whenever a request is made through TCP port 21, ftpd services that incoming request, if you have allowed it to. To ask for files from another system, you don't need ftpd. Instead, the ftp program itself connects to ftpd running on the server and retrieves the files you want. All FTP actions are in foreground with no caches or spooling.

While most UNIX and Linux systems run an FTP daemon like ftpd to service incoming requests, the same is not true for most other operating systems. You cannot retrieve files from a Windows machine, for example, unless there is add-on software configured to handle FTP requests. The same applies to Macintosh machines. Although Windows NT can be set up to handle FTP requests, it usually isn't by default.

Providing FTP services to other machines is available in two modes: normal and anonymous. In normal mode, each user connecting to your FTP server must have a valid login and password on your system. FTP checks the /etc/passwd file for each attempted login. Anonymous FTP, on the other hand, allows anyone access to the system's file transfer area. This is useful if you want to make files available to everyone on the Internet, for example, and don't want to bother adding the users to the user list. Anonymous FTP carries some security risks with it, but if properly configured, the risks are minimized.

INSTALLING FTP CLIENT AND SERVER PACKAGES

Most Linux systems use a version of the FTP server daemon called wu-ftpd. The ftpd daemon is often installed when you load Linux, but if it isn't it can be added through a configuration or package tool like RPM. There are three components of FTP to consider loading: client (FTP), server (ftpd), and anonymous FTP. These are the steps to follow to install and test FTP:

1. Install the server package.

   Use whichever configuration or package tool your Linux system employs and load the ftpd package. To install wu-ftpd on a RedHat system using RPM, for example, issue the following command replacing the package name with whatever version of wu-ftpd is supplied with your system (you can use a find command to locate the rpm library on the CD-ROM):

   ```
   rpm —i wu-ftpd-2.4.2b17-2.i386.rpm
   ```

2. Install the anonymous FTP package.

   If you want to provide anonymous FTP services, install an anonymous FTP program. Again, returning to RedHat using RPM, the command looks like this:

   ```
   rpm —i anonftp-2.5-1.i386.rpm
   ```

3. Install the FTP client.

If you want to use only the client aspect of FTP, requesting files from other machines, you don't need to install the ftpd or anonftp packages. You still need to install the FTP client package through RPM. To use client, server, and anonymous FTP you should install all three packages. Some versions of FTP for Linux include all three capabilities in a single FTP package.

USING FTP TO TRANSFER A FILE

As mentioned earlier, some graphical interfaces to FTP are available, especially on Windows platforms, but the majority of users rely on the older character-based interface. Fortunately, FTP is easy to learn and use, especially for most routine file transfers. There are some obscure commands available in FTP, but it's unlikely you will ever use them.

A key point to remember when using FTP is that once you've connected to a remote machine, you are still on your own machine as far as FTP is concerned. That means that all file commands are relative to your machine. When you issue an instruction to retrieve a file, you are retrieving it from the remote machine and storing it on the local machine.

The easiest way to start FTP and connect to another machine is to issue the IP address or resolvable name on the command line like this:

```
ftp 205.150.89.1
```

If the specified machine can be reached through FTP and the machine's ftpd answers the request, you will see a login prompt. If you are using a valid system login, enter the login and password at the prompts. Many systems allow anonymous FTP access using the logins anonymous or guest. Most systems that do allow anonymous FTP access request that you enter your e-mail address as the password. This is used for identification and logging purposes only and is not validated prior to granting you access to the system.

Before discussing file transfers, it's important to understand that FTP has two file transfer modes: ASCII and binary. ASCII is used for any text file, while binary is used for executable files or data files that use all eight bits in a byte, including the high order bits (128-256). On many FTP systems you must manually change the mode of the file transfer, while a few FTP clients can change themselves when they recognize a binary file being transferred. Transferring an ASCII file in binary mode has no effect on the contents of the file, but transferring a binary file in ASCII mode ruins the contents. Most FTP systems, including Linux's, start in ASCII mode.

Once you are connected to the remote system, the prompt changes to the following:

```
ftp>
```

At this point you can use any valid FTP command. Some valid FTP commands are shown in Table 8-1.

Table 8-1   Valid FTP User Commands

Command	Meaning
ascii	Switch to ASCII transfer mode.
binary	Switch to binary transfer mode.
cd	Change directory on the server.
close	Terminate the connection.
del	Delete a file on the server.
dir	Display the directory listing on the server.
get	Retrieve a file from the server.
hash	Display a hash symbol for each transferred block.
help	Show help information.
lcd	Change directory on the local machine.
mget	Retrieve several files from the server.
mput	Send several files to the server.
open	Connect to a server.
prompt	Suppresses y/n prompts.
put	Send a file to the server.
pwd	Display current server directory.
quote	Provide a direct FTP command.
quit	Terminate an FTP session.

The easiest way to learn to use FTP is by looking at a few examples. Suppose you want to connect to a remote machine and transfer a file. It's easiest to change to the destination directory on your machine first, although you could use the lcd command once FTP has started up.

Start FTP with the name or IP address of the remote machine and log in. Once logged in, use the cd command to change to the directory containing the file you want. If the file is not standard ASCII text, switch to binary mode with the binary command. Otherwise leave FTP in ASCII mode. Then, retrieve then file by issuing the get command with the filename. Close the session with the quit command. The entire session looks like the following:

```
ftp 205.150.89.1
331 Guest login ok, send e-mail address as password.
Enter username (default: anonymous): anonymous
Enter password: superduck@quackquack.com
|FTP| Open
230 Guest login ok, access restrictions apply.
ftp> cd ./filedir
ftp> binary
binary mode on
ftp> get bigfile
62536 bytes received in 3.4 seconds
ftp> quit
```

If you are sending a file from your system to the remote system, use the put command. You will need to have write permission to the target directory in order to save the file on the remote system.

You can send or receive multiple files using wildcards with the mget and mput commands. In this case, unless you turn prompting off, you are asked if you want to transfer each individual file that matches your wildcard. The session on the following page shows an example of one that turns prompting off.

```
ftp 205.150.89.1
331 Guest login ok, send e-mail address as password.
Enter username (default: anonymous): anonymous
Enter password: superduck@quackquack.com
|FTP| Open
230 Guest login ok, access restrictions apply.
ftp> cd ./filedir
ftp> binary
binary mode on
ftp> prompt
prompt mode off
ftp> mget *.c
file1.c 6453 bytes received in 1.4 seconds
file2.c 7364 bytes received in 1.6 seconds
file3.c 1324 bytes received in 1.0 seconds
ftp> cd ../uploads
ftp> put myfile
76253 bytes sent in 5.7 seconds
ftp> quit
```

There is no confirmation of progress with FTP until a file transfer has been completed. When sending large files, this can lead you to wonder whether anything is actually happening. The hash command is useful for solving this problem; it prints a hash symbol on the screen for every block of data that is transferred, as in the next example:

```
ftp> binary
binary mode on
ftp> hash
hash mode on
ftp> put bigfile1.foo
###########################################
21324 bytes sent in 5.0 seconds
```

At least when you see the hash marks you know something is happening!

SETTING UP AN FTP SERVER

If you have files you want to make available to others, or you need to share directories with friends or coworkers in other cities, FTP is a great way to handle filesharing. In order for others to upload or download files from your system, you must have the FTP server daemon working. The setup of the FTP daemon is easy, although configuring and setting permissions is more convoluted and time-consuming. The following steps show the process to follow:

1. Pick a name.

   Your FTP server needs a name, which usually includes your domain name, if you have one. For example, if your domain is catfood.com, your FTP server may be ftp.catfood.com. This is the most common format for an FTP server name, and others can readily identify your FTP site through this explicit name. On the other hand, if you want to prevent unwanted and anonymous logins, rename the FTP server so that only valid users know the name, hiding the most obvious name from Internet users.

2. Make sure ftpd loads in /etc/inetd.conf.

   To handle incoming requests, the ftpd daemon should always be running. The daemon is started from /etc/inetd.conf which is read by the inet daemon. By default most Linux inetd.conf files have the proper entry in them, although it may be commented out. Your /etc/inetd.conf file should have a line like this in it:

   ```
   ftp   stream   tcpowait   root   /etc/ftpd   ftpd
   ```

   If this line is missing, add it to the file. If the line is commented out, remove the comment symbol. If you want to enable logging, change the /etc/ftpd command to add the –l option.

3. Create an ftp user.

   All ftpd processes should be owned by a special ftp UID to prevent misuse. Add an entry to your /etc/passwd file like the following:

   ```
   ftp:*:205:52:FTP access:/tmp:/bin/false
   ```

   The UID and GID needs to be set properly; the UID is unique and the GID should be an existing group. Ideally you will have a separate group just for anonymous FTP access. This allows for even tighter security. If your FTP server is allowing real logins—those that are in the system's /etc/passwd file—make sure everyone who accesses your machine has a valid passwd file entry.

4. Test the FTP system.

Test the system's client and server capabilities by FTPing to your own machine. Use the following where linux is the name of the machine you are on:

```
ftp linux
```

If the FTP client and server are working properly, you see something like this, along with version numbers and a login prompt:

```
Connected to linux.tpci.com
220 linux.tpci.com FTP server
```

If you did not install the client package properly, you see a message that the ftp program can't be found. If the server daemon is not installed, you will not receive a reply and the connection times out.

If the FTP system is responding properly, you can log in to your own system using any valid login and password. The prompt will change to "ftp>". Exit FTP with the quit command. To check anonymous logins, repeat the procedure using "guest" as the login name. If anonymous FTPs are allowed, the system should respond with a message like the following:

```
331 Guest login ok, send e-mail address as password.
```

If you then enter any e-mail address, you should be in FTP again. You can log out using the quit command.

CONTROLLING ACCESS TO YOUR FTP SERVER

When the default installation of FTP is performed, security is pretty good. If you are going to be leaving your system connected to the Internet or a phone line, you should tighten up this FTP security. Access to FTP is controlled by a set of four files. These files specify who can log in, what they can access, and whether an audit trail of user transactions is retained. You only need to worry about configuring these files if you are going to act as an FTP server. This section shows how to modify these files to control access and tighten security.

MODIFY /ETC/FTPACCESS TO SET CLASSES

The /etc/ftpaccess file, as the name implies, controls who can access the FTP service. This is not a trivial file to configure, but a methodical approach to its setup pays dividends in security. The first part of the file deals with access to FTP and whether anonymous FTP is supported. There are seven commands allowed in this section of the /etc/ftpaccess file.

- ◆ **class**:   Defines the class of users who are allowed access.
- ◆ **autogroup**:   Controls anonymous logins permissions.
- ◆ **deny**:   Explicitly denies service.
- ◆ **guestgroup**:   Restricts real users' FTP permissions.
- ◆ **limit**:   Limits access times.
- ◆ **loginfails**:   Sets the number of failed login attempts before disconnect.
- ◆ **private**:   Sets special access rights.

The format of the *class* command is the keyword class followed by a classname, a list of users allowed to be in this class, and a range of IP addresses allowed to access that class. By default a class is established in ftpaccess like this:

```
class all real,guest,anonymous *
```

This creates a class called "all" with three users allowed: real, for any valid login on the system, and guest and anonymous used for anonymous FTP. Any IP address can access this class.

Since you can use classes to control access to different areas of the filesystem, you might want to create other classes that access particular directories. For example, to add a class called project_a that will eventually have access to a restricted directory, add a line to /etc/ftpaccess like the following, where login1, login2 (and any others you add) are valid logins on your system:

```
class project_1 login1,login2 *
```

Since this class grants access to a sensitive directory, don't allow guest or anonymous logins to this class. You can specify a range of IP addresses, or you can restrict to a particular netmask like this:

```
class project_1 login1,login2 205.150.89.*
```

This restricts access to project_1 to IP addresses starting with 205.150.89.

If you plan to allow anonymous access so remote users can upload or download files, you may want to create a special class just for anonymous or guest logins. These logins can then be restricted to a particular directory with very strict permissions. For example, the following class definition sets up a class called anons that allows only anonymous logins:

```
class anons guest,anonymous *
```

Of course, you should remove guest and anonymous from all other classes.

The *autogroup* command is often used with anonymous FTP sites to control group permissions for anyone logging in anonymously. The syntax of the autogroup command is the keyword autogroup, followed by the name of the group to which the user is to be assigned, followed by the name of a class (or multiple classes). Since the autogroup command deals with group permissions, the group has to be defined in /etc/ groups. For example, the next command will assign any anonymous FTP users to the group visitors (which will have suitably restrictive permissions) and the class anons:

```
autogroup visitors anons
```

By default, autogroup is not assigned in many ftpaccess files. If you are planning to allow anonymous FTP access to your system, consider setting up both an anonymous class and an autogroup command as shown here.

The *deny* command lets you deny access to FTP based on IP addresses, machine names, or unresolvable DNS names. This example of the deny command shows the syntax where the domain nasties.com is denied access and a message in /usr/lib/ get_lost is displayed when someone from nasties.com tries to gain access:

```
deny nasties.com /usr/lib/get_lost
```

The *guestgroup* command is used when you want to allow existing valid system users to use FTP but with reduced permissions. This is handy when users need to access FTP through the Internet from a hotel room, for example, but you want to ensure that they don't have complete access to all of the filesystem. The format of the guestgroup command is the keyword, followed by a group name. The group specifies the permissions for the user while they are connected through FTP. A valid guestgroup command looks like the following, where remoteusers is a valid group in /etc/groups with more restrictive permissions than the user's normal group:

```
guestgroup remoteusers
```

The *limit* command is used to control the number of users logging in to your server either by class or by time of day. This is handy for keeping the system from becoming bogged down when you want to use it yourself. To use the limit command, specify the class, the maximum number of users allowed on the system in that class, the times when that limit is in effect, and a message to be displayed if access is denied. For example, this command will only allow five users in the anons class between 6:00 A.M. and 7:00 P.M. (local time):

```
limit anons 5 MoTuWeThFr600-1900 /usr/lib/busy_message
```

If others try to access the system, they are shown the contents of /usr/lib/ busy_message. The days of the week and times are specified using the first two letters of the days, or the entire week using the shorthand "Wk". Times are specified in 24-hour format with a dash for a range.

The *loginfails* command is used to specify the number of failed attempts to log in before the connection is terminated. The default value if usually set to five. To change the number to two, use this command in the ftpaccess file:

```
loginfails 2
```

Do not set it below two as some remote systems won't show the first login prompt properly and hence will fail on the first try.

The *private* command is used when you want to share files with some users but don't want those files residing in a public directory available to all callers. To use the private option you need to use the "site group" and "site gpass" to move these callers into a different group. The syntax of the private command specifies simply yes or no to indicate whether private is on or off. By default it is off. When private is on, a special password file called /etc/ftpgroups is used to verify the special group passwords. The format of the ftpgroups file is the FTP group name, the password, and the real group name separated by colons like this:

```
project_a:Hg*@j(isll6$skahHf:projusers
```

Here project_a is the FTP group name used by the person dialing in. The real system group to which they belong is projusers and it is preceded by the proper password that must be entered. Because the Linux passwd command can't be used to change the password in the ftpgroups file, use the crypt command on your selected password, and then cut and paste the encrypted result into the ftpaccess file.

MODIFY /ETC/FTPACCESS TO SET BANNERS

When a user logs in to FTP there are four commands that control what the system tells them. These commands are used in the /etc/ftpaccess file and can be customized to show anything you want. The four commands are:

- ◆ **banner**: Specifies the sign-on information.
- ◆ **email**: Gives an e-mail contact.
- ◆ **message**: Displays messages when some action takes place.
- ◆ **readme**: Shows when a file was last modified.

The *banner* command is a pointer to a file displayed before the remote user logs in to your system. It is usually used to announce security policies and shows whether anonymous logins are allowed. You can also use it to provide information about the system and available directories, although this is best left until the user has logged in. The banner command is followed by the name of the file to be displayed:

```
banner /usr/lib/ftp_welcome
```

The *email* command provides an e-mail address so that anyone connecting to the site can send comments or questions. By default the e-mail address is root@localhost. This can be changed using the email command like this:

```
email ftpmanager@localhost
```

You can use e-mail aliases to redirect this incoming mail to whomever you want. You should usually show this in the files displayed when users log in.

The *message* command is used to send special messages to users under certain circumstances. The format is the message command followed by the path to the message to be displayed, when the message is displayed, and any classes to which the message applies. The message is triggered by a login or a change into a particular directory. For example, the following command displays the message in updir_message whenever the user changes into the directory /tmp/upload:

```
message /usr/lib/updir_message CWD=/tmp/upload
```

If the keyword LOGIN is used instead of CWD, the message is displayed when the user logs in. There can be any number of message commands in an ftpaccess file. The example above does not show any classes. These can be added to trigger a message only if the user is in a specified class, such as anonymous users. For example, the following command will display the message anon_message when someone logs in to the group anons:

```
message ./anon_message LOGIN anons
```

This is handy for explaining directory structures and policies.

There are many special characters that can be embedded in the messages to display hostnames and other information, as shown in Table 8-2. Bear in mind that when dealing with anonymous logins all paths must be relative to the FTP directory, not the root filesystem.

Table 8-2   Valid Message Characters

Option	Meaning
%C	Current directory.
%E	E-mail address (same as in email command).
%F	Free space in current directory.
%L	Server name.
%M	Maximum number of users allowed by class.
%N	Current number of users by class.
%R	Client name.
%T	Local time.
%U	User name (provided at login).

The *readme* command is used to let users know when a file in their current directory was last modified. This is useful for things like READMEs and descriptions of a directory's contents. The format begins with the readme command, followed by the path of the file to check, when to check the file, and the class for which the command applies. The latter two components are optional.

MODIFY /ETC/FTPACCESS TO SET LOGGING

Logging lets you record what visitors to your system are doing. This is helpful for seeing which files are popular downloads or which users are becoming a little too nosey. Logging is not helpful when the system has been compromised and crashed. On top of that, log files on busy systems can become quite large. Two commands control logging:

◆   Log commands
◆   Log transfers

The *log commands* command allows you to log every time a user you specify executes a command. For example, to log all commands from the guest login, you would put this command in ftpaccess:

```
log commands guest
```

To specify more than one user, use a comma-separated list.

Instead of logging a user's commands, you can log just file transfers with the *log transfers* command. The syntax requires you to specify which users will be logged as well as list in which direction transfers should be recorded (upload or download). For example, the following command logs all transfers, both uploaded and downloaded, for anyone logging in as anonymous or guest:

```
log transfers anonymous, guest inbound,outbound
```

Both lists are comma-separated. When logging is active, the log is stored in /var/log/xferlog. Formatting the file xferlog requires a line for each transaction. These lines consist of the following information:

◆   Time
◆   Transfer time
◆   Remote host
◆   Filesize
◆   Filename
◆   Type of transfer (ascii or binary)
◆   Any compression action taken on the file (C for compressed, U for uncompressed, T for tar, and – for no action)
◆   Direction (o for outgoing or I for incoming)
◆   Access mode (a for anonymous, g for guest, r for real)
◆   Local username if real
◆   Service (ftp)
◆   Authentication used
◆   Authentication user ID

MODIFY /ETC/FTPACCESS PERMISSIONS

Permissions for a user logging in to FTP are controlled by the /etc/ftpaccess file. There are a number of ways to control the permissions of a user once they are logged in, all governed by the following commands:

- ◆ **chmod**: Indicates whether a user can change server file permissions.
- ◆ **delete**: Indicates whether a user can delete files.
- ◆ **overwrite** Indicates whether a user can replace files.
- ◆ **rename**: Indicates whether a user can rename files.
- ◆ **umask**: Indicates whether a user can change permissions.
- ◆ **passwd-check**: Checks password e-mail address.
- ◆ **path-filter**: Sets acceptable upload filenames.
- ◆ **upload**: Specifies permissions a user has to upload directories.

The *chmod* command indicates whether the FTP user can change the permissions of files on the server. The command is specified with either a yes or no switch followed by a comma-separated list of anonymous, guest, or real. Real indicates a valid /etc/passwd login, while the other two are used for anonymous FTP. For example, the following command means that a valid system user can change server file permissions over an FTP connection:

```
chmod yes real
```

A number of commands control other aspects of file manipulation over an FTP connection. The *delete* command indicates whether the user over a connection can delete files. It is used in the same way as chmod. In the same manner, the *overwrite* command indicates whether an FTP user can upload files that replace existing files on the server. The *rename* command has the same syntax as chmod and indicates whether the user can rename files over the connection. The *umask* command is used similarly to indicate whether file permissions can be changed over the connection. Obviously, allowing anonymous FTP users to perform many of these actions is undesirable, but real users may in many cases find these capabilities helpful.

Anonymous FTP usually asks a client to provide an e-mail address to log in. The *passwd-check* command allows you to validate this e-mail address in a number of ways. The syntax of the command uses one of three values—none, trivial, or rfc882—to determine the strictness of the e-mail check and one of two values—warn or enforce—for the enforcement. The strictness checks are used to indicate whether you want valid e-mail addresses. A value of none indicates no check; a setting of trivial checks that the e-mail address at least looks logical (usually this means it has an @ in it); and the rfc882 setting, the strictest, tries to verify that the e-mail address adheres to address rules. None of these settings actually verify that the address is real. The enforcement setting indicates what to do in the case that a user fails the e mail address requirements. The user is either warned and let in anyway or forced to provide an address that meets the strictness requirements before gaining access. These passwd-check settings are easy to defeat as any e-mail address can be used, whether it is the user's or not.

The *path-filter* command is used to control filenames for uploads. This is often used to prevent the use of illegal characters like control codes in filenames. The command is followed by a list of affected users (anonymous, guest, real), a message file displayed if the file does not meet requirements, a regular expression valid filenames must meet, and a regular expression defining illegal values. For example, let's say you want to prevent GIFs from being uploaded. The following command displays the message in /usr/lib/bad_filename if the uploaded filename ends with "gif":

```
path-filter guest,anonymous /usr/lib/bad_filename * gif$
```

To force uploads to start with a certain character, the character could be used in place of the asterisk in the example above.

The *upload* command is used with path-filter to specify to which directories files can be uploaded. The command is followed by a directory; a regular expression to determine whether subdirectories under the specified directory can be used; a yes or no switch to indicate that files can or can't be placed there; the owner, group, and mode of the file uploaded; and one of two values indicating whether subdirectories can be created (dirs and nodirs). An example is shown in the following commands:

```
upload /home/ftp /uploads yes ftp ftp 0600 dirs

upload /home/ftp /downloads no ftp ftp 0600 dirs
```

These specify that files can be uploaded to the /home/ftp/uploads directory and any new directories that the user wants to create under it, and that files are owned by user ftp, group ftp, and have file mode 0600. The second line prohibits uploads to the /home/ftp/downloads directory.

MODIFY /ETC/FTPACCESS MISCELLANEOUS SETTINGS

The /etc/ftpaccess file can have a number of commands different from the ones already shown. These are for miscellaneous items such as path control, compression, and aliases. The miscellaneous commands supported are:

- **alias**:   Sets up short names for longer directory paths.
- **cdpath**:   Sets the path for the cd command search
- **compress**:   Provides compression and decompression for files.
- **shutdown**:   Lets the server shut down if a file exists.
- **tar**:   Provides tar compression and decompression for files.

The *alias* command lets you define directory aliases for use with the cd command. This allows you to provide shortcuts to directory paths that may be too long or convoluted to be friendly to visitors, as well as to hide the structure of your filesystem. For example, the following command will change to the long directory path whenever the FTP user types "cd stuff":

```
alias stuff /usr/tparker/file/book1/bin
```

While it is wise to organize FTP directory structures to be self-contained and separate from the rest of your filesystem, there are times when the alias command saves you from having to copy files into more than one location.

The *cdpath* command, as the name implies, provides the search path for use by the cd command. This is handy when you want to search for a directory name in several locations. For example, suppose your FTP visitor issues the command "cd book." While Linux would look only in the current directory for a subdirectory called book, cdpath lets you set up other locations in which to look for this subdirectory. Suppose your /etc/ftpaccess file had these entries:

```
cdpath /usr/temp/linux
```

```
cdpath /usr/temp/tcpip
```

```
cdpath /usr/temp/unix
```

When the user issues "cd book," it will look first in the current directory for a subdirectory called book, then in /usr/temp/linux, and then in /usr/temp/tcpip and /usr/temp/unix. Whenever a subdirectory called book is found, it changes into it.

Most ftpd packages offer the *compress* option. This allows the FTP server to compress and decompress files before or after transfer, cutting down on transfer time. It also allows compressed files to be uncompressed before transfer. While this adds to the transfer time, it does allow users without the proper compression tool to grab your files. For example, if you keep your files in .gzip format in your FTP directory and a Windows user doesn't have access to gunzip or gzip, they could use the compress option to decompress the file before transferring. To use compress you simply specify whether the option is on (yes) or off (no) with a list of all classes that can use this option. For example, the following command lets anyone in the anons class use compression or decompression:

```
compress yes anons
```

A file called /etc/ftpconversions holds information about which utilities to use to compress and decompress files. The defaults are to use compress or gzip.

The *shutdown* command is rarely used but offers a way to shut the system down if the mode of FTP has to be changed; for example, sending all FTP processes into background. Since you will probably never need to use this command, we will not cover it.

The *tar* command works like compress, allowing tar to be used to transfer files. Again, a command line with yes or no specifies whether tar is used. The file /etc/ftp conversions controls which compression tool is employed. In the next section, we look at /etc/ftpconversions.

MODIFY /ETC/FTPCONVERSIONS FOR REQUIRED CONVERSIONS

The /etc/ftpconversions file is used to control compression and uncompression, as well as file conversions as they are being uploaded or downloaded. The format of the file is any number of lines, with each line being a series of eight character sequences separated by colons. The fields are, in order of appearance:

◆ Strip prefix
◆ Strip postfix
◆ Add-on prefix
◆ Add-on postfix
◆ Command to perform conversion
◆ Type of file
◆ Logging options
◆ Description

The *strip prefix* and *strip postfix* fields are strings at the beginning and end of the filename that are removed when the file is uploaded or downloaded. The postfix is usually used to remove strings like .gzip, while the prefix is sometimes used to strip character string indicators from the name. For example, upfile1.gzip and upfile2.gzip would come across as file1 and file2.

The *add-on prefix* and *add-on postfix* fields are similar to the strip versions except they add strings to the start or end of a filename. The *command to perform conversion* field is the name of the program to use to perform any compress, conversion, or decompression, such as gzip. The *type of file* is a list of up to three possible filetypes to which this line in the ftpconversions file applies. Valid values are T_REG (regular files), T_ASCII (ASCII files), and T_DIR (directories). A pipe separates multiple values. The *logging options* field is similar to the type of file field in that it indicates one or more of three values: O_COMPRESS (compress files), O_UNCOMPRESS (uncompress files) or O_TAR (use tar on the file). Finally, the *description* is any text description you want to apply to the line for reference purposes.

The most common use of the ftpconversions file is to handle gzipped files that require no pre- or post-conversion changes except to add or remove the .gz or .gzip extension. The ftpconversions entry looks like this:

```
:::.gz:/bin/gzip —c %s:T_REG:O_COMPRESS:GZIP compression
::.gz::/bin/gzip —dc %s:T_REG:O_UNCOMPRESS:GZIP
decompression
```

The % symbols in the command line substitute the filename when the expression is expanded.

MODIFY /ETC/FTPHOSTS

FTP uses the /etc/ftphosts file to establish whether users are allowed to log on from specific machines. The ftphosts file can be used to explicitly allow or explicitly deny hosts. The format of the file requires the keywords allow or deny, followed by a user-name and an IP address. These entries are an example:

```
allow rmaclean 205.150.89.*,47.*
```

```
deny mmaclean *
```

These entries allow the user rmaclean to log in from the subnets 205.150.89 and 47 (Class C and A addresses respectively; any machine on these subnets) yet denies the user mmaclean from logging in from any host.

ADMINISTERING YOUR FTP SERVER

There are three utilities provided to help you administer your FTP server: ftpshut, ftp-who, and ftpcount. The *ftpshut* command shuts down the FTP server if it is active all the time. The format of the ftpshut command is the following:

```
ftpshut —l mins —d dropmins time messagefile
```

In this command, mins is the number of minutes before the FTP server shuts down and refuses any more FTP requests, the default being ten minutes); dropmins is the number of minutes before shutdown that the server starts dropping connections, the default being five minutes; time is the time the server will be shut down, either as a 24-hour clock time or as a number of minutes from now (as in +15, or the keyword "now"); and messagefile contains the message sent to all connected FTP users. Not all these options are required on a command line.

The *ftpwho* command shows you the users connected to your FTP server. The output of the ftpwho command shows five columns:

◆ PID, which is the process ID.

◆ Tty of the process (always a "?")

◆ Stat (R for running, S for sleeping, and Z for crashed (zombied))

◆ Time, which is how much CPU time has been used.

◆ Details showing where the connection is from and who is logged in.

The output from an ftpwho session looks like this:

```
6352 ? R 0:01 ftpd: brutus.dogs.com: anonymous/bru@dogs.com
6726 ? S 0:00 ftpd: ricecake.food.com: ychow@food.com
7265 ? R 0:00 ftpd: merlin.cats.com: anonymous/guessme@cats.com
```

The *ftpcount* command is a simplified version of ftpwho showing the total count of all the users on your FTP server as well as the maximum number of users allowed.

SUMMARY

This chapter has stepped you through the process of setting up and configuring your Linux system to act as both an FTP client and an FTP server. You may not want to be a server to others, but FTP is a handy way of sharing files. Anonymous FTP sites are often used on the Internet. Although you must carefully and properly set up permissions and user logins, anonymous FTP can be a flexible way to offer and receive files from other Internet users.

CONFIGURING NAMED (DNS)

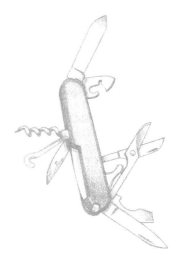

T he Domain Name System (DNS) was developed to provide a distributed database of machines. This was intended to simplify the process of one machine finding out about all the other machines to which users had to connect (originally done through the /etc/hosts file in UNIX). DNS provided a client-server model where the servers, called *name servers,* were queried by clients, called *resolvers,* to find out about other machines. Each name server contained information about a part of the larger network. If one name server didn't have the information a resolver wanted, it would communicate with another name server and pass the results back.

DNS AND THE INTERNET

In terms of the Internet, DNS provides the routing mechanism to every domain on the entire Internet system. If a local name server lacks the instructions for accessing a domain, it connects to another name server further along the line that may have the details. Name servers apply equally well in companies or organizations with a few machines that have to be internetworked. Rather than setting up and maintaining something like /etc/hosts tables on each machine, DNS provides a more simple method of maintaining the entire network's tables. While you may not have the need for DNS in a small home network of a couple of machines, as soon as you start to encounter larger networks, DNS pays dividends in long term maintenance and administration. You don't have to use DNS: there are other available name resolution systems (such as WINS).

DNS, however, is in common use and is thoroughly tested; it is necessary if you are connected to the Internet, and for a Linux or UNIX system, it's the best bet around.

In this chapter, you will get a brief overview of how DNS works. You will also see how to install BIND, the version of DNS used on most Linux and UNIX systems. While you may not need to use DNS on a very small network, as your Linux empire grows, or if you manage a company that uses Linux, you will want to employ DNS.

HOW DNS WORKS

The DNS structure is similar to a Linux file system: there is a root name server at the top, with several name servers below for subnets or other divisions. The Internet, for example, has separate name servers for each top-level domain, such as .com and .edu. Each name server may lead down the hierarchy to many other name servers, each responsible for another chunk of the network. DNS has a working limit of 127 levels of name servers in this filesystem-like structure, although there is little chance of needing this many levels even for very large internetworks like the Internet. The entire DNS structure is called a *domain name space.*

A DNS name server's database is indexed by domain name. Each domain name has a full path up the hierarchy relative to the top-level name server. A domain is a sublevel in the domain name space. If you have a large corporate domain, the details of the domain name are the same at the network's gateway to the Internet as they are within any DNS servers inside that corporation's network. There may be more details about the corporate network's contents within the network's name servers than at the gateway to the Internet, but the overall structure is preserved. A domain can be divided into several subnets or subdomains—such as brutus.com having west.brutus.com and east.brutus.com. These subnets are all part of the larger domain as far as DNS is concerned and appear like subdirectories in the filesystem-like structure. Subdomain names end with the domain name, but may have information ahead of the domain name. For example, in the subdomain name west.brutus.com, brutus.com is the domain name.

A name server may have a complete set of information about the machines it manages. For example, if you have a small domain with three name servers, each name server knows about all hosts using it for name resolution. Each name server, in this case, knows about a specific number of machines. The machines the name server manages are in part of a domain name space, called a *zone,* and the name server has authority over those machines. A name server may have authority for more than one zone.

Zones, domains, and subdomains are different entities, although in some cases they may involve exactly the same machines. Consider a small network of twenty machines. One name server may handle the entire domain with no subdomains. That name server has authority over all twenty machines, which are in the same zone. Now consider a large company with forty machines, twenty on the east coast and the rest on the west coast. Two name servers are involved in this example, one on each coast. The east coast name server has authority over the twenty machines in its subnetwork, which is one zone, and the same is true for the west coast. All forty machines are in one domain, broken into two subdomains of twenty machines.

All the data associated with domain names and the hosts inside a domain are kept in data structures called resource records (RRs). Resource records are divided into classes depending on the type of network or software in use. There are TCP/IP classes, for example, as well as several others to support older systems. The types of resource records within a class depend on the type of data to which the RR refers (see "Resource Records" on page 180). One special term you will see with DNS is *IN-ADDR-ARPA* which is a way of resolving IP addresses in reverse order.

There are two types of name servers: *primary and secondary.* Primary name servers for a particular zone get information about machines in that zone from their own database. Secondary name servers get information about the machines in the zone from another machine, called the *master server* (which may be the primary name server). When the secondary name server is started, it starts a process called *zone transfer* in which it contacts the master server, downloads the zone information, and updates it regularly. This process spreads out the workload and allows subnets to reduce overall network traffic. A third kind of name server is the *caching name server.* This machine maintains information in a cache that can handle frequent requests, again reducing network traffic.

Since the idea of DNS is to provide distributed databases, someone has to manage each database. Deciding who manages each name server on an internetwork like the Internet is called *delegation.* Large organizations usually run the name servers. Within your own network you may have one person managing all the name servers, or you may have different groups managing the name servers in different locations. Either way, the name servers are all delegated, usually by subdomain.

Any machine that needs to access a name server for information is a client to that name server and is called a resolver. The procedure is simple: the resolver sends a request to the name server, and the name server sends a reply. The resolver interprets the reply and applies it to whatever process needs it, such as e-mail addressing routines. On some Linux and UNIX systems the resolver is nothing more than a library using telnet and FTP to connect to the name server and transfer information. This is done with the BIND (Berkeley Internet Name Domain) system, which has been widely implemented as DNS for UNIX. The name server runs a daemon called named that handles a resolver's incoming requests. If that name server's named cannot resolve the query properly, it sends it along to another name server's named, and so on until a reply is sent back to the resolver. The named daemon uses a number of files to accomplish its purpose. These files are:

- **named.hosts**:   Defines the domain with hostname-to-IP mappings.
- **named.rev**:   Uses IN-ADDR-ARPA for IP-to-hostname mappings.
- **named.local**:   Used to resolve the loopback driver.
- **named.ca**:   Lists root domain servers.
- **named.boot**:   Used to set file and database locations.

Although these names can be changed, it's easiest to keep them the same.

RESOURCE RECORDS

Earlier we mentioned that resource records are used to contain the information used by BIND and DNS. There are many types of resource records, but only a few are commonly encountered on TCP/IP networks. These are:

- **A**:   Address record.
- **CNAME**:   Canonical name.
- **MX**:   Mail exchanger.
- **NS**:   Name server.
- **PTR**:   Pointer.
- **SOA**:   Start of authority.
- **TXT**:   Documentation.

Each of these records has a particular format.

Address resource records take care of the mapping of a host name to an IP address, which is the primary purpose of DNS. These records reside in the named.hosts file. The syntax of an address RR follows:

```
hostname time-to-live IN A IP_Address
```

In this syntax, hostname is the machine's name; time-to-live is the length of time in seconds that the entry is valid (usually left blank since the SOA defines this value); IN defines the Internet class or record; A defines the type of record (address); and IP_Address is the hostname's IP address.

A few examples from a named.hosts file shows the format more clearly:

```
artemis    IN    A    205.150.89.2
merlin     IN    A    205.150.89.3
pepper     IN    A    205.150.89.4
```

There will be one address resource record for each machine in the zone. Hostnames are not qualified with the domain. If you need to specify the full domain—perhaps because the name server is handling two or more domains at the same time—the fully qualified domain name must be followed by a period, like this:

```
wonderpup.brutus.com.    IN   A   205.150.89.5
superdog.brutus.com.     IN   A   205.150.89.6
bigcat.meow.com.         IN   A   205.189.23.6
smallcat.meow.com.       IN   A   205.189.23.8
```

The SOA record is kept in the named.hosts file and contains a description of the machines that are in a DNS zone. There is only one SOA record for each zone. A sample SOA entry looks like this:

```
tpci.com.IN SOA server.tpci.com
                root.merlin.tpci.com (
                2  ; Serial number
                7200 ; Refresh (2 hrs)
                3600 ; Retry (1 hr)
                151200 ; Expire (1 week)
                86400 ); min TTL
```

The fields, from top to bottom, are the domain name of the zone; the e-mail address of the zone administrator; the Serial field that contains a version number for the zone (incremented when the zone is changed); a Refresh Time which is the number of seconds between data refreshes for the zone; a Retry Time indicating the number of seconds to wait between unsuccessful refresh requests; the Expiry Time telling the number of seconds after which the zone information is no longer valid; and the Minimum Time or the number of seconds to be used in the time-to-live field of resource records within the zone. Some of the information is enclosed in parentheses: this is the command syntax that must be included to indicate the parameter order. Anything following a semicolon is a comment until the end of the line.

The pointer resource record maps an IP address to a name using IN-ADDR-ARPA format. The syntax of the pointer resource record follows:

```
IP_Address time-to-live IN PTR hostname
```

In this syntax, the IP_Address is the reverse IP address of the machine; time-to-live is usually ignored; IN is the Internet call; PTR is the pointer type; and hostname is the machine name. The IP address is reversed for IN-ADDR-ARPA records. An example pointer record is:

```
3.89.150.205.in-addr.arpa IN PTR merlin
```

This indicates that the machine named merlin has the IP address 205.150.89.3.

Name server resource records point to the name server with authority for that zone. Name server records are usually used only when subnets are used with their own name servers. The syntax for the name server resource record follows:

```
domain time-to-live IN NS server_name
```

In this syntax, domain is the name of the zone; time-to-live is usually blank because the value is in the SOA; IN is the Internet class; NS is the name server type; and server_name is the name of the DNS server for that domain. An example name server resource record follows:

```
tpci.com    IN    NS    merlin.tpci.com
```

This indicates that the DNS server for the tpci.com domain is called merlin.tpci.com. If there are multiple subnets, there will be a name server resource record for each subnet.

GETTING BIND

Practically every version of Linux is supplied with a version of BIND. BIND is available in a couple of major versions. The full-featured version of BIND is designed for large network use. At the time of this writing, the latest release was BIND 8.1.2. Few Linux systems include this version of BIND and instead opt for a subset, such as BIND 4.9.7 (the latest version as of this writing). The subset removes many features of the full system that smaller Linux-based networks probably do not need, including some security features. The latest release of BIND can be obtained from the Internet Software Consortium's web site at http://www.isc.org.

If you download a new copy of BIND, it will have to be compiled using a C compiler and the make utilities. Instructions for compilation are included with most libraries you download. Versions of BIND included with Linux CD-ROM distributions are most likely compiled already and can be installed directly. During the initial operating system load, some install routines ask whether you want to include DNS. If you did not load BIND at install time, it can be added at any point using the installation or package handler that came with your version of Linux, such as RPM for RedHat.

CONFIGURING A PRIMARY OR SECONDARY SERVER

When you choose to move to DNS, every machine on the network should be made a client, or resolver. Implementing DNS for a small part of a network is not efficient. Configuring BIND on your Linux system involves setting up the configuration files and the named daemon, which is the DNS daemon. Here are the steps to follow:

1. The main file used by BIND to tell every client about the name server is called /etc/ resolv.conf. Each client must have these instructions. The /etc/resolve.conf file needs to have entries like these added:

   ```
   search brutus.com

   nameserver 205.150.89.1
   ```

   The first line specifies the domain name of the site. The second line specifies the IP address of the name server to be used by the resolver program on this client. If you have only a single name server, all clients will have the same IP address. If you are employing primary and secondary (or caching) name servers, you can modify the IP address to reflect the zones over which each name server has authority.

2. Set up /etc/named.boot. This file is read by named when it starts. Every line in this file contains a keyword followed by domain information (comments start with a semicolon). A sample named.boot file looks like this:

   ```
   ; named.boot

   directory /usr/lib/named

   primary brutus.com named.hosts

   primary 150.205.in-addr.arpa named.rev

   primary 0.0.127.in-addr.arpa named.local

   cache . named.ca
   ```

   The directory keyword indicates where the DNS configuration files are located. The primary keyword indicates which file contains configuration information for each domain listed. The format is always to specify the domain and then the file name. A line may be added for a secondary name server, as well as a cache server. This is shown in the example above on the last line that points to the named.ca file. Another line can be added for forwarders that tells BIND which IP address receive unresolvable requests. These IP addresses are normally for a primary or secondary name server if this machine is a caching name server, or your ISP's name server if this is a primary name server.

The two lines with partial IP addresses are used to tell BIND to resolve 205.150 subnet IN-ADDR-ARPA information with the file named.rev, while the 127 local-host subnet is resolved in a file called named.local. Although these two subnet resolution lines do not have to appear, they help BIND resolve names. Note that the subnets are presented in reverse order for the IN-ADDR-ARPA lines.

If you are connected directly to the Internet, you should have a file in the cache file containing all the root servers. This can be obtained from ftp://rs.internic.net/domain/named.cache. This is unnecessary if you are not connected directly to the Internet.

3. The data file pointed to by /etc/named.boot contains information needed by the primary name server. This file is quite complex and can often be a source of frustration and errors. The file has a number of lines, each of which is a resource record, with this format:

```
name IN rrtype info
```

4. In this format, the name is the hostname; IN (in uppercase) is an indicator to specify Internet class records; rrtype indicates the type of resource record being used; and info is the associated information. The order of entries in the data file begins with a single start of authority record at the top, followed by name server resource records and then address resource records. You should have address resource records for each of the machines in your zone. Although this may sound complicated, it is easy to do. Here is a sample data file from a small network:

```
tpci.com.IN SOA server.tpci.com
            root.merlin.tpci.com (
            2 ; Serial number
            7200 ; Refresh (2 hrs)
            3600 ; Retry (1 hr)
            151200 ; Expire (1 week)
            86400 ); min TTL
tpci.com    IN    NS    merlin.tpci.com
artemis     IN    A     205.150.89.2
merlin      IN    A     205.150.89.3
pepper      IN    A     205.150.89.4
```

This continues with an address entry for each host.

5. The named daemon must be running on name servers. Naturally, BIND must be installed to properly set up named. Check to see if named is in the inetd.conf file.

CONFIGURING A CACHING SERVER

A caching DNS server needs to have a named.boot file—usually /etc/named.boot—that has entries identifying the machine as a caching server and pointing to a file with the name servers listed in it. The named.boot file for a caching server looks like this:

```
directory /usr/lib/named

cache . serverfile

forwarders 205.150.89.1
```

The first line shows that configuration files are kept in the directory /usr/lib/named. The second line identifies this machine as a caching server and point to the file that has a list of name servers used by the caching server, serverfile in this example. The third line tells the caching sever to send any requests it can't resolve to the IP address specified, which is the primary name server in this example.

SUMMARY

There is a lot of functionality to BIND and DNS that is way beyond the scope of a book like this. The details of DNS deserve their own book and there are several reference books that provide just that. Fortunately, most of us do not need to know all the details behind DNS and the different types of resource records. A simple setup like the one described in this chapter is often all that is necessary for BIND to function properly on our Linux-based networks.

# chapter 10

USING
APACHE
WEB
SERVER

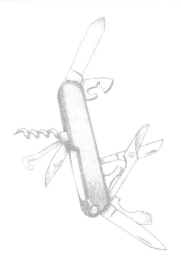

A pache is a web server package that works under Linux as well as under other operating systems. The primary advantage of Apache is that it is generally free or available at modest costs. The name Apache comes from the concept of extensive patching of existing code (cute, huh?). Whatever you think of the name, the fact remains that Apache is one of the more versatile web server systems available at any price. This chapter looks at how to configure Apache on your Linux system, and thus get into the web serving business. At the time of this writing, Apache 1.3.4 is in release and will be used as the model in this chapter.

HOW IS APACHE SET UP?

While some versions of Linux include the Apache web server software as part of the package, some don't. If you don't have Apache software already, you can download it from many different locations on the web, including http://www.apache.com, the software's official home. Updates and documentation are all available from this site. If you run Apache, check frequently for news and information about the software.

If you have a copy of Apache supplied on your Linux CD-ROM, install it using whatever installation or package manager tool your version supplies, such as RPM for RedHat Linux. For example, if your CD-ROM has Apache 1.3.4 and you want to use RPM to install the package, issue this command (substituting the full name of the Apache package, of course):

```
rpm -i apache_1_3_4.rpm
```

To upgrade an existing Apache installation to a later release, obtain the RPM version and issue this command (again substituting the name of the new package):

```
rpm -u apache_1_3_4.rpm
```

Many Linux distributions include an old version of Apache as part of their CD-ROM library. Releases 1.3.1 and higher add features to Apache that are lacking in the 1.1 and 1.2 versions, and several releases of each version are available. It is definitely worth visiting http://www.apache.com to retrieve the latest version of Apache before you install an older release. Each major release adds new features and improves both performance and security.

Apache uses a daemon called httpd to handle web requests (as do almost all web server packages). Normally the http daemon is pointed to a particular directory in the filesystem, called the web site. There are usually three subdirectories under the web site, as follows:

◆ **conf**:   Contains all the configuration files.
◆ **htdocs**:   Contains the HTML pages served by httpd.
◆ **logs**:   Contains log information.

While htdocs contains the web pages a visitor to the site sees, there are often directories below it that contain even more information. This directory and everything that resides below it is usually accessible through httpd, and hence is a security issue to be addressed when setting permissions.

In addition to the web site directory there is another subdirectory called cgi-bin in which any CGI scripts reside. These are called by httpd and HTML. For security considerations, it is inadvisable to place the cgi-bin directory inside the web site directory structure itself.

COMPILING AND INSTALLING APACHE

If you did not get a compiled version of Apache with your Linux distribution, you do not have access to a precompiled version on a web site or other resource, or you did not use an installation package tool like RPM to install an Apache binary, you can compile your own version from the source code. Most sources of Apache on the web or through FTP use gzip to compress the source code files. Alternatively, some sites make available the more widely used tar files. If the files are bundled by gzip, the file extension will be .gz, while tarred and compressed files will end with .tar.Z.

The latest versions of Apache offer you two ways to configure the tool. The older method involves manually editing the configuration files. With Apache 1.3 and later, a new Apache Autoconf-style Interface (APACI) was introduced that provides autoconfiguration for many operating systems. We will start by looking at the manual method, and then will show you the APACI method at the end of this section. The latter is much faster and does well for common Linux setups. The procedure for manually configuring, compiling, and installing Apache follows:

1. Place the downloaded files in a location that will be dedicated to the Apache files, such as /usr/apache. Uncompress the files using either gzip or tar and compress. With most Apache source files you will find a README file that explains the compilation process. In the src subdirectory created when you unpack the source files there is an INSTALL file that contains even more information.

2. You must edit the file called Configuration to set up the environment properly. The Configuration file holds a set of rules and commands. Rules start with the keyword Rule. Commands are inserted into the Makefile make file (used by the compiler). Modules are components that can be included or excluded from Apache for different purposes, and start with the keyword Module.

3. For most users, uncomment all the Modules in the Configuration file except cern_meta_module, msql_auth_module, and dld_module. Choose either db_auth_module or dbm_auth_module; they should not be used together. For other modules commented by default (indicated by a #), you can judge for yourself whether you really want their functionality included in your Apache binary. It doesn't harm the system to have modules included that are not used, but you can always recompile a new version of Apache later to add functionality.

4. You can choose the behavior of Apache by the rules settings in the Configuration file, as you will see in the section "Server Configuration" on page 192. There are only two possible values for rules which are always expressed as rule=value. The value can be yes (use this rule) or default (make a "best guess"). The most commonly available rules in Apache are shown in Table 10-1. The default settings should be fine for Linux.

Table 10-1   Apache Rules

Rule	Meaning
BADMMAP	Set to yes only if Apache compiles but doesn't run because of memory map problems.
SOCKS4	Enable the SOCKS firewall traversal protocol.
STATUS	Enable the Status module.
WANTHSREGEX	Use Apache's regular expression package instead of Linux's.

5. Create the configuration file for Linux by issuing the command "Configure". Apache's latest versions make a good guess at the native operating system and adjust the compilation options accordingly.

6. Compile Apache by issuing the make command. Of course, you must have an ANSI-standard C compiler (such as gcc) and the make utility installed and accessible for Apache to compile properly. The most common error messages encountered during compilation by Linux users concern the socket.h library. This is most likely because TCP/IP is not installed on the system.

7. The result of the compilation will be a binary called httpd. Copy this or link it into /bin or /usr/bin where it will reside in the path.

If you want to try using APACI to configure Apache, the procedure is almost trivial. It is probably a good idea to let APACI do its best guess at configuration if you have never worked with Apache before. After you've played with the web server, you can always manually reconfigure and recompile. To use APACI to configure the system, follow these three steps:

1. Start the APACI autoconfiguration utility with the following command where path is the location of the Apache files, such as /usr/apache:

```
./configure - -prefix=path
```

Two hyphens are required before the prefix keyword.

2. Issue the following command to start the make utility and build the configuration routine:

```
make
```

3. Issue the following command to build the install program that will complete the Apache installation:

```
make install
```

These steps complete the Apache autoconfiguration routine.

SETTING UP THE WEB SITE

To set up a web site to be used by Apache, you need to create a home web directory. Although the home directory can be anywhere in your Linux filesystem, it will appear to the web user as though it has its own root directory. You can choose any path you want. For example, we will set up a web site for the domain brutus.com. We will choose to create the home directory under /usr/www. Follow these steps to create the web directory and configure the Apache files:

1. Create the home directory for the web site, which will be /usr/www/brutus.

2. Create three subdirectories under the site directory: conf, htdocs, and logs. This is /usr/www/brutus/conf, /usr/www/brutus/htdocs, and /usr/www/ brutus/logs in this example.

3. Under the directory into which you installed Apache is a subdirectory called conf. Copy three files from the Apache conf subdirectory into your site's conf subdirectory. The files are srm.conf-dist, access.conf-dist, and http.conf-dist.

   If you used RPM or another package tool to install Apache, these files will be in a predetermined location such as /etc/httpd/conf. Check the documentation with the RPM package if the files are not in this location, or use the find command to locate them.

4. Rename the three files you just copied to drop the "-dist" portion of the name. For example, use the command mv srm.conf.dist srm.conf and similar commands for the other two files.

5. To prevent abuse and restrict the access permissions a web user has when they connect to your system, consider creating a special login for web users. A group specifically for web users also helps tighten security. Use the adduser command or another utility to add a user called something like "webuser," as well as to create a group with a similar name. When setting permissions for users accessing your site through Apache, make sure you specify these logins and groups for permissions.

6. Edit the httpd.conf file to specify the port number on which your web server responds (the default is 80), the user running the httpd daemon, and so on. Specify the server name, if one does not already exist, like this:

```
ServerName domain_name
```

The domain_name is your fully qualified domain name. If you do not want to have outside access to your web server and want local machine access only, you can specify localhost as the name.

Add a line that specifies the root directory for your web site (the default is httpd/htdocs), like this:

```
DocumentRoot /usr/www/ brutus/htdocs
```

Comments and commands will guide you to fill in the necessary information in this and the other two configuration files. The comments explain each option's use and proper values. Some settings will remain commented out because you do not need them. Server configuration settings are discussed in more detail in the section "Server Configuration" on page 192.

7. Edit the srm.conf file to set up the web home directory and any special internal command usage (for image processing, for example). The srm.conf file and its options are discussed in "Server Configuration" on page 192.

8. Edit the access.conf file to set a basic set of access permissions. Again, see "Server Configuration" on page 192 for more information.

9. In the htdocs directory create an HTML file for the server to read when it starts. This can be any HTML file, including one that came with the Apache distribution. The filename should be default.html, which is the default for a home page.

10. Start the httpd daemon with this command, substituting the proper path to the httpd.conf file in the command line.:

```
httpd -f /usr/www/brutus/conf
```

Test the web server by starting a browser—such as Netscape Navigator, Mosaic, or Lynx—and specify the URL http://127.0.0.1/. This uses the loopback TCP/IP driver, although you could use the IP address of the machine that is running httpd. If the system is working properly, you will see a screen with a list of files in the htdocs directory.

SERVER CONFIGURATION

Server configuration information, called directives, are contained in the three configuration files httpd.conf, access.conf, and srm.conf. Each of the three files contains in-line documentation in the form of comments. Usually reading through these files and modifying the settings to reflect such things as your machine's name, directory structure, and user and group settings is sufficient to configure the files properly.

The httpd.conf file contains directives that affect how the httpd runs. This includes the machine name, the user ID to use when running, which TCP port to listen to for incoming web requests, where log files are kept, and so on. The defaults in the httpd.conf file will be fine for almost all Linux setups with the exception of obvious directives, such as server name and filesystem structure. While you should carefully read all the comments in the httpd.conf file, the following changes will usually set up your Apache system properly:

1. Make sure the ServerType directive is set to "standalone" unless you want to use inetd to control your web site. See "Configuring inetd" on page 195 for more information on this option.

2. Check the Port directive to make sure it is set to the TCP port to which your Apache server listens (usually port 80). If you are using inetd, this option is ignored.

3. Set the User directive to either the user ID (UID) or the user name used for all web visitors. The default is usually nobody and should be changed to your specific web user login, if you created one, such as webuser. The entry in this field must exist in the /etc/passwd file. Never allow the web server to run as root if it is accessible to the outside world!

4. Set the Group directive to either the group ID (GID) or the group name assigned to all web users. The default is usually nogroup and should be changed to the group you created for web access, such as webuser. The entry must exist in the /etc/group file.

5. Modify the ServerAdmin directive to include the e-mail address of the administrator. Although the convention is to use webmaster@domain, such as webmaster@brutus.com, any e-mail address can be used. The webmaster address can be aliased to other addresses in the mail package.

6. Set the ServerRoot directive to the absolute path to the directory where all Apache resource and configuration files are stored, such as /usr/apache/conf or /etc/httpd (the latter is the default if you used RPM to install Apache).

7. Set the ServerName directive to the fully qualified domain name of your server. If a ServerName is not set, Apache will attempt to determine the canonical name of the machine on which it is running. This may not be what you want the outside world to see when attempting to access your system. You can set the name to localhost if you do not allow outside access.

The srm.conf file controls resources such as your web directory structure and CGI directory location. The defaults for most of the settings in srm.conf are fine except for those that have explicit directory path requirements. The most common changes are:

1. Modify DocumentRoot to the absolute path of the web site document directory, such as /usr/www/brutus. The default setting is usually /home/httpd/html. While this is fine for some versions of Linux, it is better to set your own tree structure as shown earlier in this chapter.

2. If you are going to allow individual users to create web documents, set UserDir to the location of the IITML files each user will make available. If you do not want individual users to offer web documents, and all documents in the site must go

through the web site's directory structure, comment this field out or leave it at the default setting of public_html. Since this is a relative directory, each user's home directory has a public_html directory underneath it for that user's files.

The access.conf file controls web visitors' access on your site as well as which documents are available to them. You can specify special security considerations in this file, too. By default the access.conf file allows unconditional access to the documents in the DocumentRoot directory, which is fine for most web sites. Although there are some settings you can tweak in the access.conf file to set up special considerations for some visitors, the default file will suffice for most Linux web sites.

The access.conf file controls global permissions to your site. You can override some settings by placing them in a .htaccess file in the server directories. This is needed if you allow user directories to be made available through the UserDir directive in srm.conf. To permit local .htaccess files to override the access.conf file you need to specify the following directive in the access.conf file:

```
AllowOverrideYes
```

The default setting is None, which does not allow .htaccess to override permissions.

STARTING AND STOPPING APACHE

If you are running Apache as a standalone server instead of using inetd, you need to start and stop the Apache process manually. This can be scripted easily, and later versions of Apache include pre-built utilities. The manual method for starting Apache's httpd process is with this command:

```
httpd —d rootdir —f configs
```

In this command, rootdir is the location of the ServerRoot directory if it is not specified in the httpd.conf file and configs is the location of the configuration file if it is not ServerRoot/conf/httpd.conf (where ServerRoot was set in httpd.conf). If you have all the configuration information set up properly in the configuration files, all you need to do to start Apache is type the following:

```
httpd
```

To shut down Apache, use ps to detect the httpd daemon's PID and use the kill command to terminate the process.

Later versions of Apache include a script that does these tasks for you. The apachectl program takes an argument such as start and stop and performs the respective action without you having to detect PIDs.

CONFIGURING INETD

Normally Apache runs as a standalone server, running in background whenever the system starts up into multi-user mode. A standalone server runs better than one managed through inetd. This is because inetd tries to start a new process every time a web request arrives. However, if you want to put a web server on a machine you use for other tasks, the standalone option can require so many resources that nothing else will work properly. Using inetd is thus a reasonable approach if your web server is used lightly. To configure Apache and inetd, follow these steps:

1. In the httpd.conf file make sure the directive ServerType is set to inetd and not standalone. When using inetd, the settings for the Port directive are ignored as inetd directly handles TCP port traffic.

2. Edit the /etc/services file to include an entry for the web server like this:

```
http port /tcp httpd httpd
```

The port is the port number to listen to for web requests (usually 80). Since inetd runs better when listening to ports in a higher TCP port range, you may want to change this number to port 8080. Anyone accessing your site by IP address instead of domain name will need to know the port number for their URL—such as http://205.150.89.100:8080 where the IP address is followed by the port number.

3. Edit the /etc/inetd.conf file to tell inetd to listen for httpd requests by adding entries in this format:

```
httpd stream tcp nowait user /sbin/httpd httpd -f /
confpath
```

The user is the UID of the user the process is to run as (usually root) and confpath is the path to the configuration files. A typical entry looks like this:

```
httpd stream tcp nowait root/sbin/httpd httpd -f /usr/
apache/conf
```

4. Restart the inetd daemon by killing the existing process. (Issue a ps -ef command. Locate the inetd process, and then issue kill PID where PID is the inetd process ID.) After being killed, inetd starts again and rereads the inetd.conf file.

CONFIGURING FOR CGI USE

Many web sites use CGI (Common Gateway Interface) scripts to perform tasks. CGI scripts are normally kept in a directory apart from the web site root, such as /usr/www/cgi-bin. For a web site to use a CGI script, the script must be executable by the web process. You should prevent web visitors from looking at the contents of the cgi-bin directory, though, to prevent security problems.

In order for Apache to find these CGI scripts, you have to specify how to find them in the Apache configuration files. The procedure to follow is:

1. In httpd.conf, modify the ScriptAlias directive to include the CGI information in this format:

```
ScriptAlias URLpath cgidir
```

   The URLpath specifies the incoming URL (such as www.brutus.com/orders/) and cgidir is the absolute directory to be run (such as /usr/www/cgi-bin/orders).

2. To log errors encountered by running CGI scripts, set the ScriptLog directive to a filename. This file will contain the log of every error encountered while processing CGI scripts. An example follows:

```
ScriptLog /usr/www/brutus/log/cgigoofs
```

   If you are logging CGI errors, you can also set the ScriptLogLength directive to specify a maximum size of the log, as well as set the ScriptLogBuffer to specify the maximum size in bytes of a POST request.

All files in the ScriptAlias directory are assumed to be scripts and do not need any special extensions, like .cgi.

VIRTUAL HOSTS

A virtual host is a web server that resides on one domain but acts as if it was on another. For example, suppose you have two domains you control: brutus.com and megan.com. Instead of setting up two web servers—one on each domain—you can set up a single machine that serves both domains. If the server is on the domain brutus.com, the server handling www.megan.com is virtual hosting. This saves on machinery and allows for a lot of flexibility in setting up web servers. It is also how many ISPs offer multiple web hosts off a single server.

Apache is capable of virtual hosting for as many hosts as you need. Instead of requiring the complex setups of some other operating systems, with Linux and Apache

virtual hosting is set up by modifying only the Apache httpd.conf file and setting up
multiple hostnames in the Linux TCP/IP configuration. Since HTTP cannot easily handle multiple domain names at the same IP address, you need to set up a distinctly different IP address for each domain, even though they are all on one machine. To set up
virtual hosting on your Linux server, follow these steps:

1. If your network uses a name server for DNS, modify it so that the domain name
   points to your web server for each domain you'll host. If you use an ISP to access
   the Internet, this will be done by the ISP in their DNS setup so that incoming
   requests all point to your server.

2. Use the ifconfig command to set up the IP address for each domain on your server.
   To add the IP address 205.150.89.60 to your existing IP address setup, the command would be the following:

   ```
   ifconfig eth0:1 205.150.89.60
   ```

   You may have to specify /sbin/ifconfig in the command line if your path does not
   include ifconfig by default. The number after the Ethernet network device is used
   to identify the host to the network.

3. Add the route to the network configuration using the route command. Following
   the above example, the command would be the following:

   ```
   route add —host 205.150.89.60 dev eth0:1
   ```

   Again, you may need to specify /sbin/route if your path does not include the sbin
   utility's directory.

4. If you are adding more virtual hosts, repeat the preceding two steps, changing the
   number after the eth0 device name. The number identifies each host's relationship
   to eth0.

5. Edit the Apache httpd.conf file to set up virtual hosting. Some templates for virtual
   hosts may already exist in the httpd.conf file, or you may have to create them from
   scratch. A complete entry, called a *block directive,* for each virtual host looks like
   the following:

   ```
   <VirtualHost www.megan.com>

   DocumentRoot /usr/www/megan/htdocs

   TransferLog /usr/www/megan/logs/access

   ErrorLog /usr/www/megan/logs/errors

   </VirtualHost>
   ```

   This defines the virtual host for www.megan.com and specifies its DocumentRoot,
   since each virtual host will have different web directories. It also specifies the files
   to use for access and error logs. If more than one virtual host is defined, the entries
   are repeated for each.

SUMMARY

There are many more configuration options possible with Apache, but they are usually used for commercial sites that require authentication or special handling characteristics. These configurations are beyond the scope of this sort of chapter in a book about Linux and belong in a detailed Apache book. If you are curious, the online documentation supplied with Apache, as well as information on the Apache web site, all help you modify your configuration to suit your specific needs. For most Linux-based web servers, though, the information in this chapter is enough to get your system running and handling web requests.

# chapter 11

LINUX CONNECTIVITY TO WINDOWS: SAMBA

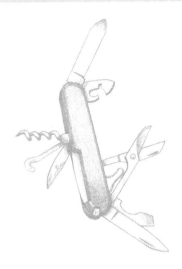

Since most of us use several types of machines on our networks, it is useful to be able to share filesystems between Linux and Windows. While this is possible with Network File System (NFS) with the appropriate Windows drivers, Linux has a better alternative: Samba. Samba is named after the Session Message Block (SMB) protocol. Using Samba, a Windows 95, Windows 98, or Windows NT machine can read the Linux filesystem. Linux can read FAT-formatted Windows filesystems, too. Even better, Samba gives you a way of sharing other resources like printers between the two operating system families. SMB was developed by Microsoft to allow files and printers to be shared on a peer-to-peer network. Adapting SMB to Linux was a matter of providing pass-though services for the SMB information. This chapter looks at how you can install Samba on your Linux machine and set it up to share filesystems and printers with Windows machines on the same network.

WHAT'S IN SAMBA?

The Samba package available for Linux has several components, all included with the available distributions. Samba is usually included with recent Linux CD-ROM compilations, as well as separately from the web.

The key component to Samba is the smbd daemon, which provides the SMB translations to allow Windows connectivity. The smbd daemon reads a configuration file called smb.conf. This file must be set up properly for Samba to work. You'll see how to configure smb.conf in "Configuring Samba" on page 200. Another part of Samba is the nmbd daemon. This provides NetBIOS-compatible name service and the ability to browse from Linux to Windows machines and vice versa.

Installing Samba is the same as with any other Linux software. If you use a package installer like RedHat's RPM, obtain the proper library and let RPM (or whichever installer you use) take care of the installation for you. Alternatively, you can obtain Samba as gzipped or tarred libraries and install them yourself following the instructions included with the library.

CONFIGURING SAMBA

As mentioned, Samba's configuration information is stored in an ASCII-formatted file called smb.conf, usually stored in /etc. The default file that comes with the Samba installation requires only a little tweaking to allow Samba to work on your network.

The smb.conf file is divided into three sections called global, homes, and printers. The global section controls the Samba service, sets the workgroup and domain name, and sets the type of printing system used. The homes section provides connections to a user's home directory, if they have one, on the Linux filesystem. Whenever a user connects to the Linux system through Samba, this section of the smb.conf file is scanned for instructions about the directories to which the user has access. The printers section controls use of Linux-configured printers on the network. The latter two sections will be examined in a little more detail in a moment.

Rather than examine each line in the smb.conf file, we'll look only at the changes you may want to make to this file:

1. In the global section at the top of the smb.conf file, add the name of your network's workgroup after the workgroup keyword. If you are using NT domains on your network, supply the NT domain name instead.

2. So that other machines can identify your Linux machine from the Network Neighborhood window, modify the comment keyword to include any notation that you want to appear, such as your machine's name or the fact that it's a Linux server.

3. The vlume keyword can be followed by any name, such as Linux. This name is used for emulation of labels on the network.

4. In the printing section of smb.conf, if you want to use the Linux printer on the network set printing to bsd, printcap name to /etc/printcap, and load printers to yes. If you don't want to share your printers set load printers to no.

The rest of the smb.conf file can be left with the default settings. Comments explain each section and keyword, so you can read through and decide if you want to change anything. This setup requires each visitor to the Linux system to have a valid entry in the /etc/passwd file in order to determine home directories. Guest logins can be set up, as can special directories for sharing, for those users who do not have a valid /etc/passwd entry.

The homes section is used in a couple of ways by Samba. First, when a user requests a share with the Linux machine, the homes section is read. After reading the homes section, Samba checks the /etc/passwd file to determine the user's home directory. Assuming it can be shared, the requested directory is then made available to the user. The homes section has a number of keywords that determine what is shared and what the user sees. The important keywords are:

◆ **comment**:   Displayed to show clients what is shared; the default is Home Directories.

◆ **browseable**:   Shows how the share is displayed in the network browser; the default is no.

◆ **read only**:   Determines if a client can add or remove files; the default is no.

◆ **preserve case**:   Determines whether case is important; the default is yes.

◆ **short preserve case**:   Same as preserve case with an 8.3 format; the default is yes.

◆ **create mode**:   Permissions attached to created files.

The printers section defines how printers are shared across the network. Normally if the printers section exists, the /etc/printcap file is used to control the printer. A number of keywords control access here, just as in the homes section:

◆ **comment**:   Displayed to show clients what is available; the default is All Printers, meaning all printers are accessible through Samba.

◆ **path**:   The location of the spool file used when accessing Linux printers through Samba; the default is usually /var/spool/samba.

◆ **browseable**:   Controls how the printers are displayed in network browsers; the default is no.

◆ **printable**:   If yes, the printer can be used through Samba; the default is yes.

◆ **public**:   If yes, then non-valid Linux users can use the printer through Samba; the default is no.

With these configuration settings in the smb.conf file, Samba knows how to make itself available to clients over the network. There are other tweaks to the smb.conf file to create special directory shares, as you'll see in this chapter's next sections, but this is usually all that is necessary to enable connectivity between Linux and Windows.

TESTING YOUR SAMBA SETUP

There are several ways you can test your Samba setup after you have modified the smb.conf file. The first step is to run the testparm program that examines the smb.conf file and verifies it for internal consistency and format. While testparm is not foolproof, it is a good first pass through smb.conf. To run the program, issue this command:

```
testparm /etc/smb.conf
```

It is worthwhile to specify the full path to smb.conf, although it is not strictly necessary if the default location is used. You can also add a machine name and IP address to the command line.

To test the printers section and the sharing of printers, use the testprns command. The format of an example command line follows, where printname is the name of the printer to be tested:

```
testprns printname /etc/printcap
```

Samba will attempt to verify that the printer is valid and can be located.

Finally, the smbstatus command can be used to report the current status of a Samba server. The command line follows, where the –d option provides verbose output and the –p option provides a list of current Samba processes:

```
smbstatus –d –p
```

Both options are optional.

STARTING SAMBA'S PROCESSES

Since two processes, smbd and nmbd, are involved in Samba, they need to be running at all times to provide connectivity to Windows machines. The easiest way to ensure these processes are running is to have init start them. You could embed the commands in the inittab file, or start and stop the processes manually or through a script. If you used a package manager, such as RPM, to install Samba, the init configuration files will have been updated automatically for you.

To manually start and stop the Samba daemons, you need to specify the following command:

```
smb start|stop
```

You may need to provide a full path to smb, such as /etc/rc.d/init.d/smb. The start option starts the Samba daemons, while the stop option terminates them.

SHARING SPECIFIC FILES OR PRINTERS THROUGH SAMBA

In the preceding section, you saw how to set up Samba to share a user's home directories across the network with any user that has a valid /etc/passwd entry. To allow access to files and printers by network users who are not valid Linux system users, you need to allow guest accounts. A section of the smb.conf file is available for this purpose and is usually commented out. If you want to allow guest access to your Linux system, this section should be uncommented and will then look like this:

```
guest account = guest

log file = /var/log/samba-log.%m

max log size = 50
```

The first entry allows anyone who is not a valid Linux system user—that is, one with no entry in /etc/passwd—to access the system with the login name guest. All guest activities are logged in the file /var/log/samba-log tagged with the name of the machine that is connecting (%m), and the log cannot grow larger than 50K.

Next, you need to create a directory for these guests to access and tell Samba how to let them access the system. The entry is in the homes section of smb.conf and is usually commented out. When uncommented and modified to suit your needs, this section will look like this:

```
[public]

comment = Guest Area

path = /usr/samba/guest

public = yes

only guest = yes

writable - yes

printable = no
```

In this entry, anyone accessing the Linux system with the guest login will be placed in /usr/samba/guest, or any other directory you specify, and only the guest account is allowed there. Guests can save and delete files in this directory.

To create a specific directory for access through Samba, you can set up a new entry in the homes section of smb.conf. For example, the following section added to smb.conf would create a new share:

```
[uploads]
comment = Upload directory
path = /usr/uploads
browseable = yes
public = yes
writable = yes
create mode = 755
```

Whenever a client browses the Linux machine, they will see the comment "Upload directory" pointing to /usr/uploads. Anyone can access this directory. To restrict access to a directory share, set public to no and add the following line:

```
valid users = tparker, bsmallwood, ychow
```

In this line, the list of logins after the equal sign are those users allowed access to this directory.

ACCESSING SHARES USING SMBCLIENT

From your Linux machine you can access Windows machine's shares and printers through the smbclient program, which offers an FTP-like interface. The smbclient program has a number of commands that can be used once the program has started up. These include the commands in Table 11-1. As you can see, many of the commands are duplicates of Linux and FTP commands, and many actions have more than one command associated with them, such as rd and rmdir.

Table 11-1   The smbclient Commands

Command	Meaning
?	Display help.
!	Execute shell command.
cd	Change directory on server.
del	Delete a file on the server.
dir	Display the directory listing.
exit	Exit the program.
help	Display help.
get	Retrieve a file from the server.
lcd	Change local directory.
ls	Display the directory listing.
md	Make a directory.
mkdir	Make a directory.
mget	Retrieve multiple files from the server.
mput	Copy multiple files to the server.
print	Print the file.
put	Copy a file to the server.
queue	Display all print jobs queued.
quit	Exit the program.
rd	Remove a directory.
rmdir	Remove a directory.

To connect to a remote machine, specify the workgroup or domain name in the command line like this:

```
smbclient '\\tpci\merlin' —I merlin.tpci.com —U tparker
```

This command connects to the workgroup or domain called tpci and looks for a machine called merlin. The –I option followed by a domain name tells smbclient to treat \\tpci\merlin as a full DNS-style entry, instead of a NetBIOS name (this is handy for compatibility with Linux utilities). The –U option followed by a username tells smbclient to use the username to log into the remote machine, which will be the server. If the remote system is found, smbclient prompts you for a password on that machine, and then you are placed inside the smbclient program with a prompt like this:

```
smb:
```

At this point, any valid smbclient command can be used, much like when using FTP.

SUMMARY

As you have seen, Samba allows you to easily share your Linux machine's files and printers in Windows-based workgroups and domains. Through Samba's smbclient utility you can also access Windows directories and other resources from Linux. The key to running Samba is to follow the steps in this chapter and ensure that the smb.conf file is created and set up properly.

INSTALLATION

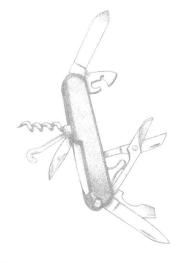

T his book is for computer-savvy readers who are "power users" on other platforms and are now becoming interested in Linux. Some UNIX knowledge is helpful, but it is not required. A good number of warnings are provided throughout the course of this chapter to assist you in your installation. As you roll up your sleeves and prepare to install Linux, get ready to have your patience tested. This will not be as familiar as the installs you have performed of other operating systems.

Note that the installation routines described in this chapter are based largely on RedHat 5.0, 5.1, and 5.2, which have the most mature and stable installation routines of any Linux implementations. Other Linux versions, particularly Caldera and Slackware, are similar. Once you see one Linux installation, you should be able to perceive any differences in other versions and should be able to deal with them.

INSTALLATION CONSIDERATIONS

Among Linux versions, perhaps the best installation is provided by RedHat Linux version 5.x. In fact, RedHat Linux' install program is comparable to Windows NT in its simplicity, stability, and comfort level. Most other Linux installations, such as those from Slackware and Debian, fail to provide effective auto-detection and use minimal installation routines. Caldera provides a substantial LISA (Linux Installation and System Administration) installation program with its OpenLinux offering.

RedHat is currently the most popular Linux distribution, and a significant reason is its more efficient installation. If you use an older copy of Linux or a more obscure version, you know installation can be maddening. It can take days of work for a basic Linux box to get up and running, particularly if you're approaching Linux for the first time. This is why RedHat's installation routines have such a competitive advantage over other Linux vendors. Using RedHat on reasonably conservative PC hardware, you can have a basic Linux installation running in less than an hour.

Regardless of the version you're installing, two key areas should always be kept in mind when choosing to install Linux on your computer:

◆   Basic hardware compatibility.

◆   The ability to partition a hard disk to properly run Linux.

Linux's roots are entirely in the public domain. Unlike Windows NT, no one software developer creates, supports, and maintains Linux. It is because of this that Linux has not made inroads into the corporate world. It is hard to justify running an entire software company on a product that is literally free. People spend money on Microsoft products because they know that having a single vendor enforces consistency and accountability. Still, there are at least five different major variants of Linux in use by potentially millions of people.

In features and functionality, Linux does indeed challenge NT, and any other existing operating system. Basically, Linux *is* UNIX, with a few minor command-line differences and considerably easier installation on the majority of PCs. Once you learn Linux, you should feel very much at home with almost any UNIX installation.

HARDWARE CONSIDERATIONS

Be conservative in your hardware choices. For example, hand-me-down systems are an ideal platform. If you have an old 486 or basic Pentium system (even a 386), Linux may install and work properly on the first try. This is one of the ironies of Linux and its stepchild origins. It breathes new life into old boxes.

You need to know the basics of your computer, such as:

◆   Type of video card

◆   Type of network card

◆   Mouse

◆   Keyboard

Do not expect to run Linux on a state-of-the-art box. If you're running a 450 MHz Pentium II or Xeon system with the latest video card and other peripherals, you may be disappointed in Linux. It can be difficult to install Linux even on a Pentium MMX or Pentium II system. This is because many of the drivers required for the latest generation of peripherals and motherboard chips may not have been distributed with your CD-ROM. Fancy SCSI, FireWire, or fibre-channel controllers and multimedia devices such as PCI sound cards or DVD drives probably won't work unless you can locate a driver someone has written. If you're a highly experienced Linux user, with substantial programming skills, you should be able to install Linux on just about any machine. Assuming that you are not that type of Linux user, don't expect to take all your new gadgets with you on your Linux journey. If you're a fairly experienced computer user who wants to try out Linux, you will have to make some choices.

Video Cards

Video cards are a particular issue with Linux. If you want to stick with basic character-mode Linux screens, any video card will work. If you want to run X for a graphic user interface, things become more complicated. Every six to twelve months, new generations of video display cards appear. Previous-generation video cards, often acceptable in quality, performance, and compatibility, are then immediately taken off the shelves.

Naturally, it's those recently discontinued cards that are often supported by Linux. As soon as an enterprising Linux developer writes a software driver for a video card, that card is apt to disappear from the market in favor of the "latest and greatest" model. If you like to tinker with your PCs, hang on to those older video cards; you may need them to run Linux. Paradoxically, if you build or buy a new machine to run Linux, installation difficulty increases.

Network Cards

Network cards are critically important. Fortunately, Linux does support most of the key Ethernet and Fast Ethernet models, as long as you stick with major cards.

Out of the box, Linux is not compatible with many Fast Ethernet networking cards.

If you're running 3Com, Intel, or Novell Eagle NE2000-class networking cards, a good Linux installation should detect them automatically. Unfortunately, a huge variety of networking cards exist, many of which are not represented in Linux's driver list.

See Chapter 3, *Configuring Devices to Work Under Linux*, starting on page 61, to set up a networking card if your installation does not detect it automatically.

Modems and Sound Cards

Sound cards and modems are another can of worms. Linux provides some basic multi-media support, but don't expect any sort of automatic setup or plug-and-play capabilities. Setting up a modem is discussed in Chapter 6, *Connecting to the Internet*, starting on page 127.

STARTING THE LINUX INSTALLATION

As mentioned earlier, RedHat Linux is used as the example throughout this chapter, although major differences between versions are mentioned. Before starting your Linux installation you need to prepare a boot and root floppy. Some systems, such as Slackware, do not need a separate root floppy, just the boot. Preparing these diskettes is a matter of using the RAWRITE utility provided on most CD-ROMs.

The boot and root floppies are used to load the Linux kernel and a bare-bones file-system for the installation routine to work with. The CD-ROM your Linux came on will have one or more directories called "images", "bootdsks.144", or some such name. These directories have several images for the Linux kernel and boot disk in them. These need to be transferred to a floppy using the RAWRITE utility, usually found in the dosutils directory on your CD-ROM. Snoop around on the CD to identify the RAWRITE and kernel image directories. Some releases of Linux, such as those from Caldera Open Linux, include pregenerated floppies for you, which makes life a little easier.

The first step in preparing the boot and root floppies is to choose the proper image. There are text files in the image directory that explain what each image does. Some systems provide only a few images, some provide many. They all differ in the type of drivers for CD-ROM and network cards that are built into the image. There are also different images for SCSI versus IDE images. For example, on a Slackware 3.5 CD-ROM, the boot images are located in the bootdsks.144 or bootdsks.12 directories for 1.44MB and 1.2MB floppies respectively.

In the bootdsks.144 directory of Slackware 3.5, there are about a dozen different boot kernel images. The most commonly used is simply called boot.i and contains typical IDE drivers. Scan through the text file in the root image directory to find the image name you need. The same applies to the root disk images. There are fewer choices for root disk images as they differ primarily in the video card controls. The most common image is called color.gz.

To create boot and root floppies, it is best to use a DOS or Windows machine. Follow these steps:

1. Open a DOS window and change to the CD-ROM's dosutils directory. The RAWRITE.EXE file should reside there. (Your directory name may be a little different, of course.)

2. Start RAWRITE by typing the utility name. It will ask you for the image name you want to write. Enter the path to the image, such as "../bootdsks.144/bare.i".

3. RAWRITE asks for the target destination diskette. Insert a formatted DOS diskette in the drive and enter its letter followed by a colon.

4. RAWRITE displays progress information. When complete, repeat the process for a root floppy if your Linux version uses one.

Use the tab and arrow keys to navigate in the requester screens during installation.

You could perform the entire procedure above from the boot and root image directories, too.

Insert the Linux boot floppy in your floppy disk drive and turn the system on or restart. The system takes a few seconds to display a simple text-based greeting screen from the floppy disk. Several function key options are provided, including an Upgrade mode to a hard disk containing older versions of Linux and an Expert mode. The simplest way to proceed is to just press Enter. From there, take the following steps:

1. After the greeting screen appears, press Enter. The system continues to load the basic Linux operating system from the floppy disk. Eventually, another Welcome screen appears. Press Enter to continue.

2. Select English as the language for installation and press Enter.

3. Select US as the keyboard and press Enter.

4. Now, you select the installation medium, which usually means a copy of Linux on a hard disk, over the network, an NFS (Network File System) image, or CD-ROM. The vast majority of new Linux users install from the CD-ROM. RedHat Linux 5.x automatically uses current IDE CD-ROM drives and works properly with many SCSI-based CD-ROMs as long as you have a SCSI controller supported by Linux. Select Local CD-ROM from the Installation Method list and press Enter.

5. Install your Linux CD-ROM into your drive and press Enter. An "Initializing CD-ROM" message briefly appears.

6. An Installation Path screen is the next thing to appear, with two options: Install and Upgrade. Select the Install option and press Enter. If you are upgrading an older version of Linux, select the Upgrade option.

If you need to upgrade a Linux installation, your previous settings will be preserved. The default method shown in this book is for a new installation.

If you have a SCSI controller installed in your system, and particularly if your CD-ROM is a SCSI device, proceed to the next section, "Installing a SCSI Controller." If you don't have a SCSI controller, skip the next section and proceed to the following one, "Using FDISK to Partition Your Disk," starting on page 213.

INSTALLING A SCSI CONTROLLER

After you go through the installation process in the previous section, a SCSI Configuration requester appears, asking the question, "Do you have any SCSI Adapters?" Three options are provided: Yes, No, and Back. The Back option takes you to the previous step in the installation. If you have an IDE-type CD-ROM drive, you don't need to worry about this.

This is where you select the drivers for your SCSI controller. In fact, newer versions of Linux provide a decent set of drivers covering most major brands of SCSI cards for your computer, including Adaptec, BusLogic, Future Domain, QLogic, Iomega Parallel Port Zip, NCR, Trantor, Ultrastor, and even the SCSI controller on a Pro Audio Spectrum sound card. You still need to know what type of SCSI controller you have to make the right selection. Look at the part number on the large controller chip on the SCSI card if you are not sure.

If you do not have a SCSI Adapter, select No and press Enter.

If you do have a SCSI adapter, select Yes by pressing an arrow key or tab key until Yes is highlighted, and press Enter.

The Adapters list appears. Follow these steps to install the SCSI controller:

1. Select the desired SCSI driver from the list and press Enter.
2. A Module Options screen appears with two choices: Autoprobe and Specify Options. For most users, the Autoprobe option is the one to select. With the Autoprobe option selected, press tab to highlight OK, and press Enter.

> **The Adaptec 2940 is a very popular Ultra-SCSI device controller that also is built onto many Pentium and Pentium II-type motherboards. Huge numbers of inexpensive 16-bit SCSI cards are built using the Adaptec 152x, 1542, and 1740 SCSI controller chips, which are listed in RedHat Linux's installation.**

3. Press Enter to continue.

If you are running a SCSI adapter with devices and it has yet to be detected, you have a device compatibility problem.

The next phase is disk setup. This is a key and potentially confusing part of Linux installation, and it's the longest section of this chapter.

USING FDISK TO PARTITION YOUR DISK

You reach the Disk Setup program once you select No when the installer asks about any SCSI controller, or once you finish the SCSI controller installation. Setup steps directly into this program to partition your hard disk.

> **You should use a minimum 1.2GB hard disk partition if you expect to do a full Linux installation.**

The assumption throughout this book is that you are using an entire hard disk and not a single partition on a larger drive. Linux OS requires at least two separate partitions to successfully install and run. If you have a hard disk that has Windows 95, Windows 98, or NT on it, repartition the disk again to start setting up Linux.

Linux installations can become complicated in terms of disk partitions. To install Linux properly, here are the minimum two partitions you need on your hard disk:

◆ Linux swap partition.

This needs to be a separate partition of 100-200 MB used by the Linux operating system as swap space for writing data to and from memory. Swap space is a form of virtual memory in Linux, and it is absolutely required for Linux to function.

◆ Linux native partition.

This is a root partition where the operating system, its applications, and any data you may create reside. You can have more than one Linux native partition on your hard disk. They show up as separate drives in your system. Test systems used for this book use a single native partition.

This is the bare minimum for a successful Linux partition. Fortunately, Linux installers, including those from RedHat and Caldera, do a good job detecting hard disks in your system.

At the Disk Setup screen, two key options are provided: Disk Druid and fdisk. Red Hat Linux provides a special program called Disk Druid that goes a bit past the typical Linux fdisk program. Disk Druid is moderately easy to use with existing partitions on a hard disk but doesn't provide as many options as fdisk. Despite its character-based nature, fdisk is quite powerful and fairly easy to use. Think of the MS-DOS version of fdisk, and the similarities are apparent.

To use fdisk to partition a disk, first select fdisk and press Enter. A Partition Disks screen appears, describing the task at hand, and any hard disks that are detected by the system. It will read something like the following:

```
To install Red Hat Linux, you must have at least one
partition of 50 MB dedicated to Linux. We suggest
placing that partition on one of the first two hard
drives in your system so that you can boot into Linux
with LILO.
```

                    /dev/hda — Model WDC AC21600H

The Partition Disks screen appears. Selecting Done in this screen brings you to the Disk Druid program that advanced users may prefer. The Disk Druid program, however, is not discussed in this book. Disk Druid is quite simple to use and you'll be able to figure it out without any help. Instead we'll use fdisk here, so select Edit and press Enter. This takes you to the fdisk program, which runs on a Linux command line.

For a quick Help list of fdisk's options, press M. The menu
options for fdisk display on the screen, in the following order:

Command action:
    A   Toggle a bootable flag.
    B   Edit bsd disklevel.
    C   Toggle the DOS compatibility flag.
    D   Delete a partition.
    L   List known partition types.
    M   Print this menu.
    N   Add a new partition.
    P   Print the partition table.
    Q   Quit without saving changes.
    T   Change a partition's system ID.
    U   Change display/entry units.
    V   Verify the partition table.
    W   Write table to disk and exit.
    X   Extra functionality (experts only).

The main options the average user needs are D, L, M, N, P, and
T. The X command displays a second list of more detailed disk
management commands, most of which should be tried only if
you know what you are doing!

The best first step in using fdisk is to check the existing partitions on the drive. If
you have a drive that contains a partition with another operating system, such as DOS,
Windows, or another version of Linux, and you don't want to erase it, definitely keep
track of things using the P command.

Press the P key to view the list of existing partitions on the hard disk. If the drive is
brand new, the chances are good that no partitions will be listed. A typical fdisk listing
appears below:

```
Disk /dev/hda: 64 heads, 63 sectors, 787 cylinders
Units = cylinders of 4032 * 512 bytes
```

```
    Device bootBeginStartEndBlocksIDSystem
```

Note the device name. The first hard disk in a Linux system will be named /dev/hda.

The most important statistic shown here is the number of cylinders in the first line.
You'll need to divide the number of megabytes in your hard disk versus the number of
cylinders Linux detects to arrive at the size of the partitions to allocate in fdisk. The
listing here is for a 1.6 GB disk, and Linux detected 787 cylinders in the drive. Your
results, of course, will differ.

The fdisk program lists any existing partitions in numerical order. If any other operating systems are on your disk, this is where they appear.

The next step is to create a swap partition and a Linux partition for your operating system. At the fdisk prompt, type <N>. Two options are provided:

```
E       extended
P       primary partition (1-4)
```

Select the primary partition type for your swap partition, and press Enter. The following prompt should appear:

```
Partition number (1-4):
```

Type the number 1 to create the first partition. The prompt refreshes to read something like this:

```
First cylinder (1-787): (For a 1.6 GB drive)
```

Type the number 1 for the first cylinder in the first partition. Then type the last cylinder for the new partition. For example, type 100 to allocate the first 100 cylinders of the disk for a swap partition. On a fairly large disk, this allocates more than enough space for the swap. The rest of the disk can be used for the main Linux partition.

If you have other OS partitions, write down their cylinder numbers and in what order they appear on the list.

To create a new partition *using a specific number in megabytes*, type a value such as +200M (for a 200 megabyte partition) and press Enter.

Once you create the new partitions, you must convert one of them to a Linux swap partition, using a few more steps in fdisk. Creating a swap partition is mandatory. You should create a swap partition of at least 100 MB, and you should do so at the very beginning of the installation.

Press T to change the new partition's System ID. Next, type 1 to select the first partition and press Enter. The following prompt appears:

```
Hex code (type L to list codes)
```

To view the list of supported partition types, type L first.

Empty		AIX bootable	PC/IX	B7 BSDI fs
DOS 12-bit FAT	A	OS/2 Boot Manag	80 Old MINIX	B8 BSDI swap
XENIX root	b	Win95 FAT32	81 Linux/MINIX	C7 Syrinx
XENIX usr	40	Venix 80286	82 Linux swap	DB CP/M
DOS 16-bit <32M	51	Novell?	83 Linux native	E1 DOS access
Extended	52	Microport	93 Amoeba	E3 DOS R/O
DOS 16-bit >32M	63	GNU HURD	94 Amoeba BBT	F2 DOS
OS/2 HPFS	64	Novell Netware	a5 BSD/386	secondary
AIX	65	Novell Netware		FF BBT

OS/2 and Win95 partitions are supported and detected by Linux's fdisk program. Type 82 and 83 are the most important for a Linux installation. Creating new partitions in fdisk automatically creates them in Linux native format, and one must be created to Linux swap format, which is Type 82. To do so, take the following steps:

1. Type 82 and press Enter.
2. Type N and press Enter to create a second partition.
3. Type P and press Enter to create another primary partition.
4. Type in the number of the first available cylinder for the partition, listed in the prompt, such as the following:

```
First cylinder (103-787): 103
```

5. Type in the last cylinder you want to use and press Enter. Cylinders are a more precise way of specifying how large a partition you want, especially if another OS is on your drive. The syntax should look something like this:

```
Last cylinder or +size or +sizeM or +sizeK ({103}-787}: 787
```

6. Type P to double-check the partition table, as shown here:

```
Disk /dev/had: 64 heads, 63 sectors, 787 cylinders
Units = cylinders of 4032 * 512 bytes
```

Device boot	Begin	Start	End	Blocks	ID	System
/Dev/hda1	1	1	102	205600+	82	Linux Swap
/Dev/hda2	103	103	787	1380960+	83	Linux Native

The example above divides the example 1.6GB hard disk into a Linux swap partition and a Linux native partition. Note the ID numbers of each partition. The blocks column shows the size of each partition in kilobytes. A 205,600 kilobyte partition amounts to about 200 megabytes of space, which is plenty for an average Linux swap partition.

7. Type W to write the partition table to disk and press Enter.

8. The Disk Partitions window reappears. After using fdisk to partition your disk drive, select Done in the Disk Partitions window.

The next exercise runs through a new phase of the installation.

Note on Caldera Linux

Caldera's OpenLinux uses a very similar installation program to RedHat's, called LISA. LISA provides the same access to the fdisk program that RedHat does, and fdisk is exactly the same on both systems. Caldera's LISA does provide some different message screens, such as:

```
You may now change any disk partitioning for your Linux
installation. Do you want to create Linux or Linux swap
partition(s) or change any existing disk partitioning?
```

When you select Yes, the hard disk selection list appears, displaying any hard disks that the OpenLinux setup program detected. The first step lists IDE/ATAPI disks in your system, including any IDE CD-ROMs that are compatible with Linux. A typical disk listing reads like this:

```
Hard Disk 1 :  /dev/hda

Model       :  Conner Peripherals 1275 MB — CFS1275A (1218 MB)

CDROM 1     :  /dev/hdc

Model       :  ATAPI CDROM CD-ROM TW 120D, Rev. V2.10
```

Caldera's LISA program provides serious warnings, too, such as the following:

```
Changing the hard disk partition table affects
partitions and the data they contain. Only use 'fdisk'
when you are familiar with its use and the way it
works.The Getting Started guide contains more
information on the use of 'fdisk.' Press <f1> for more
help. Please back up all important data before using
fdisk! Do you want to change the hard disk partitioning
now?
```

Caldera's LISA program also forces you to reboot and retrace your previous steps after partitioning your disk. RedHat does not.

SETTING THE MOUNT POINT AFTER FDISK

The next disk management process is to set a Linux native partition as the root partition for the operating system To do so, Linux uses a designation called / (forward slash). The single forward slash is a UNIX convention for indicating a root directory on a disk, and Linux follows the convention. This is called a *mount point*. The setting is defined in Disk Druid after you use fdisk. Using the mount point feature can be confusing, particularly for Linux newcomers.

FORMATTING THE SWAP PARTITION

You first need to format the swap partition so that Linux Install can use it for scratch space during file copies from the CD. If you have followed the preceding instructions, you see at least two partitions in the Current Disk Partitions screen: one Linux swap and one Linux native. To set your root's mount point and continue on the installation, follow the steps below:

1. Select the Linux native partition in the list, press tab to select the Edit option, and press Enter. An Edit Partition dialog appears.
2. In the Edit Partition dialog, simply type / for the mount point and press Enter. The Active Swap Space dialog appears. The Swap partition is listed (if it's the first partition, it appears as /dev/hda1) and selected automatically. The dialog reads:

```
What partitions would you like to use for swap space? This will
destroy any information already on the partition.


Device          Begin   End     Size (k)
[*] /dev/hda1    1       102     205600


[*]                     Check for bad blocks during format
```

3. Both options are selected automatically. Simply select OK and press Enter.

The swap space is formatted.

FORMATTING THE MAIN LINUX PARTITION

The next step is to format the main Linux partition by following these steps:

1. Press the spacebar to make sure the correct /dev/hda partition is selected for your Linux install, and also enable the Check for bad blocks during format option.

2. Select OK and press Enter. The Components to Install dialog appears. This is where you select the parts of Linux you want to install. The Everything selection is at the bottom of the list. If you have a 1 Gigabyte partition or greater, that's plenty of room for a complete Linux installation. To make life simple, I recommend installing everything.

   Yes, everything. Minimal systems are usable if you want to practice UNIX command line functions, but if you want to do any meaningful work with Linux you need to use a lot of disk space.

The X, Samba, DNS, web serving, and C development features discussed in this book rely on a full Linux install. To keep things simple, simply select the Everything option.

3. Select the options you want, select OK, and press Enter.
4. At the final dialog, press Enter.

Your installation automatically formats the disk partition and installs the various Linux packages.

AUTO-DETECTING AND LOADING DEVICES

Another critical installation phase follows: Setting up basic hardware devices such as a mouse, network card, and video.

SETTING UP MICE

RedHat's installer auto-probes for any mice plugged into your computer. PS/2 mice are the most common on current computers. Basic Microsoft or Logitech serial or PS/2 mice are usually detected after the disk is formatted and the Linux features are copied to the hard disk. Generic PS/2 mice (common on ATX-type Pentium II, Celeron, or

AMD K6/K6-2 motherboards) are also detected automatically. This is a big advance over older Linux versions.

After the disk installation finishes, the system displays a message saying that a mouse of a specific type was detected. In the Mouse Detection screen, press Enter. You may also be asked to select from a list of supported mice. If so, the Standard Three-Button PS/2 Mouse selection works for just about any mouse plugged into a PS/2 port on an ATX motherboard.

The Configure Mouse dialog appears, with your auto-detected mouse type selected. An Emulate 3 Buttons? Checkbox also appears. If your mouse already has three buttons, *leave this checkbox blank*. If your mouse has two buttons, enable this option. Press both buttons to emulate the third (middle) button in the Linux X GUI. Select OK and press Enter.

SETTING UP VIDEO CARDS

After a moment, the computer attempts to auto-detect your video card.

```
PCI probing found a:


PCI Entry: Millennium II

X Server: SVGA
```

This indicates that your video card was found successfully. As noted earlier, the type of video card has a big influence on whether you can run the X GUI under Linux. The SVGA Server is a common X server module employed for many video cards under Linux. Select OK and press Enter.

If your video card is not detected properly, you have an incompatibility problem. All current video cards are capable of handling Super-VGA screens, and you should be able to use even a generic driver to run X. Video card configuration is discussed in greater detail in Chapter 1, *Basic Interactions with the GUI*.

SETTING UP MONITORS

A few files for video support are copied from the CD to the system. A Monitor Setup screen appears, providing a significant list of monitors, and a listing should match your monitor. If there isn't a listing for your specific monitor, make an educated guess.

Monitors rely on a few key settings to determine their quality. Refresh rates and resolution are the two major determinants for a monitor's display capabilities. The higher each of these two specs are, the more likely it is to support higher-resolution X GUI screens. If your monitor doesn't exactly match a listing, consider other monitor brands and models that come close to the specs for your display. Also check your monitor's manual to make sure its settings match up with what you want in X

Select the desired monitor from the list and press Enter. A dialog something like the one below will appear:

```
Xconfigurator will now run the X server you selected to
probe various information about your video card. It is
normal for the screen to blink several times.
```

Press Enter to start the Xconfigurator. The Xconfigurator begins to autoprobe the video system in your computer. The screen blinks a couple of times, and a new dialog appears:

```
Xconfigurator has successfully probed your video card.
The default video mode will be:


Color depth: 32 bits per pixel

Resolution: 1024x768


Do you want to accept this setting, or select for
yourself?
```

You can use the default as it is shown on your screen, or choose a new setting. To start, I suggest using the defaults. You can change them later if necessary. Select the Accept option, and press Enter to accept the defaults.

INITIAL NETWORKING SETUP

You should some idea about what you want to do with Linux on the network when you approach installation. If you have general idea and connecting Linux to a small network, you have some latitude in the choices you can make. If you are in a small company or in an office department, you may have to gather a significant number of settings from your network administrator. Otherwise, your new Linux system may conflict with other networked devices.

Linux networking uses TCP/IP as its main connectivity protocol. Novell's IPX and AppleTalk also are supported to some extent.

After the video display configuration finishes, the initial Network Configuration dialog appears, as follows:

```
Do you want to configure LAN (not dialup) networking for
your installed system?
```

Select Yes and Press Enter. The Load Module list appears. A decent selection of common networking cards are provided here, including several 3Com cards, Intel EtherExpress, Novell NE2000, and HP AnyLan. Bear in mind that some networking cards can be used with a generic driver such as the DEC21040 Tulip driver or the NE2000.

The Digital 21040 (Tulip) driver supports many inexpensive Fast Ethernet cards, such as the NetGear FE310A.

Select your networking card from the list, and press Enter. The Module Options dialog appears.

Select Autoprobe and press Enter. If the card is detected properly, you go immediately to the Boot Protocol dialog, as shown below:

```
How should the IP information be set? If your system
administrator gave you an IP address, choose Static IP.


        Static IP address

        BootP

        DHCP
```

BootP (Boot Protocol) and DHCP (Dynamic Host Configuration Protocol) are widely supported standards for configuring devices over IP networks, providing IP addresses, subnet masks, and other values to workstations that request them. If your Linux system will connect to a DHCP or BootP server, select the appropriate option. (If you're not sure about this, ask your network administrator.)

To assign a Static IP address, select that option and press Enter to continue on. The Configure TCP/IP dialog appears, as shown below:

```
Please enter the IP configuration for this machine. Each
item should be entered as an IP address in dotted-
decimal notation (for example, 1.2.3.4)

        IP address:        _____

        Netmask:           _____

        Default gateway:   _____

        Primary nameserver:_____
```

To run TCP/IP on your system, you must provide the IP, the netmask, and a default gateway. When you enter the IP address and netmask, Linux automatically calculates the Gateway and nameserver addresses, as shown here:

```
IP address:          192.168.21.2

Netmask:             255.255.255.0

Default gateway:     192.168.21.254

Primary nameserver:192.168.21.1
```

If the Linux computer is your only system and you are not running a network, use the Linux computer's IP address as the default gateway. You may not have a nameserver in your installation. If, however, you are planning to run DNS services on your Linux system, you should enter the IP address for the nameserver. A sample is shown below:

```
IP address:          192.168.21.2

Netmask:             255.255.255.0

Default gateway:     192.168.21.2

Primary nameserver:192.168.21.2
```

There are so many different ways to set up IP addressing on a Linux system that knowledge of IP networking is a prerequisite for effective setup. If your Linux machine is stand-alone, any address space works for your system and you can use whatever values you want.

Type the desired values for your IP networking setup, select OK, and press Enter. The Configure Network dialog requests the domain name for your Linux system, the host name, and any additional nameservers on your network. The domain name is the DNS name assigned to servers on the Internet by InterNIC. They are also called FQDN's, for Fully Qualified Domain Name. If, as seems likely, you don't have a fully qualified domain name and simply want to experiment with DNS on an isolated system or small network, choose any domain name, as in yourname.com, as shown below:

```
Domain name:                rgrace.com

Host name:                  linuxbox.rgrace.com

Secondary nameserver (IP):_____

Tertiary nameserver (IP):_____
```

Enter the desired domain name and press tab. Linux automatically fills the Host name field with the domain name you just typed.

The host name is simply the name of your computer within the domain, as in linuxbox.rgrace.com. To run TCP/IP under Linux, you must have a host name that resides under the hierarchy of the domain name. That's why the domain name is placed in the Host name field after you enter it. Without erasing the domain name, type in the host name for your computer.

If there are no other DNS servers on your network, simply leave the Secondary and Tertiary values blank, select OK, and press Enter.

To understand more about how DNS works under Linux, please see the Chapter 9 *Configuring Named (DNS)***, beginning on page 177.**

Select the time zone for your computer, select OK, and press Enter.

A Services list displays. This is where you select the Linux networking and low-level services that start up when you boot the system. Keep the default services enabled. If you have significant Linux experience, other services can be enabled or disabled as desired. Make sure that all services you need are enabled at this point. Select OK and press Enter.

The system asks if you would like to configure a printer. If you would like to set up a printer, please read the next section. Otherwise, select No and press Enter, and pass on to the section titled "Finishing Installation."

PRINTER CONFIGURATION DURING SETUP

Setup is a good time to initiate printer configuration, because setting up print services under a working installation of Linux requires considerably more work. Going through a few fairly simple dialogs, you can set up a networked printer or local printer for use under Linux. Assuming you are continuing a normal Linux setup, select Yes and press Enter when the system asks if you would like to configure a printer. A Select Printer Connection dialog appears, as follows:

```
How is this printer connected?


        Local

        Remote lpd

        LAN Manager
```

A local printer is connected directly to your machine through the parallel port. A remote lpd printer is connected through another UNIX or Linux machine on the network. LAN Manager denotes a printer connected to an NT Server or Windows 9X system using the SMB (Server Message Block) protocol to share devices. This printer is connected to the same network as your Linux machine in some fashion. For the sake of the current installation, the assumption is that the printer is a local device. LAN Manager shared printer setup is discussed a bit later.

 Chapter 11, *Linux Connectivity to Windows: Samba,* beginning on page 207, describes the use of Linux with Windows-based networks. The SMB protocol and Linux's Samba feature are closely tied to this topic.

SETTING UP A LOCAL PRINTER

Select Local, then select OK, and press Enter. A Standard Printer Options screen appears. Most of the time, the default path and queue designation are sufficient. Simply accept the defaults by selecting OK and pressing Enter.

A Local Printer Device dialog appears, where Linux attempts to detect the parallel ports in your system. The dialog looks similar to the one below.

```
What device is your printer connected to (note that /
dev/lp0 is equivalent to LPT1:)?


       Printer device: /dev/lp0


Auto-detected ports:


         /dev/lp0:          Detected
         /dev/lp0:          Not detected
         /dev/lp2:          Not detected
```

Linux *should* detect the proper parallel port, based on the settings in your computer's BIOS. Select OK and Press Enter.

You may be surprised at the number of printers Linux supports directly. Although you may have trouble with some of the newest inkjets and high-end laser printers, Epson Stylus printers and a decent selection of the HP line are represented along with numerous others. Select the printer driver that is closest to your device, such as HP LaserJet 4/5/6 Series for a LaserJet 4MP or LaserJet 5. Select OK and press Enter.

Select the desired paper size and printer resolution, select OK, and press Enter. If the settings are correct in the Verify Printer Configuration dialog that appears, select OK and press Enter.

SETTING UP A LAN MANAGER PRINTER

Settings for a LAN Manager printer are quite similar. Again, these are printers shared from Windows machines that are typically NT Servers but could also be NT Workstations or Windows 9x machines. A primary difference between this setup and the local printer setup is that you need to furnish the IP address, the NetBIOS name of the LAN Manager host, the share name of the networked printer, and a user name and password. The dialog that appears looks like the following:

```
LAN manager host: richsbox

LAN manager IP:   192.168.21.1

Share name:       LaserJet

User name:        Administrator

Password:         _____
```

Otherwise, printer setup is identical to a Local setup.

Once you're done with printer setup, proceed to the final steps to get Linux up and running.

FINISHING INSTALLATION

The last few steps in Linux installation involve defining a root administrative password and creating a special boot floppy.

SETTING THE ROOT PASSWORD

The root password is the password for the ultimate administrator account in the Linux system. This account has privileges to modify and change everything in the system. Other user accounts you create should be named differently and use different passwords. For many Linux tasks, you do not want to use the root account, because of its sensitive nature.

While finishing the installation, you see a dialog like the following:

```
Pick a root password. You must type it twice to ensure
you know what it is and didn't make a mistake in typing.
Remember that the root password is a critical part of
system security!

     Password:       _____

     Password (again)_____
```

Type in the password for the root account on your new system, and enter it a second time to ensure it is correct. The password is encrypted when you type it in. Then, select OK and press Enter.

CREATING A BOOT FLOPPY

LILO, of course, is the Linux Loader, which is Linux's boot manager. I recommend creating a boot floppy, as there are times when hard disk partitions lose their boot tracks even when the rest of the data is intact. When this occurs, you will not be able to start up your Linux system. A boot floppy gives you a chance to fix your system and at least bypass any initial bootup problems. The screen will read as follows:

```
A custom bootdisk provides a way of booting into your
Linux system without depending on the normal bootloader.
This is useful if you don't want to install lilo on your
system, another operating system removes lilo, or lilo
doesn't work with your hardware configuration. A custom
bootdisk can also be used with the RedHat rescue image,
making it much easier to recover from severe system
failures.
```

```
Would you like to create a bootdisk for your system?
```

Select Yes and press Enter. Insert a floppy disk into your floppy drive and press Enter.

Your floppy is named /dev/fd0 in Linux device terminology.

After a moment, Linux installation prompts you to decide where to install the Linux Loader (LILO). The dialog reads something like this:

```
Where do you want to install the bootloader?
```

```
/dev/hda          Master Boot Record

/dev/hda2         First sector of boot partition
```

If your Linux system is on a separate hard disk, the best option is to use the Master Boot Record. Now, if you are running Windows NT, Windows 95, OS/2, or some other OS on the disk, those operating systems use their own boot managers. System Commander is another popular boot manager program that enables control of multiple operating systems. If this is your situation, select First Sector of Boot partition to enable continued use of the other boot manager.

Select Master Boot Record (for a stand-alone disk) or First Sector of boot partition (for a Linux root partition on a shared disk), select OK, and press Enter. A second installation screen requests special LILO boot options, including a checkbox for Use Linear Mode, needed for some IDE drives that operate in LBA mode. The vast majority of computers running Linux will never use this option, or any other boot options. Select OK and press Enter.

You have completed Linux installation! You are asked to reboot. Once you do, the LILO login prompt appears:

```
LILO:
```

Simply press Enter to start the Linux boot process.

If you have more than 64 MB of RAM in your system, there's a good chance that Linux will not make use of it automatically. The BIOS in your computer's motherboard may only allow so much RAM to be allocated to an OS regardless of how much is installed in your system.
To fix this, at the LILO prompt, type something like LILO: Linux mem=128M. This enables Linux to use 128 megabytes of RAM in your system.
Simply adjust the value according to how much memory you have in your particular system.

Every other chapter in this book builds upon this chapter. In many cases, because you installed DNS and SMB services, preconfigured your network, and set up your video display, many other process in the chapters of this book are made much simpler.

SUMMARY

It is impossible for a book of this size to cover all configuration and installation options for every Linux version. That's why only the most popular versions are shown here. Fortunately, while there are differences in the screens and step-by-step processes each Linux version follows to install the operating system, they all use the same basic approach. Read the screen information, and you will figure out how to load Linux in no time.

UPGRADING LINUX AND REBUILDING THE KERNEL

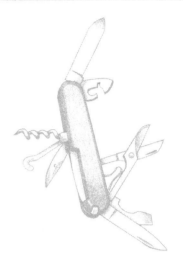

I f you are already running Linux, all the installation information is pretty useless to you. You have a system running smoothly, and you are experimenting with Linux to your heart's content. But what happens when a new release of Linux comes out? Do you bother with the new release? Do you remove your existing Linux system and load the new one from scratch, wiping out everything you have already configured? Surely there is an easier way! There is: upgrading. Linux allows you to update many parts of the system without reloading the entire operating system. The process is similar to a raw installation, but there are a few tricks and tips you need to know to preserve your existing filesystem, configuration information, and utilities. This chapter shows you how to upgrade an existing Linux system. We also look at how you can recompile, relink, and rebuild your Linux kernel to add or remove drivers. Rebuilding the kernel is a common routine with Linux, and while some users are a little worried about the process, it is remarkably simple.

INSTALLING THE LINUX SOURCE CODE

In order to load kernel patches or upgrade your operating system, you need to have the source code for Linux installed on your system. When you first install Linux, these files are sometimes installed by default. They can also be added using a package manager like RedHat's RPM or from a gzip file. To add the source code to your Linux system using a package manager like RPM, follow these steps:

1. Log on as root and place the CD-ROM in the drive. Mount the CD-ROM with this command:

   ```
   mount /dev/hdc /cdrom
   ```

   This command mounts the device /dev/hdc (use the name of your CD-ROM device) and /cdrom is the directory to which to mount the CD. You can use any existing directory as a target.

2. Change to whatever directory has the source code or package manager on the CD-ROM. For example, with RedHat issue the following command:

   ```
   cd /cdrom/RedHat/RPMS
   ```

3. If you are using a package manager, invoke it to install the code. On the RedHat system used in step 2, the command is as follows:

   ```
   rpm -ivh kernel-source
   ```

   This tells RPM to install the package called kernel-source. If you are not using a package manager, you can copy the source code using the cp command. If it is archived with gzip or tar, copy the archive file and then unarchive it.

KERNEL PATCHES

Kernel patches are minor changes in the release number of the Linux kernel, such as 2.0.12 to 2.0.13, and do not require major changes or complex upgrades to your system. Minor patches are usually released to add new support for a device, to fix a bug, or to fix a security problem in some utility. These tend to be found in code you won't run too often; if there is a need to patch commonly used code, a major release would be issued. These changes to the code modify the source code used on your system, *patching* the operating system. When you install a patch, the source code that needs the patch is updated, the code is recompiled, and the kernel is relinked and placed in the proper location for you to boot. This entire process of recompiling and relinking is mostly transparent to you, which means you don't need to know anything about programming.

You probably will not upgrade the kernel every time there is a minor release, although you should do upgrades before your kernel is too far out of date. You can determine the current release number of your kernel with the following command:

```
uname -r
```

The command will return the current version, like this:

```
2.0.32
```

In this case, the major and minor release (version number) is 2.0: 2 is the major release number, and 0 is the minor release number. The patch level is 32. Patches are issued incrementally, so the next patch would be 33, then 34, and so on. When a new major or minor release is issued—either to 2.1 or 3.0, depending on the changes in the code—the minor release and patch numbers reset to zero.

You will also see the version number and patch level when you boot your Linux system, if the messages do not scroll by too quickly. A typical boot message looks like the following:

```
kernel 2.0.32 on an i486
```

A few patch levels may pass before you upgrade. For example, if you are running kernel 2.0.30 and 2.0.33 comes out, you have missed three patch levels. Patches are not cumulative, meaning that .33 does not contain all the changes from .31 and .32. You may need to obtain every patch you skipped and install them, in order, one at a time, or obtain the complete source code for the latest release that contains all the patches. Since patching can be a tedious process if you have missed more than two or three, you may opt for obtaining the entire source code when you need some of the features that a later patch offers. The difference in size between the downloads of patches and source code is important: a patch is typically less than 100K, while the entire source code can run to many megabytes even when compressed. If you have a slow connection to the Internet, obtaining the complete source code can be a long and frustrating process. Patching incrementally or buying a CD-ROM with the latest source code on it makes more sense in these cases.

To install a kernel patch, you must have all the kernel source files installed on your system. You can obtain the patch code from a number of sources on the web, FTP sites, and newer CD-ROMs of Linux. You can also receive them from other Linux users via e-mail or on a storage media like a diskette or Zip drive.

When you are ready to use a patch, you must put it in the correct directory, unzip the file (most Linux patches come as gzipped .gz files), and use the patch command to apply the patch. These steps follow:

1. Copy the patch file to the directory in which you have stored the source code; the default is /usr/src. Then, change to that directory.

2. If the file is compressed, uncompress the .gz file using this command:

```
gunzip patch*.gz
```

3. The patch command can be used to apply the patches. Specify the patch name with the command, like this:

```
patch -p0 < patch-2.0.33
```

All error messages will be written to the screen. You could redirect them to a file if you want to save them for further study.

The message "Reversed (or previously applied) patch detected! Assume -R?" means the patch utility thinks the patch has already been applied. Answer "No" to these questions unless you have a specific reason for doing otherwise. With many Linux distributions, including RedHat, some patches are applied to the kernel but the patch level is not incremented properly.

4. If you are applying a number of patches, apply them in order. You don't need to recompile between each patch installation. However, if you don't apply the patches in the proper order, there is the potential for missing some code.

5. If you encounter an error from the patch command, it may be that the patches cannot be installed properly, probably because of a major change or the number of increments required. You should obtain a new kernel source code if this happens, and start with the new version.

REBUILDING THE KERNEL

Compiling the source code to create a new binary image is the process of rebuilding the kernel. You will have to rebuild the kernel whenever you install a new patch or add a new device driver to your Linux system. The procedure requires no knowledge of programming and the steps are really quite simple, even though the thought of the underlying activities can be daunting.

Prior to rebuilding the kernel for any reason, it is prudent to create an emergency boot floppy, just in case the kernel image becomes corrupted. If you don't have a boot floppy, you may not be able to load your system and any information stored on the filesystem could be lost.

The procedure to follow when rebuilding the kernel is the same every time. There are four steps to rebuilding the kernel:

1. Configure the kernel information files.
2. Create the modules using the make utility.
3. Create the kernel using the make utility.
4. Compile, link, and install the kernel.

In the steps above, notice that there are modules involved in the process. Modules are not linked into the kernel in the same way that other components are. This difference really matters for device drivers used to support hardware. There are two alternatives for loading a device driver with Linux: link the device driver into the kernel or load it as a module. The linked device driver is the most common and is used for any device that is used frequently. The code for the device driver becomes part of the kernel and is always available to the operating system. Linking device drivers into the kernel is the fastest way to provide support for a device, but does make the kernel grow larger with each linked device driver. Using modules is an alternative.

A module is a chunk of code that the kernel can load at any time, use it while it is loaded, and unload it when it is not needed. The advantages to using modules is that the code needs be loaded only when you need it, and the kernel doesn't have to be recompiled and relinked with every new device driver. However, using modules is a little slower than linking the device driver into the kernel.

You can easily combine both linked and modular approaches to the kernel. If you have a lot of hardware that is not always in use, such as scanners, CD-ROM jukeboxes, Zip drives, special printers, and so on, the use of modules allows you to keep the kernel smaller and faster. However, if you use the devices almost every time you use Linux, it is better to link the device drivers into the kernel. Many distributions of Linux, such as RedHat, make heavy use of the modular approach as this allows for many types of hardware to be supported in modules, with only essential hardware included in the kernel. It's a trade-off between flexibility and speed.

CONFIGURING THE KERNEL

There are several ways to configure the kernel, depending on the version of the operating system you have and the way you want to perform the configuration. During the configuration process, you will need information about your machine, such as whether to use PCI slots, whether to use math emulation, and whether to use a module approach to the device drivers. Specific information about the system is also captured.

The three choices on most systems are:

◆ Character-based menu-driven configuration using the "make menuconfig" program.

◆ Character-based one-by-one configuration using the "make config" program.

◆ X-based menu-driven configuration using the "make xconfig" program.

All three approaches allow you to specify settings for kernel parameters, but their approach is different. For X users, the xconfig routine is probably the friendliest as it prompts you for the configuration items, all in X dialogs. The menuconfig option is similar to xconfig but is character-based. Alternatively, the config program doesn't try to do everything at once, but rather steps you through the parameters one at a time. Although the latter is the slowest approach, it does allow for fine tweaking of a single parameter without going through the entire list.

Whichever configuration routine you decide to use, they all generate a file called .config which is stored by default in /usr/src/linux. This file contains all the kernel parameters necessary for recompiling and relinking the kernel.

If you look at an existing .config file, you see that it is a list of options followed by a setting value, something like this:

```
CONFIG_MODULES=y
```

```
CONFIG_KERNELD=y
```

```
CONFIG_NET=y
```

```
CONFIG_PCI=y
```

Any line starting with a pound (hash) symbol is a comment. There are three different values allowed for each of the parameters in the .config file, as follows:

- ◆ **y**: Links support for this parameter into the kernel.
- ◆ **m**: Uses a module to support this parameter.
- ◆ **n**: Skips support for this parameter.

Since most of the parameters are device drivers, you are really telling the system whether to add support for the device driver into the kernel, to use a module, or to skip the device driver altogether.

To start the configuration routine for the kernel, issue one of the make commands. To use xconfig you will need an X terminal window open. All three configuration tools—config, xconfig, and menuconfig—ask for the same information. The questions that you have to answer are shown in the following sections, divided into the type of subsystem to which they pertain, along with their meaning and usual values. This list was taken from a RedHat release of Linux, but yours will be similar.

GENERAL SYSTEM CONFIGURATION

The first series of questions from the configuration program ask about the motherboard and chipsets in use, as well as general kernel parameters. They are:

- ◆ CONFIG_EXPERIMENTAL: Linux wants to know if you want to use experimental code or device drivers in this kernel. Answer N to the question.
- ◆ CONFIG_MODULES: Do you want to support loadable modules? Normally you want loadable modules, and thus should answer Y.
- ◆ CONFIG_MODVERSIONS: Do you want to have all modules checked for version numbers? The default answer of Y is fine, although there is no harm in not loading this option, either.

- CONFIG_KERNELD: Do you want to allow a daemon to load a module when needed? Normally you will want this; answer Y.

- CONFIG_MATH_EMULATION: Do you want to have the operating system emulate a math coprocessor? If you have an 80386 or 80486SX CPU, answer Y to this question. For 80486DX and Pentium chips, answer N.

- CONFIG_NET: Do you want networking support in the kernel? If you are not networking the machine to other machines on a LAN or connecting to the Internet, answer N. Otherwise, answer Y. If you are not sure, answer Y.

- CONFIG_MAX_16M: Do you want to limit the available RAM to 16MB? This is for older systems that may not be able to access memory over 16MB, or for motherboards with less than 16MB RAM. Answer Y if either of these two cases is true; otherwise, answer N.

- CONFIG_PCI: Do you want PCI support loading? If you have a PCI bus in your motherboard, answer Y. Otherwise, answer N. Most Pentiums have PCI motherboards.

- CONFIG_SYSVIPC: Do you want to load System V Interprocess Communications? Many applications require IPC, and thus you should answer Y.

- CONFIG_BINFMT_AOUT: Do you want to generate a.out executable files (an older format used for binaries)? Answer Y to this.

- CONFIG_BINFMT_ELF: Do you want to support Executable and Linking Format, the newer system for handling executable binaries? Answer Y to this one, too.

- CONFIG_KERNEL_ELF: Should the kernel be stored as an ELF? Answer Y.

- CONFIG_M586: What type of processor are you using? Valid answers are 386, 486, Pentium, and PPro (for Pentium Pro). The default answer is 386 which allows the code to run on any processor, but if you have a Pentium or Pentium Pro, the code can be optimized for those processors by using their respective codes.

IDE SUBSYSTEM QUESTIONS

These questions in the configuration routine have to do with the type of device support (mainly hard disk and floppy drives) to be enabled in your kernel.

- CONFIG_BLK_DEV_FD: Do you have a floppy drive? Most systems do; answer Y if you have one.

- CONFIG_BLK_DEV_IDE: Do you have IDE drives? If you have IDE, EIDE, ATA, or Ultra-DMA drives (but not SCSI), answer Y. If you have SCSI and no IDE drives or CD-ROMs, answer N.

- CONFIG_BLK_DEV_HD_IDE: Does you IDE support hard drives only, with no

CD-ROM support? Unless you have an old IDE system that can't handle CD-ROMs on the IDE chains, answer N.

◆ CONFIG_BLK_DEV_IDECD: Do you have an IDE CD-ROM? If so, answer Y.

◆ CONFIG_BLK_DEV_IDETAPE: Do you have an IDE tape drive? If so, answer Y.

◆ CONFIG_BLK_DEV_IDEFLOPPY: Do you have an IDE-based floppy device, like a ZIP or Superfloppy? If so, answer Y. Don't answer Y if your device is SCSI-based.

◆ CONFIG_BLK_DEV_ISESCSI: Do you use a SCSI driver to access IDE devices? In most cases you will answer N. If you use SCSI devices only, answer N.

◆ CONFIG_BLK_DEV_IDE_PCMCIA: Do you want to support PC Cards (formerly called PCMCIA cards)? If you have a laptop or a docking station for PC Cards on your desktop, answer Y. Most users using desktops will answer N.

◆ CONFIG_BLK_DEV_CMD640: Do you want to correct problems with the CMD640 chipset? If you are sure you don't have a CMD640 chip, answer N. On the other hand, if you are not sure, it doesn't do any harm and uses only a little memory to answer Y.

◆ CONFIG_BLK_DEV_RZ1000: Do you want to correct problems with the RZ1000 chipset? If you are sure you don't have a RZ1000 chip, answer N. On the other hand, if you are not sure, it doesn't do any harm and uses only a little memory to answer Y.

◆ CONFIG_BLK_DEV_TRITON: Does your IDE system use the Intel Triton IDE interface chip? If you are using IDE drives, answer Y. It is often difficult to figure out if your system uses this chip or not, and since the overhead is minimal we may as well build the support into the kernel.

◆ CONFIG_IDE_CHIPSETS: Do you want to enable support for motherboard IDE chipsets? If you have only one hard drive and one CD-ROM connected to your IDE chains, answer N. If you have more than one drive, answer Y. If you are not using IDE, answer N.

◆ CONFIG_BLK_DEV_LOOP: Do you want to support the loopback driver to allow Linux to handle an entire filesystem through a single file? Normally you will answer N to this question.

◆ CONFIG_BLK_DEV_RAM: Do you want to use a portion of the RAM as a Ramdisk extension of the filesystem? There is no harm in answering Y to this question if you have more than 32MB of RAM. A better choice is to use a module to hold the driver so it can be loaded as needed, so answer M.

◆ CONFIG_BLK_DEV_XD: Do you have an older XT-type hard drive? Unless your PC is a very early model, answer N to this question.

NETWORKING

These questions in the config routine ask about the role of your Linux machine on a network, and any special drivers you want loading.

◆   CONFIG_FIREWALL: Do you want to use your Linux system as a firewall? If you don't plan to use Linux as a firewall to the Internet, answer N. If you want to configure Linux as a firewall, which includes proxy IP addressing, answer Y. You don't have to set up the functions right away if you answer Y.

◆   CONFIG_NET_ALIAS: Do you want to assign multiple IP addresses to a single network card? Normally you will answer N.

◆   CONFIG_INET: Do you want to enable IP forwarding using INET? You should answer Y as you always want IP forwarding.

◆   CONFIG_IP_FORWARD: Do you want to use your Linux system as a router between two local area networks? If you have configured your Linux system as a firewall (CONFIG_FIREWALL=y), then you need to set this to Y as well. If you are connecting two local area networks together through this Linux machine, answer Y. Otherwise, you can answer N.

◆   CONFIG_IP_MULTICAST: Do you want to allow multicasting through the Linux router? If you answer Y to CONFIG_IP_FORWARD, answer Y here. Otherwise, answer N.

◆   CONFIG_SYN_COOKIES: Do you want Linux to resist SYN flooding? SYN flooding is a type of network attack used by hackers to overwhelm a network. Answer Y unless your machine will never be attached to a network or the Internet.

◆   CONFIG_IP_ACCT: Answer Y if you are using your Linux system as a router. Otherwise, answer N.

◆   CONFIG_IP_ROUTER: are you using your Linux system as a router? This question ties in with others in this section. If you are using your system as a router, answer Y. Otherwise, answer N.

◆   CONFIG_NET_IPIP: Do you want to enable IP tunneling? Most of the time you will answer N unless you want to move machines from network to network without altering IP addresses.

◆   CONFIG_INET_PCTCP: Do you want to offer PC/TCP compatibility mode? Answer N for this question (the default).

◆   CONFIG_INET_RARP: Do you want to allow reverse address resolution protocol? This is best loaded as a module so it can be called only when needed, so answer M. If you want to avoid modules, answer Y.

◆ CONFIG_NO_PATH_MTU_DISCOVERY: Do you want to disable MTU path discovery? Answer N in almost all cases.

◆ CONFIG_IP_NOSR: Do you want to drop source routed frames? Answer Y, the default.

◆ CONFIG_SKB_LARGE: Do you want to allow large windows? If you have 16MB RAM or less, answer N. If you have more than 16MB RAM, answer Y.

◆ CONFIG_IPX: Do you want to support Novell's IPX protocol? Answer N unless you are on a NetWare network that insists on IPX/SPX instead of TCP/IP.

◆ CONFIG_ATALK: Do you want to support AppleTalk? Unless you are on an AppleTalk-based network, answer N.

◆ CONFIG_AX25: Do you want to allow packet-radio (X.25)? Answer N in most cases; few installations use this protocol.

◆ CONFIG_NETLINK: Do you want to allow a network link between the kernel and other processes? Normally you will answer N.

SCSI SUPPORT

These options deal with the SCSI subsystem. If you don't use SCSI, then most of your answers will be simple.

◆ CONFIG_SCSI: Do you want to load SCSI drivers? If you have SCSI devices, answer Y. Otherwise, answer N.

◆ CONFIG_BLK_DEV_SD: Do you want to enable SCSI disk support? If you have SCSI, answer Y.

◆ CONFIG_BLK_DEV_ST: Do you want to enable SCSI tape support? If you have SCSI, answer Y. Even if you don't have a SCSI tape drive, there is no harm in answering Y.

◆ CONFIG_BLK_DEV_SR: Do you want to enable SCSI CD-ROM support? If you have a SCSI CD-ROM or a SCSI CD writer, answer Y.

◆ CONFIG_CHR_DEV_SG: Do you want to support generic SCSI devices? If your system is SCSI-based, this should be Y.

◆ CONFIG_SCSI_MULTI_LUN: Do you want to probe multiple logical units on a SCSI chain? Answer N since few SCI devices cause problems and need probing.

◆ CONFIG_SCSI_CONSTANTS: Do you want verbose SCSI reporting? Answer N to this question.

◆ CONFIG_SCSI_*: This is a long list of all SCSI adapter cards that the kernel has drivers for. All will be N except for the one card that matches yours or is compatible with yours. For example, if your SCSI card is a Buslogic board, you will answer N to all the SCSI card drivers except CONFIG_SCSI_BUSLOGIC.

MORE NETWORKING

Even more references to the networking section of the kernel follow the SCSI configuration information section. Here are some guidelines for answering these questions.

◆ CONFIG_NETDEVICES: Do you have a networking card in your machine? If you have a network card, answer Y.

◆ CONFIG_DUMMY: Do you want the dummy interface (localhost) setting up on your system? If you are using PPP or SLIP to connect to the Internet over a modem or a LAN, answer Y. If you are running TCP/IP on your machine, answer Y. In fact, since some Linux applications refer to the dummy interface even if there is no network installed, you can safely answer Y to this question.

◆ CONFIG_EQUALIZER: Do you want to enable serial line load balancing on two or more phone lines used by your system? If you use two or more lines to connect to the Internet at the same time, answer Y. If you use only a single line, or don't connect to the Internet, answer N. (Load balancing requires software at both ends of the connection to function properly.)

◆ CONFIG_PLIP: Do you want to configure the Parallel Port Internet Protocol, a means of connecting two machines together over the parallel ports? In most cases you will want to answer N. There are better ways to connect machines together.

◆ CONFIG_PPP: Do you want to use Point to Point Protocol? If you are connecting to an ISP over a modem, answer Y.

◆ CONFIG_SLIP: Do you want to use the Serial Line Interface Protocol (a slower protocol than PPP) to connect to an ISP? If you are not sure whether you use PPP or SLIP, say Y to both.

◆ CONFIG_NET_RADIO: Do you want to use the packet radio interface? This is not in common use, so you should answer N.

◆ CONFIG_NET_ETHERNET: Do you want to use Ethernet for your network? If you have an Ethernet card, answer Y.

◆ CONFIG_*: A series of network cards are now displayed. Usually these are displayed in two parts. First, the vendor is displayed (such as CONFIG_NET_VENDOR_3COM or CONFIG_NET_VENDOR_SMC) and if you answer Y to any vendor, all the supported cards are listed. As with the SCSI adapter earlier, answer N to all except the one item that matches your network card's name and ID or is compatible with it. For example, if your network card is a 3Com 3c503, answer Y to CONFIG_NET_VENDOR_3COM and then Y to CONFIG_EL2 (the 3c503 option). Your network card box usually has an identifier for the card, instead of a common name (such as Etherlink II).

◆ CONFIG_NET_EISA: Is your network card an EISA card? If it is answer Y. Otherwise, answer N.

◆ CONFIG_NET_POCKET: Is your network card a pocket or portable adapter? In most cases answer N. For some laptops you will answer Y.

◆ CONFIG_TR: Do you want to configure token ring support? In most cases, you will answer N.

◆ CONFIG_FDDI: Do you want to use FDDI (fiber) support for networking? Unless you have a FDDI card, answer N.

◆ CONFIG_ARCNET: Do you want to add ARCnet support to the networking? In most cases answer N.

◆ CONFIG_ISDN: Do you want to add Integrated Services Digital Network to your kernel? If you have an ISDN modem or a direct connection to an ISDN ISP, answer Y.

FILESYSTEM SUPPORT

The next series of parameters have to do with filesystems that will be supported by your kernel. The section also asks about different characteristics of each filesystem. You can support many different filesystem types, but remember that each adds overhead to the kernel and slows your system down a little.

◆ CONFIG_CD_NO_IDESCSI: Do you have a non-IDE and non-SCSI CD-ROM? In other words, do you have a nonstandard CD-ROM, such as one hanging off a sound card? If you do, answer Y, otherwise, answer N.

◆ CONFIG_QUOTA: Do you want to use disk quotas? Disk quotas allow you to limit the amount of disk space alloted to a user. If you have a system with limited disk space and many users, you may want to answer Y; otherwise, answer N.

◆ CONFIG_MINI_FS: Do you want to support the Minix filesystem? This filesystem is still used on some floppy disks. Install it as a module for loading only when needed. Answer M.

◆ CONFIG_EXT_FS: Do you want to support the extended filesystem? This filesystem is no longer used, so you can answer N.

◆ CONFIG_EXT2_FS: Do you want to use the second extended file system? This is the current standard filesystem for Linux, so answer Y.

◆ CONFIG_XIA_FS: Do you want to support the XIA filesystem? This filesystem is rarely encountered, so answer N.

◆ CONFIG_FAT_FS: Do you want to support the DOS FAT filesystem? If you want to access your DOS or Windows 95 (non-FAT32) filesystem from Linux, answer Y. Otherwise, answer N or M.

◆ CONFIG_MSDOS_FS: Do you want to support MS-DOS filesystems? This filesystem is used on DOS-formatted floppies, so answer Y.

◆ CONFIG_VFAT_FS: Do you want to support the VFAT filesystem from Windows 95? If you have a VFAT filesystem you want to access from Linux, answer Y.

◆ CONFIG_UMSDOS_FS: Are you using the UMSDOS filesystem to store Linux on a DOS partition? If you are not using UMSDOS, answer N.

◆ CONFIG_PROC_FS: Do you want to provide support for the /proc virtual filesystem? The /proc filesystem doesn't actually exist on disk; files are created in the filesystem when you access them. You should enable this option, so answer Y.

◆ CONFIG_NFS_FS: Do you want to allow NFS (Network File System) mounts from other machines on your Linux machine? If you are running NFS, answer Y. Most people don't bother with NFS unless they have several UNIX or Linux servers. Unless you do, you can answer N.

◆ CONFIG_SMB_FS: Do you want to support SMB (Server Message Block) to allow Linux to access directories on shared Windows machines? If you use Samba or a similar tool, or want to use networking to access Windows-based drives, answer Y.

◆ CONFIG-SMB_WIN95: While this is similar to CONFIG_SMB_FS, it bypasses some bugs in Windows 95's shared directories. Answer Y if you said Y to CONFIG_SMB_FS.

◆ CONFIG_ISO9660_FS: Do you want to provide support for the ISO 9660 (previously called High Sierra) filesystem used on CD-ROMs? If you are using a CD-ROMs on the system, answer Y.

◆ CONFIG_HPFS_FS: Do you want to provide support for OS/2's High Performance Filesystem? If you do not access HPFS filesystems, answer N.

◆ CONFIG_SYSV_FS: Do you want to provide support for the System V filesystem used by UNIX systems like SCO OpenServer? If you access a System V UNIX system, answer Y.

◆ CONFIG_UFS_FS: Do you want Linux to read (but not write) the UFS filesystem used by several versions of UNIX? If you access a UFS system (such as SunOS, NetBSD, or NeXTstep), answer Y.

MISCELLANEOUS CONFIGURATION ITEMS

The rest of the config routine questions cover everything that doesn't fall into another category, including multiport cards, special devices like touchscreens, and non-SCSI tape drives.

- CONFIG_SERIAL: Do you want to configure the serial ports for use by Linux? Answer Y to this unless you never use a serial port.
- CONFIG_DIGI: Do you have a Digi International multiport card? If you have, answer Y.
- CONFIG_CYCLADES: Do you have a Cyclades asynchronous mux on your system? If you have, answer Y.
- CONFIG_STALDRV: Do you have a Stallion Technologies multiport card? If you have, answer Y.
- CONFIG_SDL: Do you have an SDL RISCom multiport card? If so, answer Y.
- CONFIG_PRINTER: Do you want to provide support for a parallel printer? You will normally answer Y to this one.
- CONFIG_SPECIALIX: Do you have a Specialix 108+ multiport card on your system? If so, answer Y.
- CONFIG_MOUSE: Do you have a bus or PS/2-style mouse, instead of a standard serial mouse? If so, answer Y.
- CONFIG_ATIXL_BUSMOUSE: If you have a bus mouse, is it an ATIXL mouse? If so, answer Y.
- CONFIG_BUSMOUSE: If you have a bus mouse, is it a Logitech busmouse? If so, answer Y.
- CONFIG_MS_BUSMOUSE: If you have a bus mouse, is it a Microsoft busmouse? If so, answer Y.
- CONFIG_PSMOUSE: Do you have a PS/2 style mouse, instead of a bus or serial mouse? Answer Y if you have.
- CONFIG_UMISC: Do you have light pens, touchscreens, or other devices you want to support? If so, answer Y. Most users will answer N.
- CONFIG_QIC02_TAPE: Do you have a QIC (Quarter Inch Cartridge) tape drive? Is so, answer Y or M. Use M if you will not use the device often. This will free up memory space.
- CONFIG_FTAPE: Do you have a Travan tape drive in your system? Travan tape drives can be connected to the IDE interface or to a SCSI chain. If you have a Tra-

van tape drive, answer Y or M. Use the M option if you will not use the tape drive often. This keeps the kernel smaller and requires less RAM.

♦ CONFIG_APM: Do you want to support Advanced Power Management? APM is used on laptops and some desktops to allow the system to conserve battery or electrical power. Because Linux doesn't like to be interrupted, answer N.

♦ CONFIG_WATCHDOG: Do you want to use the watchdog feature? Watchdog tries to write a particular file once every minute. If it can't, the system is rebooted. Answer N for this option in most cases. Watchdog can be handy for monitoring a high-availability server such as a web server. It will reboot the system if it locks up for any reason.

♦ CONFIG_RTC: Do you want to access the PC's real-time clock through a special device driver? Unless you have multiple processors and you are running a symmetric multiproccesor (SMP) version of Linux, answer N.

SOUND CARD SUPPORT

The penultimate section in the config routine asks about your sound card. There are many sound cards on the market, many of which will not appear in the list config offers. However, most sound cards will emulate another card, such as the Creative Labs SoundBlaster. The options and choices for them follow.

♦ CONFIG_SOUND: Do you want to configure a sound card? If you have a sound card, the answer is Y. You could load the sound driver as a module only when needed, which frees up some memory. If you do load the driver as a module, any other sound-related option below should be loaded as a module, too.

♦ CONFIG_AUDIO: Do you want to use the /dev/dsp and /dev/audio drivers for sound and digital signal processing? If you have a sound card, answer Y.

♦ CONFIG_MIDI: Do you want to configure a MIDI device? If you have a MIDI card or MIDI support on your sound board, answer Y.

♦ CONFIG_YM3812: Do you want to enable FM Synthesizer support? Many sound boards (especially older ones) use a Yamaha chip to provide sounds using FM synthesis. Answer Y if you have an FM synthesizer chip on your sound board.

♦ CONFIG_PAS: Do you want to enable ProAudio Spectrum support? If your board has this chipset, answer Y. Most sound boards do not have this chipset.

♦ CONFIG_SB: Do you want to enable SoundBlaster support? Many audio cards support SoundBlaster drivers, as do all Creative Labs cards. Answer Y if you have such a card.

◆ CONFIG_ADLIB: Do you have an older Adlib card or a card supporting the OPL2/OPL3 FM synthesizer chip? If you have an Adlib board, answer Y.

◆ CONFIG_GUS: Do you have a Gravis Ultrasound sound card? If so, answer Y to enable support for its features.

◆ CONFIG_PSS: Do you want to support the PSS ECHO ADI211 chip? Most sound boards do not use this chipset, so answer N unless your card has the set. The documentation will tell you if this chipset is used.

◆ CONFIG_MPU401: Do you want to enable the Roland MPU 401 MIDI card support? Many cards emulate the MPU401 set, so answer Y if you have such a MIDI board. Do not answer Y if you have a SoundBlaster 16. Also, if you are using the serial port version of the MPU401, do not answer Y.

◆ CONFIG_UART6850: Do you want to enable the UART 6850 MIDI support? Some MIDI cards and sound boards use the 6850 UART. Answer Y if yours does.

◆ CONFIG_UART401: Do you want to enable support for the Roland MPU401 serial port version? If your MIDI board uses the serial port, answer Y.

◆ CONFIG_MSS: Do you want to enable support for the Microsoft Sound System? Microsoft's sound board has been unavailable for many years, but it is still in many older systems. Answer Y if you have one in your Linux machine.

◆ CONFIG_SSCAPE: Do you want to enable support for the Ensoniq SoundScape system? Some high-end audio boards use the Ensoniq chipset, including boards from Ensoniq. Answer Y if you have such a board.

◆ CONFIG_TRIX: Do you want to enable support for the MediaTrix AudioTrix Pro board? If you have one, answer Y.

◆ CONFIG_MAD16: Do you want to enable support for the MAD16 or Mozart cards? If you have such a card, answer Y.

◆ CONFIG_MAUI: Do you want to enable support for the Turtle Beach Wave Front synthesizers? This system was used in several boards, including the Maui and Tropez from Turtle Beach. Answer Y if you have one of these cards.

◆ DSP_BUFFSIZE: What size audio DMA buffer do you want to use? Options are 4K, 16K, 32K, or 64K. The latter (default) setting is best.

◆ CONFIG_LOWLEVEL_SOUND: If you are using a sound board, answer N to this question. The sound board drivers will handle all sounds for you.

PROFILING THE KERNEL

The last question of the config routine is about profiling the kernel. A profile lets you determine how much time the kernel spends with each component and driver and can be useful when debugging drivers.

◆ CONFIG_PROFILE: Do you want to profile the kernel. Most users should answer N to this question unless you want to examine device driver performance.

BUILDING MODULES

If you decided to use modules in any of the configuration questions, you will need to build and install the modules before you complete the kernel installation. Making the modules is easy:

1. Log in as root and change to the /usr/src/linux directory or whichever directory your source code is kept in.
2. Build the modules by issuing the command:

   `make modules`

   You will see a set of messages and perhaps some error messages. When the shell prompt returns, the process of building the modules is complete.
3. Modules will be kept in a directory named after the version of Linux that you are running. For example, if you are running level 2.0.32 there will be a directory called /lib/modules/2.0.32 that contains all the modules. Install the modules by issuing the following command:

   `make module_install`

After the make routine is finished, the modules are ready for use. You can now compile and install the kernel.

COMPILING THE KERNEL

When you have finished completing the configuration questions using xconfig, config, or menuconfig, the routine tells you the next three steps to complete the compilation of the kernel. There are three commands you need to issue separately or on a single line, separated by semicolons. The three commands are:

`make dep`

`make clean`

`make boot`

The make dep command checks dependencies, ensuring that only code that has changed is recompiled. This dramatically cuts the amount of time required for a compilation. The make clean command deletes old, unneccessary files from the system, such as old copies of the kernel. Finally, the make boot command creates the new kernel. The kernel is given the name zImage and is stored in the /usr/scr/linux/arch/386/boot directory on most systems. To use the new kernel, it needs to be copied to the /boot directory using cp. You may also want to modify LILO if you have added new filesystem support.

Issuing the three commands on a single line separated by semicolons is handy. It means you can leave the Linux system alone, rather than having to wait for the shell prompt to return. On the other hand, if any errors are generated, they might scroll past the screen when the other commands on the command line are executed.

Compiling the kernel takes a few minutes on a Pentium system, and much longer on slower machines. On an 80386, for example, it can take a half hour or longer, depending on the number of drivers loaded.

INSTALLING THE KERNEL

After the kernel code has been compiled and the modules are built, you can install the new kernel on your system. Depending on the version of Linux, your routine may differ from the one shown here, but most versions of Linux use LILO to install the new kernel. The configuration file /etc/lilo.conf lists the name of the kernel that LILO is to run. By default, the /etc/lilo.conf file will look for a file with the name specified in this line:

```
image=/boot/vmlinux-2.0.32
```

In this case, LILO will look for the file /boot/vmlinux-2.0.32. The newly compiled version of the kernel doesn't have this naming convention; it is instead called zImage. You could simplify the entire installation process and avoid any changes to the /etc/lilo.conf file by simply copying zImage to the /boot directory and overwriting the existing vmLinux kernel with the same name. If you don't need to backtrack to other versions of the kernel and don't care about keeping track of the kernel release as part of the boot image filename, this technique is fast and works flawlessly.

If you want to do things in a more proper way, you need to copy the new kernel image to the /boot directory and modify the /etc/lilo.conf file to contain the new name. Use any text editor to modify /etc/lilo.conf, changing the line mentioned above to reflect the new kernel name. You may want to change the kernel name so that it reflects the patch level which will also require a very minor change in /etc/lilo.conf.

REBOOT THE SYSTEM

After modifying the /etc/lilo.conf file, you need only reboot your system for the changes to take place. When you boot, you should see the new patch level name in the diagnostic messages, or you can use the uname command to display the version.

UPGRADING REDHAT LINUX WITH RPM PATCHES

As mentioned earlier in this chapter, you may receive errors when trying to install a new kernel patch using recent versions of RedHat Linux (particularly version 5.X and 6.X). This is because RedHat likes to handle everything as a package with RPM (RedHat Package Manager). Even patches can be handled by packages, and this is the approach RedHat prefers.

To install a new patch using RPM, follow these steps:

1. Download the RPM-compatible package for the kernel patch from RedHat's Web or FTP site. You will also need to download the kernel-modules package. If you do not have the source code on your system, you will need to download it, too, as both the kernel-source and kernel-headers package.

2. Install the packages using the following command, where pkgname is the name of the package to be installed:

```
rpm -i pkgname
```

3. Modify LILO as mentioned above to allow it to boot the new kernel image. Then reboot the machine.

SUMMARY

As you have seen, the process for upgrading the kernel version and rebuilding the kernel is not difficult. As long as you follow the steps mentioned in this chapter, you will find everything proceeds smoothly. Of course, you should always have an emergency boot disk handy, as well as a complete backup of your filesystems. Applying patches to the kernel is a good way to keep your Linux release current, bug-free, and free of any security holes.

LINUX
AND
WINDOWS

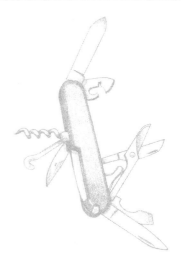

N ow that you have a Linux system up and running, there are ways you can access it from other machines. One of the most common uses for Linux is as a mail, web, or X server on a network of Windows machines. Connecting the Windows machines to the Linux server is straightforward once you understand how the two operating systems communicate. Some tools, such as Samba, remove much of the complexity that was once inherent in cross-operating system work. See chapter 11, *Linux Connectivity to Windows: Samba* starting on page 199 for more information on Samba. This chapter shows you how to set up several Windows versions to run with a Linux server, how to access the Linux server, and also how to configure Windows to use Linux as a DNS server or a gateway.

TCP/IP NETWORKS

Linux, like most versions of UNIX, uses a network operating system called TCP/IP (Transmission Control Protocol/Internet Protocol). While it is possible to set up Linux to use other network operating systems like Novell's IPX/SPX or Microsoft's NetBEUI and NetBIOS, it is much easier to instead configure Windows to use TCP/IP. There are a number of advantages TCP/IP has over other operating systems, not the least of which are that it has been around for decades and is the protocol of the Internet and UNIX. TCP/IP is also supported by network devices such as printers, mass-storage arrays, and multifunction devices. Also, TCP/IP is fast, efficient, and tends to cause the least number of problems in a heterogeneous network.

Microsoft didn't provide TCP/IP support with Windows 3.X. Users of this platform could only use TCP/IP by purchasing third-party products from companies like Net-Manage and FTP Software. With the development of Windows NT and Windows 95, Microsoft started adding TCP/IP support for the Windows package. This trend continues with Windows 98 and Windows 2000, as well as with Windows NT 4.0 and Windows 2000 Professional. All of these have improved and efficient TCP/IP drivers as part of the operating system. Just as Microsoft's Windows NT has replaced many Novell NetWare servers, TCP/IP has supplanted IPX/SPX as the default for most Windows-based networks. Indeed, TCP/IP is now the most commonly used network operating system in the world.

If you have a small network at home, maybe with two or three machines, the difference in speed between the different network operating systems won't make much of a difference to you. For a larger network, such as for a business, TCP/IP provides better throughput than NetBEUI and is easier to configure on multiple platforms.

NETWORKING HARDWARE AND CABLING

Since TCP/IP is the network protocol, it doesn't matter what type of network cards or cabling you use, as long as they support the TCP/IP protocol on them. Most network cards do allow TCP/IP to be used, although there are a few that do not. The most common network setup for TCP/IP is through Ethernet, which is available in a classic 10Mbps version and a newer, faster 100Mbps release. Most modern Ethernet cards support both speeds, although only one is in use at a time. Since Ethernet is so common, we'll concentrate on it in this chapter.

There are two kinds of cables used to connect TCP/IP machines together in most networks: coaxial cable and twisted pair cable. The difference in configuration between coaxial and twisted pair is important and different connectors are used on the network cards for each. It is also important to note that many network cards do not support coaxial cable connections.

Coaxial Cable

A network using coax cable is similar to your cable TV connection. In fact, TV coax can be used for coaxial cable networks, although there are standardized coaxial cables you are supposed to use instead. When connecting machines together with coax, a single cable runs from one end of the network to the other, connecting all the machines together along the way. The back of a coax network card has a BNC connector, which is connected to the coax cable through a T connector.

The two ends of the T are connected to cables running to other machines, except at either end of the run where terminating resistors are used. A coax cable network, then, runs from machine to machine, through T connectors, with no other hardware required. If you have only two machines on your network, then all you need are two BNC-equipped Ethernet cards, a single length of coax cable long enough to run between the machines, and two terminating resistors (often included with the network cards or coax cable packages). For three machines, you need three cards, two coax cables, two terminating resistors, and so on, adding a card and a length of coax cable for each additional machine.

The problems with coax-based networks are twofold: the coax cable itself and the layout of the cable required to interconnect your machines. The coax cable is fairly thick and inflexible and can be difficult to bend along the contours of your wall or floor. Sharp corners are virtually impossible with coax cables, and hiding them under carpets and rugs is difficult because of their thickness. On the other hand, the thickness itself is a benefit as it prevents electrical losses in the cable and resists breaks caused by twisting and bending. The second problem is that properly connecting machines in many locations with a single long chain of coax cables can be awkward.

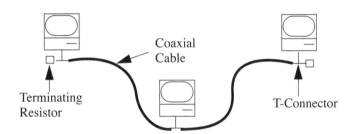

Figure 14-1   A network using coaxial cable has lengths of coax running from machine to machine, with terminating resistors at the two end points.

UTP Cable

The alternative to coax is twisted pair cable, also called unshielded twisted pair, or UTP. Inside Ethernet UTP cables are four pairs of wires totally eight conductors in all, of which only two pairs are usually used. UTP cable is a little thicker than typical telephone cable, but has the advantage of being flexible, easy to run, and easy to hide along walls and under carpets.

The connectors on a UTP Ethernet cable look like a wide telephone jack and have eight pins. These are called RJ45 connectors, and most network cards have an RJ45 connector on the back plane. UTP Ethernet cables are not run end-to-end like coax.

Instead, from the network card, a single length of UTP cable runs to a hub or switch, which can be hundreds of feet away. There is no direct machine-to-machine connection. Instead, the hub or switch handles the transmission of signals to all the machines connected to it. This also means that there is no need for terminating resistors using UTP cabling.

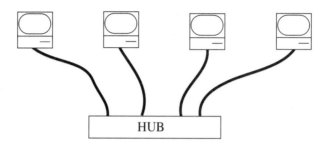

Figure 14-2   A UTP-based network has individual cables running from each computer to the hub or switch.

UTP Ethernet networks have a number of advantages over coax, the most important of which is the ease of running the cables. You do need to buy a hub or switch, which can range in price from fifty dollars to many thousands of dollars, depending on the type of hub or switch and the number of connectors it supports. To set up two PCs at home—one Windows and one Linux—on a UTP Ethernet network, you need two Ethernet cards, two lengths of UTP cable, and a hub or switch. For every machine you add to the network you need another network card and another UTP cable. Most Ethernet hubs or switches support eight or sixteen connections. If you need more, you can connect hubs and switches to provide more ports. Most hubs and switches allow this daisy-chaining between specific ports, or a special cable can be constructed to allow connections on hubs that do not have a port dedicated to hub-to-hub connections.

To set up a Windows-to-Linux network, you need to install Ethernet network cards in each machine. For Windows machines, many inexpensive network cards are available, often in bulk packs of five or ten cards at heavily discounted prices. These network cards are usually plug-and-play devices. These work well with Windows 95 and later, but not with Windows NT 4.0 which lacks true plug-and-play capabilities. Install the network card per the instructions, and either let Windows recognize the card or you can provide configuration information. Don't worry about the network protocol for the moment, just install the card and ensure that it is recognized. After the card is properly installed, it is time to install TCP/IP on the Windows machines.

INSTALLING TCP/IP ON A WINDOWS MACHINE

When you install your network card in a Windows 95, Windows 98, Windows NT 4.0, or Windows 2000 machine, the system asked for the network protocol you want to use. It doesn't matter if you specified TCP/IP at that point or not; you can always install TCP/IP after a reboot. The procedure to install TCP/IP on a Windows machine follows.

1. Open the Control Panel and select the Network applet. The window that appears should have your network card listed along with one or more protocols. If your network card does not appear, Windows did not recognize the card when you installed it, and you need to reinstall. Your window will look something like the one shown in Figure 14-3.

Figure 14-3   The network applet shows a network card installed but no TCP/IP protocol.

2. Highlight the name of the network card in the list, and click the Add button. You are asked what you want to add in a window like the one shown in Figure 14-4.

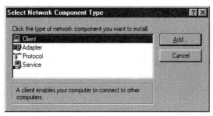

Figure 14-4   After choosing the Add button, you must tell Windows you want to add a protocol.

Select Protocol, and you are presented with a list of manufacturers in the left-hand side of a new window. Select Microsoft. The right-hand side of the window shows a list of drivers and services available from Microsoft. Select TCP/IP.

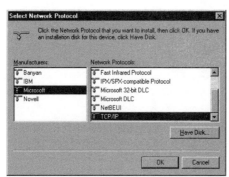

Figure 14-5   Select Microsoft in the left - hand window and TCP/IP in the right-hand window.

3. The dialog box that appears has several page tabs across the top. The first page asks for your IP address. If your system has a method of assigning IP addresses dynamically when the machine is booted, the default setting of "Obtain an IP address automatically" is fine. However, if you do not have DHCP (Dynamic Host Configuration Protocol) or a similar IP address assignment service running, you must assign the IP address manually. Select the "Specify an IP address" button and

two fields become highlighted. Choose a unique IP address that is in the same sub-net as your Linux server. Although the netmask depends on your IP address, it is 255.255.255.0 for most Class C IP addresses.

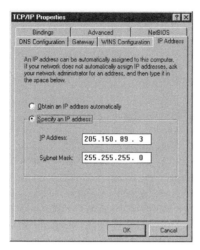

Figure 14-6   Most Linux-based networks require IP addresses to be specified in the TCP/IP Properties window.

4. If you are not using a gateway or a DNS server, that is all that is required to enable TCP/IP. Click the OK button at the bottom of the TCP/IP Properties window, then OK again at the network applet, and Windows will bind the TCP/IP driver to the network card. When you reboot your system and reopen the network applet, you will see TCP/IP bound to the network card, as is shown in Figure 14-7.

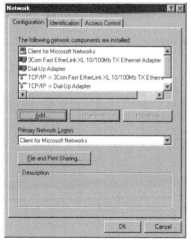

Figure 14-7   If TCP/IP has been properly added to the network card, you will see a line in the Applet showing the TCP/PI name followed by the card name.

5. If you are using a gateway on your network, such as your Linux machine, another UNIX server, or a Windows NT server, you can instruct your Windows machine to use the gateway for access out of the local area network. To add a gateway machine's IP address to your configuration, highlight the TCP/IP entry bound to the network card, and click Properties, or simply double-click the bound TCP/IP entry. The TCP/IP Properties window appears. Click the Gateway tab at the top of the screen and a window like the one shown in Figure 14-8 appears.

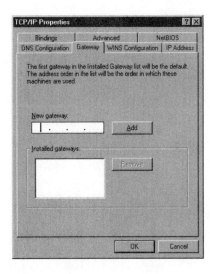

Figure 14-8   The Gateway page in TCP/IP Properties allows you to specify the IP address of your network's gateways.

6. Enter the IP address of your gateway machine and click Add. The IP address appears in the list. If you have multiple gateways, you can add the IP addresses one at a time. When Windows needs to connect to a gateway, it tries all the IP addresses listed, from top to bottom, until one of the gateways answers.If you have no more changes to the Properties window, click OK, then OK again at the applet window, and after a reboot the gateway information is available to Windows.

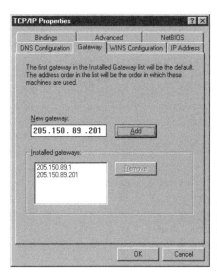

Figure 14-9   Multiple gateway IP addresses can be specified and are queried in order from top to bottom when needed.

7. If your network uses a DNS server (usually UNIX-based although Linux can easily act as a DNS server), you can add the information about the DNS server through the DNS Configuration page tab in the TCP/IP Properties window.

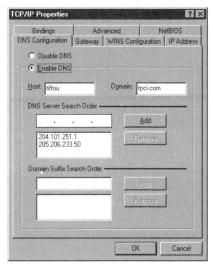

Figure 14-10   The DNS Configuration page lets you add the IP addresses of any DNS servers your Windows machine uses.

8. Enter the IP address of the DNS server as before, and click Add to include the server in the list. Specify your host name and the domain name in the top portion of the window for DNS to function properly. In the example shown in Figure 14-10, there are two DNS servers that are queried to resolve names and IP addresses.

After completing any of these TCP/IP configuration steps, Windows rebuilds its driver database and the binding of protocol to network card, and usually requires a reboot for the changes to become effective. After configuring TCP/IP on your Windows machine, test the network and see if your Linux machine can be reached. The easiest way to quickly test the configuration of your TCP/IP drivers and the network is to use *ping,* which stands for the rather obtuse "packet internet groper." Open a DOS window or use the Run command to issue the command ping, followed by the IP address of your Linux machine (which you should have preconfigured, of course). If the network is working and Windows is configured properly, you will receive diagnostic messages telling you how long it took for the packets to travel to the Linux machine and back.

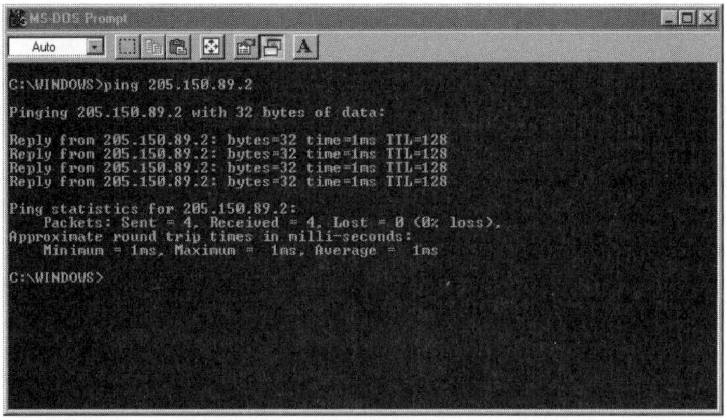

Figure 14-11   Using ping to test the network.

If you do not see output like this, or you receive a message about the host being unreachable or that the request timed out, then either TCP/IP is not configured properly on your Windows machine or the network is not functioning.

You can also ping your Windows machines from the Linux system using the IP addresses of the Windows machines.

SUMMARY

Connecting your Windows machines to your Linux machine over a TCP/IP network is uncomplicated, as you have just seen. The inclusion of TCP/IP drivers with all the recent Windows operating systems has made the task even easier. Now, using Samba or a TCP protocol like FTP and Telnet, you can quickly communicate between your Linux machine and Windows machines. It sure beats SneakerNet!

LINUX

ON

LAPTOPS

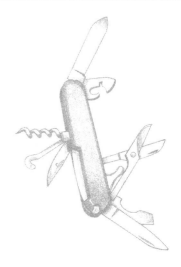

A lthough most Linux users want to run the operating system from a desktop machine, Linux is equally at home on a laptop or other portable computing device. Installing and configuring Linux on your laptop can take a little more effort than the same process on a desktop. Still, if you are willing to experiment a little, it is not too onerous a task. Indeed, running Linux on an older laptop is a great way to use equipment that can't keep up with the increasing speed and memory requirements of Windows systems. You may also feel a satisfying smugness when opening your laptop to run a complex operating system like Linux, while everyone around you is messing with Windows. (You'll be amazed at the comments you will receive at airports!). This chapter looks at what you need to do to install and configure Linux on a portable device such as a laptop, and how to configure the PC Card slots if you have them.

CHOOSING A PORTABLE COMPUTER FOR LINUX

If you've been using computers for a few years, you may have an old laptop or lugable computer—such as the Compaq "lunchbox"—sitting around, unable to run anything but DOS or Windows 3.X. Most of the older laptops ran on 80386 or 80486 CPUs, or on their equivalents from other manufacturers such as Cyrix and AMD. They seldom had more than 16MB of RAM in them. Since these machines are unable to run Windows 95 or Windows 98 with acceptable speed, most users let them gather dust in a cupboard or give them to relatives who want only simple word-processing capabilities.

Instead of wasting these older machines, they can be put to much use running Linux. As you know, Linux's system requirements are modest, so an 80386 or 80486 is fine for this operating system. One problem with many of the older laptops is the lack of RAM and video capabilities, often preventing you from running X or forcing you to run it in lower resolutions, like basic VGA-only. Still, if you work from the character prompt most of the time, older machines are ideally suited as Linux workstations. The other problem with very old laptops is disk space. Some laptops came with 40 MB drives; thus, a subset of Linux is required. Even so, these machines work well, in most cases.

Installing and configuring Linux on new laptops is much easier, mostly because these new machines are designed to run many different operating systems. While most manufacturers bundle their Pentium-class laptops with Windows 98, they are tested with other operating systems like Windows NT and SCO UNIX. As a general rule, if the laptop can run Windows 98, it will be able to run Linux. Again, the graphics sub-system is usually a limiting factor, as some laptops still use proprietary graphics chips that may not have Linux drivers.

Dual-boot systems are popular with laptops, as well. It is entirely possible to have multiple operating systems loaded on a single laptop, assuming the hard drive is suffi-ciently large. One of the author's machines, for example, provides a simple menu when the machine restarts allowing a choice of booting into Windows 98 (for games), Win-dows NT (for high-end Windows applications), or Linux. The machine's 8 GB hard drive gives plenty of room for all three operating systems.

KNOWING WHICH PORTABLES SUPPORT LINUX

It is difficult to predict exactly which laptops support Linux. However, there are a few web sites that try to collect information about laptops that have been proven to support one or more versions of Linux. The lists maintained in these sites tend to be a little old, as many manufacturers don't test Linux on their newest machines. Instead, it is users who have tried to install Linux on their machines who alert these webmasters about their success in doing so.

The two most complete sources of Linux-compatible laptop information are found at web sites like the Linux Laptop site at http://www.cs.utexas.edu/users/kharker/linux-laptop/ and the Linux on Portables site at http://www.queegueg.ifa.hawaii.edu/linux/ portables.html. These sites provide lists of laptops known to work with Linux, broken down by manufacturer and then model. Some web pages are specifically tai-lored to a model or series of laptops, such as the IBM ThinkPad, which is supported by the web page at http://www.wwsi.com/linux-tp.html. Just because your laptop doesn't appear on one of the supported laptop lists doesn't mean you are out of luck. Many laptop models are compatible with others; if a similar model is listed, there is a good chance that your model might work, too.

Most modern laptops have fairly standard designs internally, using PCI bus and common video chips. If you have a recently purchased machine, the chances are good that Linux will run on the system. Older machines are a little tricker, though, because many companies used proprietary hardware requiring specific devices. Of course, the best way to tell if Linux will run on your laptop is to try and load it. You may have to repeat the process several times, but the experience will help you determine which problems are being encountered (and solved) with each successive attempt.

PC CARDS

The PC Card interface (formerly known as PCMCIA cards) is available on many laptops and is often the only way to support network cards and similar devices. A special package called Card Services is required to allow PC Cards to work with Linux.

There are several versions of Card Services available, some commercial and some public domain. Most of the PC Card controllers are manufactured by a limited list of companies like Intel, Cirrus, Ricoh, VLSI, and Databook. They are all supported by Linux's free Card Services package, available from many web and FTP sites as well as in some Linux CD-ROM distributions. The main exceptions to Linux PC Card support are the proprietary controller found in many Hewlett-Packard Omnibook subnotebooks and some Hyundai laptops with Motorolla controllers.

Loading Card Services is usually simple. The drivers are added to the Linux kernel in the usual way, and after a reboot, the PC Cards are recognized as valid devices. Most PC Cards work through Card Services, including the majority of network cards, modems, and multifunction cards. Some hard drive PC Cards do not work, and some SCSI PC Card controllers are not recognized properly.

NETWORKING A LAPTOP

Few laptops have an Ethernet port built in to the body of the unit. Usually, networking is added through the PC Card slots. Once Card Services are loaded, identify the card to the operating system. While some cards require special configurations, most commonly used PC Card network cards from manufacturers like SMC, 3Com, and Linksys work well under Linux. Some manufacturers are starting to bundle Linux drivers with the network cards they sell, adding extra value to their packages. Check the manufacturer's web site or read the network card's packaging to see if Linux drivers are included.

The network interface for a PC Card Ethernet card is configured as normal. You can use your laptop for any Linux networking role, including as a proxy server, web server, gateway, and so on. As far as Linux is concerned, the machine's type does not matter.

TOUCHPAD SUPPORT

Instead of a mouse or the IBM-popularized mouse button, some laptop manufacturers opt for touchpads. These are common in laptops by Sony, Compaq, Dell, and Gateway. Touchpads do not behave the same as a mouse and thus need a special driver.

The majority of touchpads are based on a design by Synaptics, and a Linux driver has been written specifically for this device. The driver can be downloaded from the web site at http://www.pdos/lcs/mit/edu/~cananian/Synaptics/. The driver runs from the command line, not as part of the kernel, and cannot be used when a mouse driver is loaded through the kernel. Still, it works well on most laptops with touchpads.

INSTALLING AND CONFIGURING LINUX ON A LAPTOP

The installation procedure for Linux on a laptop is almost identical to the process on a desktop machine. Many laptops cannot boot off the CD-ROM drive. For these laptops, boot and root floppies are required. If you have no specific instructions about the kernel and root images to use for your laptop, choose those that are the most generic. For newer laptops, the IDE interface is customary and the root image should be for a standard VGA system, unless you know otherwise. These images provide the safest bet for installing Linux on a laptop. Once you have made sure that Linux loads on your system, you can experiment with other, more powerful images if you want.

The amount of disk space you allocate to Linux is up to you. The same rules apply for disk usage on a laptop as on a desktop. To run X, you need a video chip that can be handled by an X driver, and the chips in laptops are often not detected properly by the X autoconfiguration routine. You can usually identify the graphics chip through a startup message, from the owner's manual, or sometimes from the BIOS. Most laptops, even the earliest models, support generic VGA emulation, so at worst you can run X in VGA 16-color mode. Higher resolutions and more colors require specific drivers. Many 80486 and Pentium class laptops easily run SVGA and XGA drivers without special software. The only way to make sure is to experiment with the configuration routine (and reboot a lot!).

All Linux software runs just as well on a laptop as on a desktop, once the devices are configured. Device names are similar to those of a desktop, especially for serial and parallel ports. Once X is running, any X application functions just as well on a laptop screen as on a desktop, although the smaller screen makes some applications hard to read. There are several public domain utilities available to help correct minor problems like this by altering the contrast of the screen and changing the behavior and shape of the cursor. A little research at one of the Linux web sites will provide you with many utilities designed specifically for laptop Linux users.

SUMMARY

Running Linux on a laptop is not only possible, but usually quite easy. Possible problems you may encounter include proprietary chips are on the motherboard or supporting hardware. On older laptops you will also have to juggle the features you load, especially X. Still, Linux works just as well on a laptop as it does on a desktop. With the support of Card Services, you can network your laptop and add as many peripherals as you wish.

LINUX

SYSTEM

SECURITY

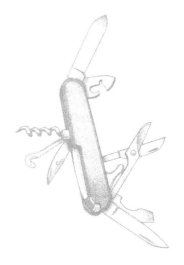

Since this book is aimed at the more advanced user, you know all the basic system administration procedures. You know how to add users to your system, mount and unmount floppies and CD-ROMs, and use utilities like GZIP. You probably know the basics of good security, too, such as always using a strong password, not leaving accounts wide open, and setting file and directory permissions. Enhanced security, though, is one of those subjects that is hard to fully understand unless you have been working with an operating system for a while. Since many of our machines are in some way connected to the Internet, we have to be aware of our machine's security features. This chapter looks at how you can button up your Linux system, preventing unwarranted intrusions and attacks from hackers. While the subjects in this chapter do not give you a foolproof security system, you will have a machine that catches all the most common break-in attempts.

SECURITY BREACHES

There are a number of ways that hackers try to break into Linux systems. To understand why hackers try to break in, you need to understand what they are doing once they do get in. For the most part, there are two ways hackers behave once they have broken into a new system. The first is to act curious, nosing around to see what software you have installed, how your system is set up, what type of user load you have, any neat hardware you are using, and your system's connections to other machines. These types of hackers are benign, usually more curious than anything else, and very seldom do they cause problems beyond intrusion.

The second type of behavior is the one we hear about the most, causing direct or indirect damage to the system. Sometimes hackers take files from your system and then hide or delete them. Sometimes they poke around in your databases and applications, stealing what they want or can use elsewhere and then trashing the system completely. Others use a technique called a "denial of service" attack. In this scenario, hackers do not erase anything, but rather render the system nonfunctional by using up the memory or CPU. Sometimes they use networking software to overload the TCP/IP systems on your machine. Whatever their methods, these hackers are out to do damage to any system they can access.

The methods of accessing a system without being a valid user are manifold, most arising from the early days of UNIX systems and the earliest PCs. The methods to gain access can be broken down into a few simple categories:

◆   Intrusion.

◆   Trojan horses.

◆   Viruses.

◆   Backdoors.

◆   Program spoofs.

While there are some other methods, these five account for almost all the attacks recorded by Linux administrators.

INTRUSION

Intrusion is, as the name suggest, the technique of trying to log in using someone else's login name and guessing the passwords or using open logins like anonymous FTP. There are thousands of software programs available on the Internet that hackers can use to guess passwords. Many of these routines simply work through dictionaries and all permutations of dictionary words until they acquire a password. If a hacker knows a user's name, they can often guess a user login. For example, Bob Brown's login is most likely bbrown, bob, or bobb. There is always the root login to try, too. Some system logins are well-known to the hacker community, such as guest and satan. These are all attempted with simple password-cracking routines.

TROJAN HORSES

Trojan horses are programs with a hidden program inside. For example, you might download a game from the Internet called "x_tetris" which runs a Tetris game under X. However, underneath all that game code is another program that is snooping through your password file or recording logins from users. Typical targets for trojans are programs that actually use a login and password from you, such as Telnet and FTP. It is simple to write a shell script called "telnet" in which the user executes what looks like a normal a Telnet session with a disconnect message at the end, but which has also stored the user's login and password in a file available to the hacker. Although these are classic, well-known hacks, they still catch all but the most alert system administrator. An excellent tool for finding trojan horses is called Tripwire, available from http://www.visualcomputing.com. Another such tool is available through FTP at ftp://coast.cs.purdue.edu/pub/tools/unix/trojan.

VIRUSES

Viruses act like trojan horses in the sense that they are programs that trap user logins and passwords and then send them on to the hacker. However, a virus is a little more involved in that it can spread itself from machine to machine over a network, letting the chunk of code gather information from every system it touches. Viruses are difficult to find under UNIX because most run as daemons, not user processes, and hence require a very alert system administrator to notice the process.

BACKDOORS

Backdoors are holes in operating systems or applications that can be exploited for access. A typical UNIX backdoor program watches a TCP port and records all the activity going on through that port. Every time someone logs in through that port, the login and password are copied to a file for later access. Other backdoors don't record anything, but grant immediate access to the system when a password is typed. Backdoors can lie dormant for a long time, often working without you knowing they are there. Typically a backdoor is placed on a system after someone has broken in. After gaining access, the hacker sets up the backdoor and then leaves the system, secure in the knowledge the backdoor will be there to let them in again.

PROGRAM SPOOFS

Program spoofs are similar to trojan horses in that they are a way of getting the user to type a login and password and then recording that information. Spoofing works with applications that run well over a network, as they can see traffic from many users and sites. Spoofing also refers to taking advantage of specific holes in applications that users run. Since Linux is made up of thousands of smaller programs, there are lots of holes to be exploited by an unscrupulous hacker. By using one of these holes, information about the user or the system can be obtained. The list of susceptible applications is huge: sendmail, apache, rsh, quake, finger, and many others all have documented holes. The only way to prevent the exploitation is to secure the holes with system patches or configuration information. This type of information is often made available through Linux web sites and Usenet newsgroups, as well as through sites like the Computer Emergency Response Team at http:www.cert.org.

DENIAL OF SERVICE

Denial of service attacks have become routine over the Internet, particularly since they require little knowledge and most people who use them are copying instructions verbatim from hacker web sites or newsgroups. The most common denial of service attack uses the ping command with the flood option. For example, if you are on a local area network, you could issue one of the following commands:

```
ping -f IPaddress 80

ping -f http://www.servername.com:80
```

IPaddress is the IP address of some web server and servername.com is the name of a server on the network or Internet. The number 80 tells ping to use TCP port 80, commonly used by the web daemon httpd. The -f option tells ping to flood the site with ICMP (Internet Message Control Protocol) messages, essentially causing the port to become so clogged that the server has no choice but to shut the port down and stop receiving requests. The web server now becomes unavailable to other, legitimate users. You have denied that service to others.

Don't do this unless these are your own machines. It is illegal and prosecutable. You can be traced through the ICMP messages.

Protecting yourself completely from denial of service attacks is difficult unless you shut down all the TCP-based daemons. This isn't practical when you want to run a web or FTP server. However, you can do a lot to prevent this type of attack. Typical preventative measures include:

◆ Checking the daemons.

◆ Scanning TCP ports.

◆ Disabling weak applications.

CHECKING THE DAEMONS

Checking the daemons running on your system verifies that everything executing on your system is known to you and is supposed to be running. The easiest way to check the daemons is to use the ps command. Filtering out the daemons run by root lets you see these daemons more easily, like this:

```
ps -aux | grep root
```

Most of the daemons that appear do not have a port assigned to them, but do have a question mark in the TTY column. Of those daemons, most are system processes. The main daemons that run on a Linux system are summarized in the list below. Although these are taken from a Slackware system, the names are similar in other Linux versions:

◆ **crond**   A cron utility for scheduling jobs.

◆ **ftpd**   FTP server.

◆ **httpd**   Web server.

◆ **imapd**   IMAP mail server.

◆ **in.telnetd**   Server for telnet sessions.

◆ **inetd**   Starts networking services.

◆ **kflushd**   Kernel memory utility.

◆ **klogd**   Kernel logging utility.

◆ **kswapd**   Controls the swap space.

◆ **lpd**   Printer control.

◆ **mountd**   Handles mounts.

◆ **named**   Domain name server.

◆ **nfsd**   Network file system server.

◆ **popd**   POP3 mail server.

◆ **pppd**   Point-to-point protocol server.

◆ **sendmail**   Mail utility.

◆ **sshd**   Secure shell for inbound requests.

◆ **syslogd**   System logging utility.

◆ **xntpd**   Network time protocol.

Although there are other daemons on some systems, these are the main ones. The important thing to look for are daemons without ties to some protocol or utility you need. For example, if you are not using NFS on your network, you should not be running the nfsd daemon (which has a number of well-known security holes in it). If you are not using the POP3 mail system, don't run popd, and so on. Getting rid of the processes you don't need simply removes them as a source of intrusion and denial of service on your server.

SCANNING TCP PORTS

TCP ports are assigned fairly standard numbers for each protocol, such as 80 for web servers. However, a clever hacker can use your open TCP ports to get into your system. There are a couple of ways you can scan your ports to see what is genuinely used by some protocol and which are open and exploitable. The nmap utility is one of these ways. The nmap program scans the /etc/services file, where the utilities and daemons that use a TCP port are listed. The nmap system has a many options that control how scan is performed, allowing you to examine port usage in a number of ways. If your system didn't come with a copy of nmap, you can obtain it from many Linux web and FTP sites.

The strobe command is another way of monitoring port usage. The strobe utility scans all the ports looking for specific types of information. Both nmap and strobe will produce a list of known ports your system is using. If you don't need the port for something your server is running, then close the port down, usually by removing the offending entry in /etc/services. For example, if you are not providing FTP services to the network or the Internet, close down the ftpd daemon in /etc/services and allow ports 20 and 21 to stay closed. They can't be entered that way. As with nmap, you can obtain a copy of strobe at many Linux web and FTP sites.

DISABLING WEAK APPLICATIONS

Some applications have been around for years and are known for security problems. The most common applications in this category are the Berkeley r-utilities: rsh, rlogin, and rcp. Through these, a hacker can gain root privileges quite easily. It is best to completely disable and remove these types of applications.

Some of the best ways to keep on top of these intrusion techniques are through the CERT web site (http://www.cert.org), through the Bugtraq mailing list (http://www.geek-girl.com/bugtraq), and through the Linux security mailing list (http://www.oslab.snu.ac.kr/~djshin/linux/mail-list/index.shtml).

SATAN AND ITS ILK

A lot of fuss was made about the Satan utility a few years ago. The popular media would have us believe that this system administration tool was a license for all hackers to break into networks. Far from it. Satan is an extremely handy and useful tool. Satan stands for Security Administrator Tool for Analyzing Networks and is a security tool developed by programmers at Silicon Graphics (who subsequently left the company because of disagreements about the distribution of the program). Satan is available through the Internet and many user support groups and is free of charge.

What does Satan do? It essentially scans a complete network for any of the well-known holes in UNIX security. These holes have been well-documented and most system administrators know about them, although many systems may not have fixes in place to protect against security problems caused by these holes. Satan scans the network, from the primary gateway to all subsidiary machines, looking for any of these holes and sends a report back to the person who ran Satan. The report includes a description of the hole and how a hacker could exploit it. The idea, of course, is to make it easy to plug security problems on a network by providing a complete list of all the holes that still exist. Satan can be run only by a user with root access, which usually limits it to system administrators.

Satan's interface is extremely easy to use. It is also very cleverly programmed, designed so that new descriptions of holes ("rules") can be added easily to help detect new gaps in security as they arise. Satan is completely passive as distributed. It snoops around the networks and does not leave any trace of its presence.

So far, Satan sounds like a really useful tool, right? So why the fuss? The most common fear is that unscrupulous people will obtain a copy of Satan on their home machine, will run it against other networks accessible through the Internet, and will obtain a list of all the holes in that network. The hacker can then exploit those holes and gain access to the remote network. This is a real possibility, and it can be assumed that many hackers have obtained a copy of Satan to try this out. Since they have root privileges on their own machine, they can then launch Satan against any other network accessible to them. The report will include all the holes the gateway to the remote network possesses, as well as holes in machines further inside the network to which Satan could gain access.

The modular design of Satan means that a knowledgeable programmer can also add new material to the code, exploiting holes in security that Satan detects. A hacker could, for example, instruct Satan to use a hole it finds to plant a snoop program that records passwords and logins, retrieving the file at a later date.

Satan is a double-edged sword for many system administrators. It is the most useful and powerful tool available for verifying a machine's security from hackers. This also makes it usable by hackers to detect holes. Since it would be impossible to restrict access to Satan, there is no easy way to keep it out of hackers' hands. One proposal was to make the software available only with a high purchase price to discourage hackers. The authors of Satan vehemently disagreed with this approach, wanting it available to everyone free of charge. The logic, presumably, is that if every system administrator on the network used Satan to plug their holes, hackers would be out of luck. Of course, not every system administrator will bother, as only a small percentage of system administrators actually know much about their systems beyond the basics.

So we have a security tool that offers ideal behavior for the system administrator: an easily executed program that generates a nearly complete list of problems with the system's or network's security. It also can be used by others to detect those same holes and exploit them. There is no easy solution, except to strongly suggest that every system administrator obtain a copy of Satan and make sure their systems are buttoned up. Maybe the threat of a break-in, inspired by the thought of a hacker equipped with Satan, will be enough to make system administrators do what they should have done a long time ago. You can get a copy of Satan from many web and FTP sites, especially those dealing with security, like http://www.cert.org.

Satan isn't the only such tool available to system administrators. There are several tools that allow administrators to scan their networks, looking for holes and vulnerabilities. Again, a visit to a decent web site dedicated to security is a good place to start.

SUMMARY

Covering everything to do with Linux security could take a whole book (and some books are out on this exact topic). However, a little common sense, a little prudence, and some vigilance on the part of yourself as the system administrator will make your system much safer and less vulnerable to hackers. If you don't have a dedicated Internet connection, don't assume you are safe: if you dial in to an ISP, you are vulnerable as long as that connection is alive.

index

G

H

I

Keep Up-to-Date with
PH PTR Online!

We strive to stay on the cutting-edge of what's happening in professional computer science and engineering. Here's a bit of what you'll find when you stop by **www.phptr.com**:

@ Special interest areas offering our latest books, book series, software, features of the month, related links and other useful information to help you get the job done.

Deals, deals, deals! Come to our promotions section for the latest bargains offered to you exclusively from our retailers.

$ Need to find a bookstore? Chances are, there's a bookseller near you that carries a broad selection of PTR titles. Locate a Magnet bookstore near you at www.phptr.com.

! What's New at PH PTR? We don't just publish books for the professional community, we're a part of it. Check out our convention schedule, join an author chat, get the latest reviews and press releases on topics of interest to you.

✉ Subscribe Today! Join PH PTR's monthly email newsletter!

Want to be kept up-to-date on your area of interest? Choose a targeted category on our website, and we'll keep you informed of the latest PH PTR products, author events, reviews and conferences in your interest area.

Visit our mailroom to subscribe today! **http://www.phptr.com/mail_lists**